T0302917

The Path
of Kabbalah

By Rav Michael Laitman PhD

The Path of Kabbalah

LAITMAN
KABBALAH PUBLISHERS

By Rav Michael Laitman PhD

Executive Editor: Benzion Giertz
Editor: Claire Gerus
Translation: Chaim Ratz
Compilation: Shlomi Bohana
Layout: Baruch Khovov

Laitman Kabbalah Publishers Website:
www.kabbalah.info
Laitman Kabbalah Publishers E-mail:
info@kabbalah.info

THE PATH OF KABBALAH

ISBN: 0-9732315-9-9
FIRST EDITION: DECEMBER 2005

The Path
of Kabbalah

TABLE OF CONTENTS

Part One: The Beginning

CHAPTER 1.1
THE GREAT ILLUSION

Thou shalt have no other gods before Me. Thou shalt not make unto thee a graven image, nor any manner of likeness (Exodus 20:3).

Judaism forbids idolatry and any kind of fetishism. This prohibition envelops the most fundamental principle in Judaism: that everything we see is only a figment of our imaginations.

Over the years, many of us have consciously or unconsciously adopted this principle after realizing that, by changing our perspective, we might be able to better cope with our day-to-day problems. This perspective determines our reactions, our feelings, and ultimately our reality. What, then, is the actual reality around us?

Today, Kabbalists can state a principle that Jews concealed for thousands of years: that there is no reality at all, but something called "His Essence," the "Upper Force." This Force operates in such a way that one sees Him as an image of a certain reality, which we call "my world."

We are all able to see and feel varying images and sensations depending on our sensory organs and inner properties. All our sensations are subjective and exist only with regard to our feelings.

However, because the sensory organs of non-human creatures would differ from ours, they would see the world as completely different from us. In fact, it is possible that another creature's sensory organs would be so different from ours, it might exist in a different dimension without ever encountering us.

The closer one's properties are to the properties of the Upper Force, the closer the image of "my world" comes to the actual reality, and the less distorted it is by one's egoistic attributes. Since the property of the Upper Force is altruism, when one attains that quality and bonds with the Upper Force, one learns to feel reality as it is. All of the above is mentioned only to emphasize that all our sensations are personal and might change in time.

The only way for us to approach the right perspective of reality is by studying Kabbalah, since it is the only study that deals with the part of reality that humanity has yet to attain. But it is not enough to merely study the text because we are reading about the unknown. We must also direct ourselves to the right vision and be prepared for a truer, and as yet concealed, feeling.

Everything exists inside us. Outside us there is only the Upper Force, the Creator. We cannot feel Him in any other way than by how He works on our sensory organs. Only through these sensations can we guess anything about the Creator.

Hence, the study of Kabbalah must be correctly directed; thoughts must be focused on studying the inner attributes that we are still unable to see in ourselves.

All the worlds, *Partzufim*, *Sefirot*, names, everything the Kabbalah speaks of, exists in us and will be revealed in us, depending on the degree of our correction. We will find our inner Moses and Aaron, King David and the angels, the evil, the righteous, and the degrees of attainment called "Jerusalem," "the Temple" and more. Every word in the Torah speaks of our own forces and our levels of ability to sense the Creator.

That is the only topic of discussion of the Torah. That is also the only thing we speak of in our daily lives, because we talk about our feelings. In fact, all we feel is the influence of the Creator. Everything around us is no more than the influence of the Creator on each and every one of us.

Hence, to discern the actual picture of the world, we must find what we read inside us, as we read the Torah, because every written word exists within us—it just hasn't been discovered.

We feel what the books speak of in accordance with our spiritual growth, hence the importance of the study from genuine sources of Kabbalah: the *Zohar*, the writing of the Ari, and the writings of Ashlag. This is the safest way to attain the correction of our feelings and attributes, and our spiritual ascent.

The best way to make progress is to study while remembering that these books actually speak of what is within me, that all this already exists somewhere inside me. All these worlds and *Partzufim* are things that I must discover within. They are my own properties.

The more we acquire control over these attributes, the more we will feel how the Creator operates inside us. Although we will never be able to feel Him "outside" us, we will understand how He operates inside us because, "By your actions we know you."

And since we sit together as a group, studying our still-concealed real properties, we are collaborating in the study of how the Creator operates inside us. We have a common goal, a common thought, and one area of experimentation—our own feelings.

This results in a collective goal, thought, and desire that in time creates in the group the feeling of one body and common properties—a feeling that there are no separate entities, but only one, "man," and before him, the One Creator.

This thought must be directed inwardly toward changing our qualities in search of the Creator within us. Instead of the ordinary reading of the Torah, we discover the Torah "as a spice," as a means for correction. It is also called a "potion of life," for it pours into us the sensation of the Creator, the Light of eternity and wholeness.

People who study from the wrong books are denied this remedy and remain with their properties. They do not discover the Creator, and their Torah becomes dry, concealing the purpose of Creation even more than before.

CHAPTER 1.2
BETWEEN CREATOR AND CREATURE

The question, "Who am I?" exists in everyone. But when that question can no longer be put aside, then it relates to the Creator: "Who is He?" This is because the Creator is inside us, the Source of the human "self." Hence, no matter how many times we ask ourselves, "Who am I?" the question still relates to the Creator. The "self" is a consequence. Our desires, our every movement, everything we do is, in fact, created by the Creator.

The notion that everything we say and think, even when we speak of the Creator and ourselves, is the work of the Creator, is virtually impossible for us to perceive.

So where is the "self"? There is no "self." The "self" is the work of nature, created by the Creator. The "self" clothes us, yet everything we do is actually His doing. The question, "Who am I?" can only exist outside the Creator. We are different from the Creator only in wanting to resemble Him and to attain His degree.

The will to receive is essentially the desire of us creatures to enjoy, corresponding to the abundance and pleasure that come from the Creator. We feel that will to receive and the Creator wants us to enjoy it. If we feel an abstract will to receive, it is not a creature, it is nature, God. If one works according to nature's guidance, one is like a beast that hasn't even a spark of a Godly soul.

Only if our will to receive is clothed with an intention that monitors its use and corrects it, can we regard ourselves as creatures enlivened intentionally by the Creator, and not just another rock, animal or bird. But that depends on us.

Our desires to drink, eat, sleep, marry, and have children are natural and come from the Creator. We can't escape or altogether change them. However, we can robe the will to receive with an aim and build a correct way to use that desire. The extent and depth of this aim depend

PART ONE: THE BEGINNING

solely on us. That is what we call, "Creation." We must search for the right way to use our natures, our desires.

Nature comes from the Creator, and our job is to know how to use it. The "point in the heart" is the way we relate to our nature as given to us by the Creator, as well as our ability to use it correctly. The heart itself consists of our desires, our yearning for pleasure.

Anything that is not the Creator is regarded as "the creature," limited by nature and divided by four degrees of desire: still, vegetative, animate, and speaking (man). Man is the only degree that can use nature with a special, self-created aim. It is called the "point in the heart."

The first phase is the "fetus," the root coarseness: when one nullifies oneself completely, melts, so to speak, in the Creator. After that, the creature must gradually rise to the degree of the Creator and overcome the differences that exist between the Creator and the creature.

Using this aim, we seemingly build the Creator within us, but all along we feel the "self," because the "self" is really the Creator. By attaining the Creator and equalizing in form with Him, we attain our own unique "self."

The Creator wants a Creation that can retain its independence even when it feels the Creator, seemingly producing a "dual Creator"— the first being the Creator Himself, and the second, Creation, operating precisely like the Creator.

The creature's will to receive is completely identical to the Creator's Will to bestow, also named "bestowal in order to bestow." The will to receive does not vanish or becomes lost, and the creature retains its independence by using the desires that it wants to return to the Creator. That is where they are equal. The creature's purpose is to attain complete wholeness while retaining its nature. The Creator couldn't have created an incomplete creature. He had to create a creature equal to Him. And the way to do it was by creating a creature and giving it the possibility of attaining the degree of the Creator by itself.

13

That is the meaning of "perfection." When that is attained, there is a clear sensation that there is nothing other than the Creator and the creature. The creature discovers that it doesn't exist without the Creator, but the Creator cannot be called a Creator if there isn't a creature, just as a woman cannot be called a mother if she doesn't have a child.

It is only possible to attain spirituality when there is a desire for it. But where does one find it if one doesn't even know what it is?

Let's say that we are pushed a little to awaken in us an interest in spirituality, but in the end, the truth is that we still know nothing. If we knew what it was, and still wanted it, at least to a certain extent, things would have been easier.

But spirituality is purposely hidden from us. If we were to enter it with our current will to receive, we would never be able to change it. In order to enter spirituality, we must want it. But wanting means knowing, trying, feeling how good it is. There is a law that states that, "The expansion of the Light, and its departure, make the vessel fit for its task."

In order to attain spirituality one must turn to the Creator with a special prayer to discover spirituality, not for self-gain, but for the will to bestow. After that, that desire to discover spirituality must be used correctly through the work with the group and the teacher.

Thus, there must first be a great desire for spirituality. It is not given as a choice, but extends from the Creator. There will come a time when more and more souls will be ready for spirituality. Man always follows his desire. Before the study of the wisdom of Kabbalah, one is led from Above, and when one opens a book, the Creator seemingly steps away from the student, like a parent teaching an infant to walk. At first, the mother holds her baby, but she slowly backs off when the child begins stumbling toward her. We approach spirituality in much the same way, gaining more and more independence.

There are things we can and cannot work with. I can't say that something doesn't hurt me when it does. I rely on my feelings, and no philosophy will help me in this case. This is the limit of my "self." It is impossible for me to realize my desires if I only rely on my feelings without any concrete basis.

When one attains spirituality, it is a different feeling altogether. We discover that our inner feelings arise from the actions of the Creator. We learn that man and the Creator are one and the same thing. There is no contradiction between them; they want the same thing, and there isn't even a cause and consequence. This is called the "unity of the degree."

Yet we must act as we actually feel. On the one hand, we read inspiring essays that say, "He is One and His name is One," but we still have to act according to our current levels of spirituality.

There is nothing missing in spirituality. For example, when an experience is over, it still remains, although it is no longer present in my current feeling. This is called "there is no absence in spirituality." Any situation that is experienced remains and is stored until the end of correction.

In fact, I am already at the highest degree, or the lowest, depending on my feeling. I cannot imagine any other situation, let alone feel it. Our beastly nature should know that redemption can only come from Above. Then we can advance.

We have a will to receive. That will comes from Above and is constantly increasing, growing farther from the Creator through the impure worlds, and acquiring its final shape of egoism. That state is called "our world."

One begins one's advancement within the impure system and acquires the aim to bestow. With this aim, one begins to correct the will to receive until reaching one's *Bar Mitzvah* age (thirteen years old, a certain spiritual degree).

The Light comes from Above, depending on the correction of one's desires, and fills the creature. This means that the soul—the Light of Correction—clothes the body (the will to receive). The soul, or Light, passes through the holy worlds, and this is the time of correction. If we render pleasure to the Creator in the act of reception, it is called "bestowal." The Talmud states that if a respectable man marries, he doesn't have to give a ring to his bride. On the contrary, his willingness to marry her is sufficient because she respects him.

Such reception is tantamount to pure bestowal. If man works in this way toward the Creator when receiving from Him, with the aim of bringing contentment to the Creator, it is called "equivalence of form."

At first, one restricts oneself, saying, "I don't want to receive anything for myself unless the Creator wants it and it pleases Him." Only under that condition is man willing to receive pleasure. The desire that the Creator created and the pleasure that He gives serve as a condition upon which the relationship with the Creator is based. Man agrees to receive from the Creator only if he is certain that he will please the Creator by receiving from Him.

However, in order to do that we must first meet the Creator, feel Him, and build a connection with Him. There is an inconceivable difference between receiving for self-gratification and receiving to bestow to the Creator. Such a contact is a gift of God.

Two things come from the Creator: body and soul, or Light and vessel. The Light helps the body receive the soul, becomes the giver, and turns the will to receive into bestowal until the will to receive is filled with Light. The situations we go through over the 6,000 degrees move us at any given moment toward the end of correction. At the end of correction, we will attain eternal and perfect pleasure and unity with the Creator.

Without attaining equivalence of attributes with the Creator, we will only be able to experience pleasures of the "still" degree, but not of the "vegetative, animate, and speaking" degrees. An impure system is necessary to increase the will to receive, so that afterwards, using the aim to bestow, it will be filled with Light exactly according to its intensity.

CHAPTER 1.3
THE EVOLUTION OF THE SOUL

A person in this world has no soul. There is only one thing to do if we want to understand and realize our true essence, and that is to embark on a spiritual quest with all the zest, eagerness, and willingness to change that we can summon—a quest to discover the soul. The journey begins at the exact place where we felt our very first desire for spirituality, the "point in the heart."

This point is the embryonic soul that demands our return to our spiritual roots. The soul is drawn to the Creator and takes us along. We don't know where we are being pulled because the Creator is as yet concealed from us. But this point in the soul urges us on to an unknown destination, even though it is still not a "real" soul. When we begin to work on our spiritual side, the point gradually expands and grows. However, it remains dark because we feel a greater and greater desire for something, hence the darkness.

When this point finally grows to the right size, we acquire a screen to surround it, the aim to give, and the Light enters this point. The Light sorts the desires in the point to five parts that correspond to the attributes of the Light: *Keter, Hochma, Bina, Zeir Anpin,* and *Malchut.* Thus, one acquires a soul.

The smallest desire is in *Keter* and the greatest is in *Malchut.* The attribute of reception is smaller in *Keter* and *Hochma* than in the other desires; therefore, *Keter* and *Hochma* are considered "giving" desires. When one is in that state it is called *Katnut* (smallness, infancy).

If we in this world have only beastly and corporeal desires, then we live like everything else on earth. Our next state begins only when the "point in the heart" appears in us. Then, we begin to feel a mysterious attraction to spirituality that we cannot ease, even though we do not know what spirituality is.

If we study Kabbalah at that state, we cross the barrier and enter the spiritual world. This is the third situation. At that stage, a screen with *Aviut Shoresh* (root coarseness) replaces the "point in the heart." It is called *Galgalta* with the Light of *Nefesh*.

That state is regarded as the "embryonic state." Much like an embryo in our world, the seeker wants nothing but to lie inside the maternal womb, inside a higher *Partzuf* that will raise the developing spiritual seeker. After that, the embryo takes nine months to develop its own nine *Sefirot* in *Malchut*, from *Nefesh* of *Nefesh* (*Keter* of *Malchut*) to *Yechida* of *Nefesh* (*Malchut* of *Malchut*).

At this point, the fetus is born and acquires a vessel of *Hochma* with the Light of *Ruach* (*NRNHY* of *Ruach*) with *Aviut Aleph* (1st degree coarseness). This period is called "infancy" and lasts two years, or twenty-four months. In infancy, the *Partzuf* attains a state called *Katnut*, or *Galgalta* and *Eynaim*, a complete screen in first-degree coarseness. The infant is different from the embryo in that the embryo wants nothing, but the infant sucks the Light with its own independent desire, just as a baby sucks from its mother.

How does the milk become food for the baby? When menstruation stops, the mother's blood is used for the development of the embryo. During labor, blood pours out; this blood is "impure" and cannot be corrected. It becomes impure desires, denied of any desire to give, to bestow. But there is a part of the blood that turns into milk after labor. It rises from the *Sefira* of *Yesod*, where the womb is, to the *Chazeh* (chest), which is in the *Sefira* of *Tifferet* of the *Partzuf*.

Everything that happens in the spiritual world and every spiritual law automatically applies to our world. Thus, by studying the processes of impregnation, the evolution of the embryo, and labor, as well as the infancy and growth of the spiritual *Partzufim*, we can understand the processes that occur in our world and their origins.

The state following infancy is the state of *Gadlut* (adulthood). The *Partzuf* receives *Mochin* (Light of Wisdom) in its vessels of *Bina* in the *AHP* (*Awzen, Hotem, Peh*) of coarseness 2, 3, and 4. They are filled correspondingly with the Lights of *Neshama, Haya,* and *Yechida*.

We needn't do anything, just stay out of the way and let the Creator do His Work in us, regardless of what He does. We mustn't exit the boundaries of the Creator's governance under any circumstances. If we can do that, then we have attained a state called "the spiritual embryo."

In a state of infancy, we can already make requests and have a dialog with the Creator. After two years of infancy, we need the guidance and education of the Creator and can receive some Light of Wisdom, the first of which is called "the Light of *Neshama.*"

The entire spiritual relationship between the Creator and the creature in the state of *Katnut* is built exactly like the relationship in our world between mother and child. We can solve all the problems that arise in physical relationships by understanding the root relationships that exist in the spiritual world between the Creator and the creature.

The Creator sends us obstructions on purpose, so that we will begin to want to approach Him through our efforts. Without obstructions in our corporeal life, we would not feel any need or desire for Him, and would never be able to advance.

If the soul of the First Man hadn't been broken, it would have remained a single soul, uncorrected and with very little chance of correcting itself. The correction is the reunification of the broken pieces, after which the pieces can unite with the Creator.

Our work is basically to correct our approaches to what we receive from the Creator, and the consequence of that work is our unification with the Creator, the justification of His every move.

A group of students can attain total unification between themselves. Beginning from the preliminary state, they can build a framework that is comfortable for egoists. Such a framework would suit all those who come for the sole purpose of attaining connection with the Creator. No one should suffer because of this framework, and it need not be turned into a cage or a prison.

The framework should keep changing and improving, according to its members' inner states, and it should always support the goal. The tighter and stronger the connection between the members of the group, the stronger the foundation for connecting with the Creator.

When we begin to advance spiritually, we actually lose the desire for it. It would be more correct to say that we are given additional egoism, with such a will to receive that we can no longer resist it. In that case, there is nothing we can do except continue to move our egoism from the corporeal to the spiritual level by studying and working with members of the group.

All our thoughts must be analyzed and marked as having come from the Creator. They must be catalogued and determined that they will not contradict our goals and aspirations. We must ask ourselves, "Do I follow that thought or do I resist it? Is the Creator now calling me by this thought, or does He want to provoke me by rejection?" There is a difference, but in both cases He still wants to bring us closer to Him.

CHAPTER 1.4
THE AWAKENING OF THE "POINT IN THE HEART"

The study of the wisdom of Kabbalah is research into man's relationship with the Creator. It explores man's every thought, desire and in fact, the entire reality one attains with one's senses. Even in our world, below the spiritual world, there are degrees of attainment. At the beginning of our preparation period for spirituality, we begin to understand the connections and relationships between spiritual properties, although this understanding cannot be compared with the actual sensation when spirituality is attained.

When the *Zohar* says, "Go and ask Rabbi Shimon and Rabbi Abba," it means that you should ascend to their degree and ask why they present things the way they do. When the *Zohar* writes that a certain person met Rabbi Shimon, it means that that person rose to the degree of Rabbi Shimon, and can therefore see and understand what Rabbi Shimon can.

This is how a degree gets its name, and when we ascend to it, we are called by that name. If we attain only a part of that degree, we are regarded as "a son to it." That is why we are considered the sons of Adam, because we are all parts of the degree called "Adam," and our task is to attain that part individually.

A person who rises to a certain degree feels what happens in it, attains its characteristics, and sees the Creator accordingly. By climbing higher, the pictures that were seen in the previous degree will change, as well.

It is not like a movie theatre playing 125 different films, one for each degree, because there is only the Simple Upper Light and the person rising to a certain spiritual degree. We acquire certain spiritual attributes, and thus feel a part of the Upper Light. That part is what we call, "world." We can even feel a tiny part of the Upper Light in our egoistic attributes, which we call, "our world."

All that really exists is the will to receive this or that attribute of the Creator. The acquired attributes present us with a certain image. Different people who attain the same attributes of the Creator will see the same picture, despite their different desires, but from different angles. It is like a debate where the number of opinions is equal to the number of participants.

Because of different thoughts and ideas, we also have different perspectives on the world. However, the general picture remains the same. It is also the same regarding our varying personal experiences, although we agree about the appearance of things.

If we try to understand one another with our attributes or our will to receive, we only grow farther from each other. We can understand each other only through the attributes of the Creator that we will attain in spiritual degrees.

The First Man was created with nothing but altruistic desires, meaning vessels of bestowal. He tended to all the trees in Paradise because he could use all his altruistic desires. If so, then how could he have corrected his egoistic desires (vessels of reception), if he didn't have them, or to be more accurate, if he didn't feel them within? The sin of the First Man was premeditated. He had to sin, to taste of the Tree of Knowledge, and mingle with the egoistic desires (vessels of reception) in order to create a complete mixture of the vessels of bestowal and the vessels of reception. Only afterwards would there be a gradual correction of the vessels of reception.

There seems to be no sin here because it was premeditated by the Creator. But in fact, there is still a breach of the rules, whether knowingly or unknowingly. Did Adam know? No, he did not. Did he want to commit a sin? No, he did not. But did he break the law? Yes, he did.

Even corruption in spirituality is no coincidence; everything is always done for one purpose—to correct egoism and unite it with altruism. If an altruistic spark, a vessel that appeared there at the moment of the sin of the First Man, were not in every egoistic desire, egoism would have been incorrigible and spiritual ascent made impossible. Thus, the First Man's sin was a necessity.

We live in complete spiritual darkness. The Surrounding Light shines on the outside and awakens our egoism, our will to receive, yet cannot penetrate this egoism. This is how we are awakened to spirituality.

To further awaken us, not necessarily to spirituality, but to any personal achievement, a part of the Surrounding Light must (seemingly) be inside us. For that purpose, the "point in the heart" is inserted into our selfish hearts. This point is a gift from Above. It is the lowest point of a higher spiritual object, the posterior of a higher *Partzuf*.

Looking from Above, there is nothing but a vessel, screen, and *Reshimot* (reminiscences). But if we look from below, we find that the soul has three lines: right, left, and middle. Man must gradually overpower each of the lines and unite them. This process consists of the suffering of the left line, the ability to cope with it through the forces of the right line, and the reception of the Light of the Creator in the middle.

There is a certain duality here. From the Creator's perspective, everything is clear and foreseen, including the sin of the First Man and its detailed process of correction. Everything has its place and time. In fact, everything is already at the end of correction. But for us, it is all a secret. Man has yet to discover the rules governing the hidden. We must move ahead with faith above reason, with the unknown pressing and encouraging us to strain to find the Creator and maintain constant contact with Him of our own choice.

But we and the Creator have opposite characteristics, and because of our egoism we are afraid to connect with Him because we don't know what the good inclination is, let alone pure altruism!

From the perspective of the Creator, nothing ever changes; everyone is at the end of correction, delighting in the Light of the Creator. What changes is the anguish that we begin to feel as a result of our egoism and our continuing attempts to correct it from the starting point to the world of *Ein Sof*, from reception to bestowal. If a person in our world does not get this altruistic point, this spiritual attribute from Above, it will be impossible to perform any spiritual acts.

It is written that at the moment of one's spiritual birth, one immediately gets the "posterior of the holy soul," meaning the last (and lowest) degree of the soul, referred to as a "point" because of the restriction. This is placed in our hearts, in the midst of our selfishness.

Without that point, people remain in the animate degree. Their desires do not reach beyond the level of this world. Such people can be attracted to pseudo spiritual ideas and philosophies, predict the future, and be extremely sensitive, but there is nothing that connects them with spirituality. Only the "point in the heart" can bring us out of the beastly state and raise us to the spiritual.

These people may appear alike on the outside, but you can see the difference only when you have equivalence of spiritual attributes, when the "point in the heart" becomes a whole *Partzuf*. Sometimes such a point can remain dormant in the heart for many life cycles. If that point is absent, a person can study Kabbalah for years and be with a group, write everything down, and do everything necessary to attain spirituality, but to no avail.

Even if one joins a group to become a teacher and takes pride in the knowledge attained, if there is no inner desire for unification with the Creator, the group will spiritually reject this person. Thus, success in achieving spirituality depends on the presence of the "point in the heart."

Rav Laitman asked his teacher if the "point in the heart" could be acquired if it wasn't there to begin with. His teacher replied that if a person enters a group and sees that everything revolves around one desire—to find the Creator—and if that person sees others arriving from afar with only this objective, then, with the right books and the right teacher, the person without a "point in the heart" can pick up the general desire, even if the point has not yet been awakened.

However, it is known that an extremely strong desire can awaken the "point in the heart." Even the Ari mentioned it.

In order for an individual to be included in the united desire of the group, that person must be in complete agreement with that desire. This is because even when this point does exist, its attributes vary from person to person. For instance, it is known that Rabbi Yosef Karo, who wrote the *Shulchan Aruch* (the Jewish code of laws), a priceless piece of work, slept during his Kabbalah lessons with the Ari.

Of course, there were people who absorbed the Lurianic Kabbalah (the Kabbalah of the Ari) naturally, and there were people who could not understand it and had troubles disconnecting themselves from the Kabbalah of the Ramak (Rabbi Moshe Kordoviro). The Ari introduced a fundamental change in the method of the study of Kabbalah, enabling us to study Kabbalah from below, meaning from the perspective of the vessels, the souls.

Ramak's study method examined the world from the perspective of the Lights, meaning from the perspective of the Creator, whereas we study it from the perspective of the screen, which helps the Light expand.

Rav Laitman studied Kabbalah with many teachers, but could find no answers until he was shown the books of the Ari and Baal HaSulam.

The Upper Degree is the Creator, our own future state. The lower degree is the creature in his current state. The degrees are like an accordion, opening up to us as we progress.

What is time? Is it a changing, living concept? And if so, does it exist outside or inside us? Does each degree keep its own time?

The concept of "time" is a consequence of the work of the shells. We continue to feel "time" just as long as we refuse to agree with the Creator about everything that happens to us. But time disappears after our complete correction, when nothing further needs to be changed and everything is at complete peace.

The root of time is the discovery of deficit and the need for correction. The First Restriction created an empty space intended for correction. The restriction happened because the desire, which is opposite to perfection, and the contradictions could not be reconciled immediately. That is what created "time" and "space" in our world. These two contradictions can be brought together by changing either time or space. Before the First Restriction, there was no "time" or "space."

If there were a special timer that could be connected to man's heart, we could see the axis of the spiritual life in different people. Some live a thousand years, and others live only for a minute. Our ordinary clock shows only the "still" time, meaning the pace of progress of the still toward the purpose of Creation.

CHAPTER 1.5
KABBALAH AS A MEANS OF ATTAINING SPIRITUALITY

Kabbalah revolves around the spiritual worlds. Therefore, the student attracts spiritual Lights during the study. Studying other parts of the Torah also awakens a certain spiritual illumination, but the intensity of the Light during the study of Kabbalah is much stronger than when studying other writings.

However, we must make sure we are studying in the right path of instruction, otherwise the opposite result may be achieved: the more we study, the more we will feel righteous instead of feeling our own evil (which is the desired result). Feeling our own evil would make it easier for us: just imagine studying for several months, each month feeling that you are becoming meaner and meaner. Can you really call that sensation pleasant?

Not at all! However, this is the truth! If you keep feeling better about yourself, you are learning a lie, a pleasant one, but still a lie. On that basis, society can be divided to two opposing groups: "Homeowners" and "Torah Owners."

Homeowners are those who study Torah and are content with the study. They feel that they accumulate merit for the world to come. This world already smiles at them and they are confident that they will be happy in the next life.

The Torah Owners, however, are people who wish to do something with themselves. These two groups are in complete opposition to one another, although their outward appearance is the same. They consist of an entirely different spiritual substance, just as two computers can appear identical but use two different operating systems.

All religions rely on one's efforts to receive rewards in this world and the next. A Kabbalist, however, can only give no significance to reward, striving instead to find Truth. Granted, there are very few such people, but the numbers increase significantly with each passing generation. There are cases where one comes to a certain point in one's quest for Truth, and then gradually loses interest. The reason for that will be explained in further detail in the study of reincarnation.

All the worlds (this world included) are states that reside within us. We will find them nowhere outside us. In other words, it is not we who are inside the worlds, but the worlds that are inside us. Outside us there is only the Creator, the Upper Light.

People in our world are convinced that they are inside some kind of existence, a reality that was created before we came inside it. But this is an illusion. There is nothing outside us but the Light of the Creator. That Light affects our senses in such a way that we feel it as solid, liquid, or gas, as vegetative or as animate. Everything we can imagine and can see around us is built inside our own senses, making us feel as though everything exists outside us. But the truth is that there is nothing outside, only the Creator.

This world is the lowest point that a Kabbalist attains. It is the total opposite of the Creator and is termed, "the exile in Egypt." The natural power that works on us in that state, the power of our egoistic nature, doesn't allow us to advance anywhere except to care for ourselves. This is called "the state of Pharaoh."

Our egoism doesn't let us feel the sublime and perfect state. It is egoism, man's inner and vicious force called "Pharaoh," that the Torah speaks of at length, whereas the force that frees one of that state is called "Moses." Pharaoh, Moses and everything that is written about the exodus describe spiritual states and emotions.

Our current state is the lowest possible. It is a state of absolute slumber and even unconsciousness. We have no sensation whatsoever of who or where we are. It is even a lower state than "this world," since defining our state as "this world" implies that we are already aware that there is another world. It is so low that we cannot feel any spirituality.

The Torah is not a historic epic, though there is a correlation between the text and human history. But this is only because the construction of the worlds is based on the same principle: everything that happens in one spiritual world is reflected in its adjacent lower world, down to our own.

Everything that humankind will have to go through during its ascent through the worlds must be felt by each and every individual in each of the worlds, especially our own. Our ascent in this world is done while in our current state and with our egoistic substance of this world.

There is a law for the spiritual nature that states that, "Every spiritual root must touch a corporeal branch." This means that every spiritual origin and spiritual force must hang down and build its final corporeal manifestation in our world.

For instance, there is a negative force in the world of *Atzilut* named Pharaoh and a positive one named Moses. These forces must materialize at least once in our world. In principle, everything that happened or that is happening in the spiritual world has already happened in ours, everything except the coming of the Messiah and our ascent and exit from this world to the spiritual world. This is all that still awaits us. But the times to come before the ascent are also the hardest, darkest, and most painful.

When we "work on ourselves" with Kabbalah, we enter a state called "the exile in Egypt." During this process, we feel that we are becoming less virtuous, that we were better before we began our studies. This is incorrect; it is through our studies that we discover our true nature. As we continue to study and be influenced by the Light and our correct study of Kabbalah, we develop a strong desire to cross this barrier and enter the spiritual world. We long to resemble the Creator, even in the smallest manner.

CHAPTER 1.6
LANDMARKS

We might be amazed to find along our spiritual paths that not only are we not evolving, but we have come to a halt, or are even retreating. We will find that our chances to enter the spiritual are rapidly dimming. But it is at that precise stage when we feel our inability to cope with the obstructions that we are making our most impressive progress.

If we only stop for a moment, we will see that we are actually advancing more rapidly. However, we are trying to measure our progress with senses that are just beginning to evolve. Any correction and change that we perform brings us closer to acquiring the aim to bestow. But for that we need to go through a great many changes. We must discover what our "self" really is and what it wants from us, what "the will to receive" means, the discovery of the substance of Creation, and the meaning of life and death.

We come to the conclusion that life means feeling the Light, and death is the sensation of darkness, the absence of the sensation of the Creator. We go through many different situations until we know the true meaning of "good" and "bad."

A barrier is a curtain that hides the Light from our world. How is a barrier different from the screen? The nature of the screen is completely different than that of a barrier, in that the entire Light stands before the screen and nothing hides it but man, who rejects it with the power of his desire to not receive for self-gratification.

The barrier, unlike the screen, stands outside us, covering the Upper Light. The screen is something we erect inside us from our understanding and consciousness of the desire to resist the egoistic reception of the Light, prevent it from entering us in an egoistic form. If we do let the Light in, we want our objective to be to give to the Creator. When there is a screen, there is no need for the curtain, because the screen can resist the Light.

THE DIVISION OF THE 125 DEGREES
THAT CONSTITUTE OUR WAY

There are 125 degrees of attainment between our world and the world Ein Sof. But all we need for our correction is to reach the world of Atzilut, meaning the end of the Second Restriction. We have to cross the worlds of Assiya, Yetzira, and Beria, each consisting of 2,000 years (states, degrees). Thus, the sum total of the corrections we have to go through is 6,000, after which we enter the corrections that belong to the First Restriction.

Our souls consist of five parts: Keter, Hochma, Bina, Zeir Anpin, and Malchut. They are divided by the intensity of their will to receive, and form two groups: *Galgalta* and *Eynaim* (*Keter* and *Hochma*), and *Awzen, Hotem, Peh* (*Bina, Zeir Anpin,* and *Malchut*). *Keter* is called *Galgalta* (skull), *Hochma* (wisdom) is called *Eynaim* (eyes), *Bina* (intelligence) is called *Awzen, Zeir Anpin* is called *Hotem* (nose), and *Malchut* (kingship) is called *Peh* (mouth). The structure of all souls is identical: the first part of the soul enjoys giving, while the second enjoys receiving.

We should only concern ourselves with correcting our *Galgalta* and *Eynaim* (GE), our vessels of bestowal, the desires to give. Our spiritual path begins with an ascent above our world. An ascent is a gradual correction of our *Galgalta* and *Eynaim*. By ascending to the world of *Atzilut*, we confirm that our vessels of bestowal are corrected. We cannot correct our vessels of reception.

So what can we do? We can gradually raise our vessels of reception (AHP) from the worlds of BYA to the world of *Atzilut*. We first raise the AHP from the world of *Beria*, which is the AHP with the least amount of egoism. After that we raise the AHP from the world of *Yetzira*, which are more egoistic, and finally we raise the AHP from the world of *Assiya*, the most egoistic of all vessels. We don't actually correct the vessels/desires, only connect them with their corresponding GE, and combine them with the altruistic desires.

After every correction we receive more Light. The correction is called an "ascent." There is an ascent from each of the places of the worlds of *Beria, Yetzira,* and *Assiya*. The AHP that rise to the world of *Atzilut* are not "real" desires to receive (vessels of reception), they are not our "self," our "stony heart." We are incapable of correcting that part. The only part we can correct is a small portion called AHP *de Aliyah* (raised AHP). But no greater correction is needed. As soon as this correction is made, the Creator Himself will correct the stony heart.

In order for us to know what we must correct, we have to see and feel what it is that needs correction. For that there are ascents and descents that do not depend on us, called "an awakening from Above." These are the holidays, the Shabbat (Saturday, the seventh day of the week), and the beginnings of the month. They are given to us only because we have already corrected our vessels of bestowal, want nothing for ourselves, and are already in the world of *Atzilut.*

The first act—the ascent—will be the joining of the *AHP de Aliyah* of the world of *Beria*; the second will occur by adding the *AHP* of the world of *Yetzira*; and the third will be the adding of the *AHP* of the world of *Assiya.* When a person has already ascended these three degrees, the stony heart is corrected, constituting the End of Correction.

We can feel pleasure either from receiving or from giving. The pleasure from giving is felt in the vessels of bestowal, while the pleasure from receiving is felt in the vessels of reception. But both types of vessels are corrupted in us.

The easiest to correct are the vessels of bestowal. We correct these by giving not for our own pleasure, but to please the receiver. These vessels are easier to correct because the act (giving) and the purpose (for another) are in the same direction.

The vessels of reception allow us to enjoy only when we receive. They are much more difficult to correct because we have to please another by receiving. This demands a much tighter connection with the Creator because receiving runs through the core of the "self," the human ego.

For that reason, the *AHP* are corrected gradually, following the correction of *Galgalta* and *Eynaim.* Thus, it is not as difficult to ascend to the world of *Atzilut* with vessels of corrected *GE*, as it is to add the *AHP* to them, because the correction of the *AHP* contradicts the aim.

All five worlds are like curtains hiding the Light of the Creator. The lower the world, the more it covers the Light. The worlds/screens end at the barrier, which hides the Light completely from our world. Only a tiny spark called "Minute Light" enters our world. It is just enough to sustain life on earth. The Creator made it so we could live without a screen. In the absence of Light and having only a minute amount of Light, there is no necessity for a screen.

That feeble Light is divided into many particles. It turns the atoms, moves the molecules, creates every substance, and urges it towards development and growth. It revives every degree of existence, the still, vegetative, animate, and speaking—our own degree.

And if we acquire a screen over even the smallest will to receive, through our studies, our groups, and our teachers—a screen over root coarseness—then we are already able to resist the dimmest Light—the Light of *Nefesh*, that however small, is still far greater than the "Minute Light." At that point, we are able to stay in that Light without receiving it for ourselves. The screen, in that case, functions like the barrier—the transition from this world to the spiritual world.

For example: if we have been taught not to steal and someone puts a $100 bill before us, we will not steal it. But the minute we face the temptation of a larger sum than the sum we'd been taught not to steal, we will not be able to resist; all our previous education will be insufficient to resist that amount.

The same applies to spirituality: where there is the Light of *Nefesh*, we work for the Creator without any difficulty, feel Him, maintain contact with Him, and enjoy ourselves because we want to please Him. We have a sufficient screen for this degree that protects us from receiving for ourselves. That state is called "the world of *Assiya*."

Then, as a result of our studies and the additional efforts we make, we acquire a screen over a greater amount of egoism, that of *Aviut Aleph* (first degree of coarseness) and can now receive the Light of *Ruach* in order to bestow. Accordingly, we have protection against stealing a larger sum of money, say $1000. In such a case, we pass from the world of *Assiya* to the world of *Yetzira*. In the same way, when acquiring a screen for the second degree of coarseness, we ascend from *Yetzira* to *Beria*.

By passing from one world to the next, the curtain falls off the previous world and instead we place over it a screen that suits the coarseness of that world. The screen that covered the higher world moves into the vessel and the higher world appears. When that happens, we are able to keep the law of the world we are in, and therefore do not need the law. We rise above it and keep it of our own conscious will.

Since our souls consist of five parts, we must acquire five separate screens in ascending degrees of power, according to the coarseness of the egoism. We cross the barrier when we acquire a screen of root coarseness and attain the spiritual degree of the world of *Assiya*.

A screen for first degree coarseness raises us to the degree of the world of *Yetzira*. A screen for second degree coarseness raises us to the degree of the world of *Beria*. A screen for third degree coarseness raises us to the degree of the world of *Atzilut*. And finally, a screen for fourth degree coarseness raises us to the degree of the world of *Adam Kadmon*.

Above *Adam Kadmon*, the soul ascends to the world of *Ein Sof*. There are five *Partzufim* in every world, comprised of five *Sefirot*. Each time a person acquires five new *Sefirot*, he acquires a new degree, a new *Partzuf*. If it is in the world of *Assiya*, the first five *Sefirot* give us the ability to attain the *Partzuf* of *Malchut* of the world of *Assiya*. The next five *Sefirot* raise us to *Partzuf Zeir Anpin* of the world of *Assiya*. Five more *Sefirot* and we come to *Partzuf Bina* of *Assiya*, five more and we are in *Partzuf Hochma* of *Assiya*, and the last five *Sefirot* render us *Partzuf Keter* of the world of *Assiya*.

In this way, the soul acquires the screens in the root coarseness of the world of *Assiya* and goes over to the first screen of the first degree of coarseness of the world of *Yetzira*. The soul continues this way until it crosses all the worlds and all 125 degrees.

When we are in the world of *Assiya* with our root coarseness, our soul evolves through a number of degrees like a fetus in its mother's womb (*Bina*). The conception lasts nine months, the same time it takes for a woman to give birth in our world.

The birth of the soul is the transition from root to first degree coarseness, from the world of *Assiya* to the world of *Yetzira*, which corresponds to the birth of a baby in our world. In the world of *Beria*, the soul undergoes a two-year phase of "suckling," during which the soul evolves and receives Light that gradually increases its screen.

But in the world of *Beria*, the soul is still in a state of *Katnut* (meaning it only has vessels of GE). Beyond the world of *Atzilut* begins the gradual process of the growth of the soul, the acquisition of the vessels of *AHP*. Growth continues until the age of thirteen, the *Bar Mitzvah* age. At this stage the soul becomes independent in *Atzilut*, and has the screens with which it can commence receiving in order to bestow by adding the vessels of reception denominated *AHP de Aliyah*.

There are two *Partzufim* called *Zeir Anpin* and *Nukva* (*Malchut*) in the world of *Atzilut*. They relate to one another in various ways, depending on whether the soul is in *Katnut* (smallness) or in *Gadlut* (greatness). These states are called *Zivug* (spiritual mating).

The term, *Eretz* (land) in the spiritual world refers to where you are or the place you are headed. The word, *Eretz* comes from the word, *Ratzon* (desire). Our souls consist of one big desire (*Eretz*) with many smaller "lands" inside them. There are desires called the "nations of the world" or "abroad" and there is the Land of Israel, which is the closest desire to the Creator. The neighbors of this *Eretz*—Jordan, Egypt, and Syria—want the Land of Israel because that is where the Creator can be found.

The correction process begins with the finest desires, called "Israel" or *Galgalta* and *Eynaim*. On the one hand, they are the closest desires to the Creator, but on the other, they are the farthest. This is because of the law of the oppositeness between Lights and vessels.

For us to return to the Creator, we must be the greatest egoists, because we must feel that there is something very important missing in our lives. On the one hand, egoistic vessels are far from the Creator, but on the other hand, when we invert our intentions, we will become the closest to Him.

When we begin to study Kabbalah, we slowly learn to sort out our desires in order of coarseness. When the sorting is done, we determine which of our desires we can begin to correct. When we begin the work with our desires, we begin to see where we are on the spiritual map.

CHAPTER 1.7
FROM ABOVE TO BELOW

The study of the Kabbalah focuses on studying the structure of the worlds as they evolve from Above down to our world. One would think that since we are in the corporeal world, we would be taught how to climb along the spiritual path from below upward, not the other way around.

But the truth is that it is the exact path that the Kabbalists write about. A Kabbalist is a person who lives in our world but has attained spirituality from below upward. None of the writings of Kabbalists speak of a person who hasn't attained spirituality.

Our purpose is to build an additional sensory instrument with which to feel the spiritual world and the Creator. That is how it was done before and that is what Kabbalists describe. There is no other revelation of the Creator to man. We can feel the spiritual world and the Creator only by changing ourselves. That is what we can write about and convey to others.

The First Man wrote about his attainments. Abraham the Patriarch followed in his footsteps, which in turn was followed by Moses, who named his attainments of the Creator and Creation, "Torah." The Kabbalists that followed wrote about their feelings and attainments in additional books, the Mishnah, the Talmud and so on. Every Kabbalist describes our world and how to enter the spiritual world. We call these books, "Holy Books," or "Torah," from the Hebrew word *Ohr* (light) and *Hora'a* (instruction), meaning instructions for entering the spiritual world.

These books didn't arrive "out of the blue." They were not carved in stone by an Upper Power and were not written by the Creator on papyrus. There was always a Kabbalist who sat down and put spiritual research on paper. That research is done from below (our world) upward.

The fact is, the ascent from below upward is personal and differs from one person to another. There are certainly common methods, general rules, degrees and phases in the ascent, but though the ways are common to all, each person experiences them differently. The spiritual world is attained from below upward. But in order for this instruction to be suitable for everyone, Kabbalists wrote it from Above downward, not from below. It is actually the same road, but when looking from Above, it is described in more general terms, more uniform.

Light descends from the Creator, building five worlds on its way down—*Adam Kadmon, Atzilut, Beria, Yetzira,* and *Assiya.* Below the world of *Assiya* there is the barrier—a partition that separates this world from the spiritual worlds. There is another partition between the world of *Atzilut* and the worlds below it. It is called *Parsa.* Between the world of *Ein Sof* and the world of *Atzilut,* there is the restriction.

Thus, from the highest state—the world of *Ein Sof*—down to the lowest, where we are, there are five worlds—*Adam Kadmon, Atzilut, Beria, Yetzira, Assiya,* each consisting of five *Partzufim* and each *Partzuf* of five *Sefirot.* In total, the number of degrees that stand between our (necessary) future state and our present state is 125.

These degrees are not carved in stone, but are inside us. They are degrees of internal spiritual development. When we change something inside us, we ascend by one degree. When we change another, we climb another degree and so on. All the degrees are levels of equivalence with the Creator.

The world of *Ein Sof* is in complete equivalence of form with the Creator, while our world is in complete oppositeness. The degrees between our world and the world of *Ein Sof* are measurements of equivalence of man with the Creator, phases of closeness to the Creator.

The goal that the Creator set for us is that while being in this world, we will work on ourselves and gradually correct our inner properties, so that while we are in our worldly bodies, we will be in the world of *Ein Sof* in our inner soul, our inner properties.

This means that we must resemble the Creator while living in this world. Until we accomplish that, we will keep returning until we suc-

PART ONE: THE BEGINNING

ceed. We will have no choice, and will be pushed to do it. This is true for each and every person. This helps to explain why we are often confronted with pressures and unpleasant situations. These are to make us understand that there is a reason for the anguish, that the suffering is not meaningless, and that the Creator wants to do something with humanity.

CHAPTER 1.8
CAUSE AND CONSEQUENCE

Our lives are really learning experiences. Sometimes the world appears so dark and bitter that we think the end of the world has come and there is no way out. But as we continue to study, we see it isn't so, that these are only exercises sent from Above. Only after they are over can we understand and appreciate the necessity for those exercises while in our "pre-correction" phase.

For that reason, we should endure as long as we can and stick with the purpose of our progress without losing our heads. If we are given situations when we feel we are in the middle of a fire and there is nothing we can do to save ourselves, it is only to show us once again that we are not running the show.

There is no way around these situations, but they can be made much shorter and less painful. To do so, we need to join a group of students who work together, to read and to study. We must follow the verse, "Whatsoever thy hand attaineth to do by thy strength, that do" (*Ecclesiastes* 9:10).

How does one who is concerned with doing inner work deal with one's surroundings? Is the person's environment supportive of this quest?

Sometimes, situations at work or at home make us feel hostile to the apparent source of the troubles. Then we quarrel, blaming the boss, our colleagues, spouse, children, and so on. We feel trapped and angry, and think we can't go on. But afterwards we realize that all this was given to us from Above in order to experience a certain series of emotions.

37

We realize that we were the ones who exaggerated and misperceived the problem. Eventually, it is resolved, but soon a new situation will arise. The sooner we escape these situations and tell our group about it, the better it is for us. The worst thing is to remain immersed in the situation, drowning in our own emotions.

When we feel good, we should remember that there were bad situations in our lives and relate to them as cause and consequence, as good that comes after the bad. This brings us closer to completeness and eternity.

We begin to look at things as opposite sides of the same coin; we cannot have one without the other. Then, evil can also be accepted as good, because it is only in our corrupted vessels (emotions) that we feel evil as dark. If our vessels were corrected (in order to bestow) we would perceive both good (Light) and bad (dark) as Light.

As long as our natural attributes (pride, greed, and desires for power and sex) don't disturb us, as long we are not ashamed of them and don't understand that they are, in fact, the barrier between us and spiritual progress, these attributes will not perform the tasks for which they were created. We will have no choice but to be ashamed of what we have inside, and understand that until a Force comes from Above that enables us to own our desires, we will not be happy. The important thing is to focus our desires in the right direction. There is not a single negative attribute in us. Only the way we use these desires can be negative.

When we face certain situations in life, the first thing we need to say to ourselves is, "Look what the Creator is doing with me." That will maintain our connection with the Creator, meaning with the One who is really creating these situations. If we can hold onto that thought, the connection will not let us fall back to a lower degree. A fall is when the Creator disappears from our feelings. In that case, we can connect with a book or connect with the group. Within a short time, we will feel a change for the better.

However, every situation should be taken as an ascent to the next degree. If the time has come for the soul to correct, there is no escaping. Any attempt to do so will only make the pain worse.

All we can feel before we cross the barrier are beastly desires. As we approach the barrier, while in it and across it, we discover the desires of the Creator. In none of those desires will we find man. The only desire in which we have free choice is that of agreement with the Creator's Providence.

The soul of *Adam ha Rishon* (The First Man) broke into 600,000 parts that are interconnected, but have a different coarseness, from the root to the fourth degree. From us to the Creator there are 6,000 degrees/years.

In the first two millennia, the root degree souls were corrected. All they had to do was simply live a little in this world and endure some suffering (wild animals, enemies, famine etc.). For them, attempting to escape the pain was enough to correct the root degree coarseness.

In the third and fourth millennia, the first degree coarseness was corrected in the souls. Then came the second and the third coarseness degrees. (At the end of the sixth millennium (our time) the time had come to correct the souls with the fourth degree of coarseness.

This is a very general description. But today, we are nearing the conclusion of the sixth millennium, and the time of the spiritual redemption begins, the time of the coming of the Messiah.

CHAPTER 1.9
WHAT EXISTS BETWEEN THIS WORLD AND THE NEXT?

It is quite possible that there are other worlds that exist in the same space as ours that we simply don't make contact with because these worlds are in a different dimension. But if we remain confined to the boundaries of our own nature, we will never be able to discover them. These other worlds are where our roots are, the reasons for everything that happens in our world. There we will find the reasons for our own life and death.

There are some among us who succeeded in acquiring a new sense—one that imparts the ability to feel a broader reality than we generally see. The expansion of the limits of their senses allows them to skip the boundaries of time and see everything that happened before they were born and what will happen when they are gone.

These people can remain outside the bounds of their normal emotions and see the general and real picture of Creation. They are able to connect causes and their consequences, while the rest of us are able to see no more than a tiny part of this reality. We cannot see the reasons for what happens to us, let alone the consequences of our actions.

Although such people are just as human as we are, they have succeeded in developing additional sensory organs. They are called "Kabbalists" because they are able to receive the Upper Knowledge, eternal pleasure, and the force of the Creator. The method that allows them to move beyond the boundaries of our nature and its limitations is called "the wisdom of Kabbalah."

Such wisdom reveals how any person can understand the reality beyond our world and perceive the actual reality, the seemingly external one. Kabbalah is called "the wisdom of the hidden" because this wisdom is hidden to everyone who is confined to the framework of our five senses.

This method enables us to receive additional desires to the ones we are born with, and in them receive the actual sensation of reality. Although this method is complex, serious, and profound, it is one that anyone can understand and use.

Furthermore, Kabbalists claim that until we attain the real sensation of our existence and reach beyond the boundaries of our physical world, we will have to be reborn into this world over and over again.

Kabbalists live and feel our world and the spiritual world at the same time, and pass their knowledge and insights on to us. They say that there are many other worlds besides our own. These worlds are like circles that surround one another. Our world is at the innermost circle. We call this tiny circle our "universe."

Each of the circles is a world in itself. There are five circles altogether, or five "worlds." Each circle can sense itself and the lower ones, but not the upper ones. For that reason we, who are in the lowest circle, can feel only our own world. But if some of us can ascend with our senses to the spiritual world, to a higher circle, we become able to feel that world, as well as the worlds below it.

Thus, Kabbalists live in several worlds at once, and are therefore aware of all the reasons for and the consequences of the events in our world. With the wisdom of Kabbalah and their additional sensory organs, such people begin to perceive the broader picture through every feeling. Their thoughts and acts become clear because they discover their origin, their spiritual roots.

We can see a wider picture of reality in every new degree, which we call "this world," or "my world," because it becomes "our world." Our "next world" is what we have yet to attain, meaning the segment of the picture to be discovered in the next spiritual degree. The name, "next world," indicates that this is the picture we will see in the next degree, which might be in the next instant.

The way to enter the spiritual world and understand it clearly is based on a single spiritual attribute: because there are no boundaries in the spiritual world, the difference between spiritual objects is measured in attributes. If two objects are identical in every property, they unite and become one. Thus, the spiritual world is a world of attributes and desires. The separation or unity of two spiritual objects/desires is measured by the degree to which they are identical.

The spiritual sphere is not a physical one, but one of desires, the highest being that of the Creator, and the lowest, its total opposite. There are five principal spiritual degrees between these opposing desires, called "worlds." We can traverse them according to the changes in our attributes and desires. When our desires become identical with those of a certain spiritual degree, we immediately bond with that degree on a feeling level.

We are born in the lowest spiritual degree, one of absolute egoistic desires, called "this world." But our goal is to climb all the spiritual degrees of the worlds and bond with the attributes of the Creator, the highest spiritual degree, while living in our physical, corporeal bodies. Thus, after having equalized in form with the Creator, we will contain all the worlds and desires within us. Indeed, the purpose of Creation is to be like the Creator.

Much as in the Upper World, we, too, feel what happens "outside us" by the principle of equivalence of attributes. In order to feel something external, an organ must have identical attributes to the phenomenon it feels. It is like a radio receiver where the wavelength in the radio must be the same as the wave that one wants to receive. One can only feel a transmission with an identical wavelength as that of the receiver. Thus, we only feel the environmental phenomena that correspond to our sensory systems.

Moreover, we cannot really feel anything outside us, only our responses to external influences. For example, we cannot perceive actual sounds, only the movement of our eardrums resulting from the pressure of the wave in the air that pressures our eardrum, coming from the generator of the sound.

Therefore, it is not the wave itself that we feel, but the response of our eardrums to the pressure of the wave. All our sensory organs operate by reacting to an external stimulus. In the end, we only feel ourselves.

But in order to react to an external stimulus in such a way, we must have the same properties as the stimulus. For example: a person would respond to an insult, but a mouse would not, because a mouse doesn't have the property to perceive this kind of stimulus.

Thus, if we acquire spiritual attributes, we will immediately begin to receive the spiritual forces that correspond to the acquired spiritual attributes. A person can feel the new, spiritual world only by receiving new spiritual attributes.

CHAPTER 1.10
FAITH ABOVE REASON

A ll that people want out of life is to satisfy their own needs, but when they are dissatisfied with their situations, they begin to want to reach the actual source of their situations, meaning the Creator. Our desire for the Creator is the highest degree in our desire to study the self. In order to attain this degree, one must stand face to face with one's egoism, which operates like a sophisticated obstacle between the Creator and oneself.

In order to allow people to study themselves and attain this degree, Baal HaSulam was prepared to speak to anyone, if only to have more students. He even published a paper that later on became the basis for the book, *Matan Torah* (*The Revelation of Godliness*), but there was hardly anyone who would listen. The irony of it is that in the past, there were many Kabbalist teachers but hardly any students, whereas today there are many who wish to study, but there are almost no Kabbalists.

The situation we are in today is the first in history. There is a growing need and desire from below, while at the same time we are being pushed into deeper spiritual darkness. But in fact, this is a very good situation because it means that once we have the desire for real spirituality, we will receive an immediate favorable response from Above.

The intensity of the love between a person and the Creator is determined by the agony of one's longing. The agony is a consequence of the absence of the Light from the vessel, and the longing comes from the sensation of fulfillment by the Light of the Creator when one is in adhesion with Him. Thus, if only one could collect the genuine desires for spirituality the appropriate answer would come.

The difficulty that faces people who try to break through the barrier and feel spirituality through intellectual study, is that they are undeterred by the fact that the mind is but a product of their egoistic natures. That is why they are unsuccessful in their efforts to attain spirituality with their intellects. Most beginning students of Kabbalah tend to stride that path, because it is customary to think that we can attain spirituality using our intellects.

But when one learns to go above reason, one begins to understand that the egoistic vessel is basically a desire to enjoy every kind of pleasure. The spiritual vessel, on the other hand, is initially directed at pleasing the Creator through us.

Human beings open a book, read it assiduously, and try to understand it with their intellects. But it is impossible to feel what the book speaks of through the intellect. It is impossible, with mere understanding, to cross the barrier that separates the spiritual world from our own.

All that students can do is gather around the teacher, dedicate their desires to the collective melting pot, and receive a unified desire that is dozens of times greater in return. Each member of the group must be considered a valuable force that can help us shorten our spiritual paths by dozens of worldly lifetimes.

Baal HaSulam writes in item 155 of *The Introduction to the Study of the Ten Sefirot*, that only students who delve into the same book can extract from it that for which their aching hearts yearn, and only if they understand why they want it. All of them must nullify themselves before each other. When they get together, they should always keep in mind why they are there.

Such attitudes must be formed in the very first stages of the construction of the group in order to create physical closeness. This will later lead to spiritual closeness, just as great Kabbalists have done in the past. If each and every member of the group longs to be together, and if that longing burns in each heart like a fire, then that need will soon be realized.

Our brains and even our consciousnesses are only secondary factors. They process and support the fulfillment of our desires. The mind is but an accessory. As soon as one understands that it is the feeling that should be cultivated, not the mind, one will immediately begin to see the path that leads to the spiritual world. The problem lies in our habits and our lack of trust.

We are not accustomed to relying on our feelings. We want to understand first, and only afterwards to feel and act. But if our brains are the obstacles, why then were they given to us?

They were given to us so that we would develop them and then go above them, above our reason, meaning that we must follow our feelings. The "above reason" route is based on trial and error. Everyone who starts to walk in that direction must stumble in it and rise again with one's own strength, and begin to perceive daily circumstances as assistance from Above for one's spiritual progress.

There are many forces that were created by the Creator, such as the "evil eye," slander, etc. Their one and only purpose is to teach us to control ourselves. The Golden Rule states: "Walk humbly with thy God" (*Micah* 6:8). One must hide one's goals even from one's own egoism, let alone that of others.

However, this does not mean that we should dress or act any differently than is customary where we live, or refrain from contact with people. But when around strangers, conduct only general conversations (small talk).

When Kabbalah students gather, they should not talk about their love for the Creator and for one another. This is only expressing their personal feelings and their private opinions. They should rather speak in more general terms about the greatness of the Creator, the greatness of the goal (spirituality) and the greatness of the friends in the group.

People who study Kabbalah get together with the help of Superior Forces, Forces of the Creator. They obtain a collective goal for their lives that becomes clearer and clearer every day. The only question that remains then is how to speed the attainment of that goal.

There is a very clear hierarchy between the Creator and us: we are at the bottom and the Creator is at the highest point. We must climb the rungs of that ladder from our current location to that of the Creator's.

There are different ways to ascend. One of them is called an "Awakening From Below," where, through influence from Above, we begin to want spiritual attainment and ascent. We begin to read books, join a group, and so on. There is also another way: an "Awakening From Above." That happens when the Creator Himself chooses to lift a person up.

The difference between those paths is that the "Awakening from Above" is the slow and steady ascent of our entire world, regardless of our personal ambitions. However, those who appear to have a personal desire are brought to study Kabbalah. If those people do not use what they are given, the Upper Forces begin to demand it of them. Consequently, one must take the spiritual work one is given from Above very seriously.

There is something in us called "the Stony Heart." This refers to our egoism. It can only be corrected when a Collective Light, called Messiah, comes to our world. Only that Light can correct it, but we must first crave the correction of that part of the egoism in our world. When there is such a desire, the phenomenon called "the coming of the Messiah" will occur instantly, and will deliver us forever from the torments of this world.

CHAPTER 1.11
FREEDOM OF CHOICE—TO OPERATE ABOVE NATURE

There is no point discussing freedom of choice before we acquire spiritual forces and the ability to operate above our natures. Freedom of choice is the freedom to operate against our desires. Only then can we decide freely.

The Light from the Creator created the desire for pleasure in four phases. Those phases constitute the creature. This creature then gradually begins to materialize until it enters our world, where it is shattered into a multitude of small fragments. Each fragment is called a "soul." As souls ascend to higher levels, they gradually change their attributes, using a special system that constantly moves the souls from one place to another so that they will help one another correct.

The Torah, the Kabbalah, and all the Holy Scriptures were written by people who climbed the spiritual ladder and wrote their instructions from there. Many Kabbalists climbed these steps, but there are conditions that limit the number of people permitted to write. There are only three Kabbalists who attained the final degree and were permitted to describe the system. They are Rabbi Shimon Bar-Yochay, author of *The Zohar*, the Ari, author of *The Tree of Life*, and Rabbi Yehuda Ashlag, author of *The Sulam* Commentary on the *Zohar* and *The Study of the Ten Sefirot*.

These books were all written after their authors ascended to the degree of the Creator in every property and capability. When one acquires the attributes of the Creator, one becomes free. Such a person is not limited in any way, but is above everything.

Kabbalah rarely mentions one's ascent in the degrees, though it is the most important thing for us. The books speak primarily of one's descent from the worlds Above. The descent is described in detail in the *Zohar*, in the writings of the Ari, and in *The Study of the Ten Sefirot*. We learn about the ascent from below from letters and articles that Baal Ha-Sulam and Rabash (Rav Baruch Ashlag) wrote to their students.

There seems to be a shortage of material that describes the ascent. But the reason is that the complementary material should only serve to encourage us to attain the state of "this world," and act as a springboard for the ascent to the spiritual world. Once we are in the spiritual world, the books that speak of the worlds from Above downward, their structure, the *Partzufim* and the *Sefirot*, serve as "manuals" for ascent, because the path from Above downward and from below upward is the same.

If a person who studies *The Study of the Ten Sefirot* is at a certain spiritual degree, and that person learns about the attributes of a higher degree, it makes no difference if one is studying about the concatenation of the worlds from Above or the ascent from below. The important thing is for one to study the attributes of a higher degree to know what to equalize with and then aspire to it, determine what requires correction, and so on.

A world is an empty state of the soul. Consequently, "this world" is only a concept. A world is *Malchut*, a vessel, a soul. The term, "this world" indicates that the soul is completely empty, in utter darkness.

There are only five spiritual worlds. And although "this world" is not considered a spiritual world, it is a conscious, quasi-spiritual state that precedes the entrance to the spiritual world. In such a state, a person already acknowledges one's insignificance with regard to the spiritual world.

It is most important for us to push ourselves from our current state to the state of "this world," our descent to the state of Egypt. The acute sensation of that state is called "the exile in Egypt." Then we will push ourselves into the spiritual world. Once in spirituality, our troubles are over because we will have the Creator to guide us.

At that stage, we will already have a close connection with the Upper Force; we will be in close contact with it and connect with it as we connect with each other in this world. All the questions of this world disappear instantly the minute we cross over to the spiritual world.

Each degree poses new questions. The answers to those questions come in the form of knowledge and strength. The problems of this world disappear once a person attains the first spiritual degree. It is written: "One's soul shall teach him." This means that the soul teaches us how to advance. From that point on there is no darkness; we have a "map" to guide us in this new "spiritual country."

The word *Olam* (world) comes from the word, *Ha'alama* (concealment). It means "the inner state of the soul." There is nothing in reality except the soul, the "self," and the Creator. Everything that we perceive as real is only a reflection of the corruption of our attributes on our senses. If our attributes were corrected, we would feel nothing but pure Light filling the vessel. This is the state of *Ein Sof* (infinity).

A world is a transition phase, when the soul is only partially corrected. The soul perceives the Creator according to its measure of correction. Its corruption makes it feel that there is something that can go against the Creator. This apparent "power" or "influence" is called the *Sitra Achra* (Other Side). In such a state, the soul is seemingly trapped between two forces—pure and impure. This state is called *Olam*, meaning "concealment."

It occurs when the Creator is only partially revealed. This partial revelation is necessary because there cannot be a sensation of concealment if there is not some disclosure. There is no way to know you're in the dark without knowing there is Light.

The greater the disclosure, the greater the sensation of the Creator; the greater the concealment, the greater the sensation of the *Sitra Achra*. If the Creator is totally concealed in our world, then all our forces turn against Him. The truth is that the impure forces in our world are very weak compared to the impure forces in spirituality. Our egoism, our evil force, is tiny. The higher we climb and the greater the disclosure of the Creator becomes, so grow the forces that oppose the Creator.

These dark forces continue all the way from this world through the world of *Atzilut*. The Pure Forces (the Creator) and the impure forces (the *Sitra Achra*) remain parallel throughout the climb from bottom to top.

CHAPTER 1.12
QUESTIONS & ANSWERS

Question: Why study Kabbalah?

Answer: To answer that, we must read not only the explanations of the Kabbalists regarding the Upper Worlds, but also the connection between the Upper World and ours.

There seem to be two separate parts to Kabbalah: the first speaks of the creation of the creatures as a consequence of the thought of the Creator (the Thought of Creation) and the evolution of the worlds. The Thought of Creation relates to the emanation of the Light from the Creator, the only power existing in the world. That Light builds a vessel for itself, a will to receive, that wants to take pleasure in the Light.

The relationship between the Light and the vessel constitutes the basis for the entire Creation. The only thing that was actually created is the vessel, and the Light keeps working on it, changing it in order to bring it to the best possible state.

Why, then, did the Creator not build a complete vessel to begin with? Because in order to be in a perfect state, we must first feel that state, and feeling it is only possible if we experience the complete opposite, the most incomplete state.

Thus, each creature consists of two parts: The first is a descent, an estrangement from completeness, from the Creator. It is the lowest possible state, which is our world. But here in our world is where we find the best conditions for attaining the purpose of Creation. If we are created with the worst possible properties, the complete opposite of the Creator, then with a little bit of free choice, and with the help of the wisdom of Kabbalah, we will begin the ascent in the exact degrees by which our souls descended.

We will continue to explain which, if any, freedom of choice we actually have, how to use it, and who possesses it. We will see that we are all servants of our own egoism and that only the Kabbalists who climb the spiritual degrees have real freedom. Furthermore, the more they correct themselves, the greater is their capability to lead the world.

We learn about the descent of the Light from the Creator down to our world in *The Study of the Ten Sefirot*, in the *Zohar*, and in the writings of the Ari. The other part of Kabbalah, which talks about our ascent from our world back to the degree of the Creator, is described quite vaguely in the books. This work is called the "work of God," a work by which we equalize our form (properties) with those of the Creator.

Q: Is Kabbalah the only way to feel the Creator, and if so, how can that be proven?

A: Yes, it is. Start studying and you will see that there is nothing as logical or scientific that provides a fuller picture of our world, and places all the sciences and other "wisdoms" in their place. There is nothing more realistic than Kabbalah. Thus, now that science has reached a dead end, the only true wisdom of Creation appears from Above. That is why Kabbalah is referred to as "the wisdom of truth."

Q: Will Kabbalah save the world?

A: The *Zohar* states precisely that this is so. What is Kabbalah? It is a spiritual force that rules our world. We will attain correction only if we draw the force down here for that purpose.

Q: Certain mystical things are, in fact, a kind of drug that people try in order to escape their problems. Drug addicts are normally very quiet people, but the entire world seems to be against them. Why?

A: The reason is that drugs cut a person completely off from the purpose of life. They prevent us from reaching our destination. When people take drugs, they completely deny their existence in this world, are cut off from it, from the very place they were put by the Creator. The Creator wants to lead every person in a unique way, and drugs detach them from it. There are many questions involved in this issue. For example: if this is so, why then does the Creator place these choices in our hands?

There is another question: why do we have the ability to rid ourselves of problems through ordinary medicine, instead of resolving our problems only through Kabbalah? But because there is a purpose to our being here, drugs and other elements that detach people from the purpose of Creation will never be accepted by mankind.

SPIRITUAL EVOLUTION

Q: What are the situations one goes through during one's spiritual evolution?

A: The Creator created the creature in only one state, called *Ein Sof* (No End, Infinity). That state exists forever in the same form. The creature merges perfectly with the Creator in that state. However, from the perspective of the creatures, meaning from the point of view of the creatures' feelings, that state discloses itself as a gradual process, consisting of a beginning, middle, and end.

The beginning is considered the existence of that state at the moment of Creation. The intermediate situation is the concealment of the Creator, and the final, the complete disclosure of the Creator before the creatures. Those situations are numbered respectively as 1, 2, and 3.

In situations No. 1 and 3, there is no room for any appearance of evil. The absolute good prevails as the sole attribute of the Creator with regard to the creatures. In the second state, the creatures feel there is evil, although it is, in fact, only disguised good.

The good appears gradually in the intermediate state, but not through the revelation of additional good, but quite the contrary, through the revelation of greater evil than before, its rejection, and the discovery of the good that actually stands behind it. That system is applied because the revelation of the ultimate good is possible only through the discovery of the lowness and harm of evil.

Q: What are the degrees of one's spiritual development?

A: A person's spirituality evolves through the (spiritual) degrees of still, vegetative, animate, and speaking.

1. Still: the desire for physical pleasures, such as food and sex.

2. Vegetative: the desire for money and wealth.

3. Animate: the desire for respect and power.

4. Speaking: the desire for science, self-awareness, and learning about the surrounding world.

5. The spiritual: the degree where the desire for spirituality appears. In fact, this is no longer a degree, but a "meta-degree," as the object of desire is outside this world.

Q: How is progress in spirituality expressed?

A: Spiritual progress consists of being in two opposite situations: right and left intermittently. It is as though we walk on two legs, stepping on our right leg and then on our left. Each step provides us with further knowledge and faith. (In Hebrew, the word, *Raglaim*, means legs, but it also comes from the same root as the word, "spy," meaning one who provides information).

Q: What does the degree of one's spiritual attainment depend on?

A: The degree of one's spiritual attainment depends on one thing only: the willingness to endure in order to achieve one's goal. There are no shortcuts.

Q: How can I change my current spiritual degree, and what happens with my soul afterwards?

A: Regardless of the name you give it—Creation, Soul, Man—the preliminary state is always uncorrected. The soul must be corrected by itself and ultimately attain the spiritual degree at the end of correction. Imagine a state where you have a broken tool that you are supposed to work with. The first thing you'd do is fix it. Only afterwards would you be able to use it. The Torah explains exactly how to fix that broken vessel, which is the soul we received from the Creator.

During the process of correction, one lives in two worlds, the Upper and the lower, where the soul obtains the knowledge and the experience necessary for its advancement. Most important, one begins to feel new feelings and obtain different spiritual attributes. When the process of correction is complete, the person is equipped with spiritual properties for entering and remaining in the Upper World in a state of calmness, eternity, completeness, and peace.

That spiritual degree (at the end of correction) is not described anywhere in Kabbalah or the Torah, simply because there is no language with which to describe it. Beyond the end of correction is a realm that is not described anywhere. It is there that we find the secrets of Torah.

There are subtle hints of this in the *Zohar* and in the Talmud. That spiritual state is called *Maase Merkava* and *Maase Bereshit*. But those are all very subtle hints. It is actually impossible to describe these spiritual feelings in words because the words and the letters in our language are valid only in the correction zone (until the world of *Atzilut*), since that is from where they are taken. We cannot feel anything above the system of correction, and therefore cannot describe those feelings in words or define it in terms and concepts that we understand.

The first verse in the Torah speaks of heaven and earth. The two terms relate to two properties: an egoistic and an altruistic property. The egoistic property of "earth" (the soul) is corrected through the altruistic property of "heaven." The entire process of correction is performed in seven spiritual degrees called "seven days."

Of course, this does not refer to our earthly days, nor does the text relate to earthly nights and days, or Light and darkness as we normally interpret them. The terms relate to spiritual degrees, spiritual sensations that one feels when one experiences the phases of correction. It is a system that corrects our souls when they are still in an earthly spiritual degree.

The soul must be raised from the degree of *Malchut* to that of *Bina*, meaning the egoistic trait of *Malchut* must be turned into the altruistic trait of *Bina*. That process occurs through seven gradual corrections called the "seven days of the week."

Q: Will everyone eventually have to come to Kabbalah?

A: Absolutely, if not in this life, in the next, so why wait? Our lives are not sweet enough for us to keep returning here.

Q: What is the reason for suffering?

A: Suffering exposes the lowness of our situation. It forces us to look for a solution, grow smarter and reassess the situation. A person who has everything seeks for nothing. At that point, pains come and turn the apparent fulfillment into emptiness and hunger. We grow wiser as a result of suffering, which begins to show us where to go and what to do with our lives. But if the same result can be reached without the pain, then why suffer?

Kabbalah points to how we can approach the Creator through the keeping of the spiritual laws. It is what we call the "path of Torah." It is not a physical keeping of Mitzvot, but keeping the spiritual laws of Creation. All we have to do is to choose it.

Q: What do I do if I feel that a certain situation is being forced on me?

A: There are clear rules with regard to that situation: if someone threatens you, you should react accordingly, but not in the Christian way, meaning by turning the other cheek. Never wait for the second hit. For as long as you are here in this world, you should behave according to the acceptable rules of society. Those rules are a revelation of the Creator in our world. There is no shame in matters that concern your basic livelihood. Should we be dying and need a piece of bread to survive, we will feel no shame, neither in how the Creator relates to us, nor in how we relate to the Creator.

We were created that way and it is not our fault that we must have our thousand calories a day. There is no shame in what concerns the elementary livelihood. However, as with anything beyond the necessary, shame appears automatically. Here is where one is compelled (willingly or unwillingly) to take society, family, and oneself into consideration.

The highest spiritual degree is that of reciprocal love between man and the Creator. But this can be attained only if a degree of fear precedes it. It is called "the Mitzva of fearing God." The last and highest Mitzva that is built on top of the fear is that of the love of God. One cannot exist without the other. Because we are made of a single egoistic desire that conducts and moves us, only fear can force the ego not to carry out its desires without consideration.

Q: Can a person be pushed into studying Kabbalah?

A: No. It can only be done passively. Give that person something to read and let things evolve naturally.

Q: How does the recognition of evil appear in me? Is it different in a person who has committed a crime?

A: In an ordinary criminal, the evil inclination appears as a negative desire that is not connected with anything else. But Kabbalah portrays your evil in comparison with the good. Because of that, you begin to feel your evil inclination as such.

If you speak to a murderer or a rapist, you will always find a person who thinks that what he did was just. Simply thinking that a certain person is evil is still not considered "the recognition of evil." The recognition of evil is when one sees one's *self* as evil. When comparing the self with the Creator, meaning when one can already feel the Creator to a certain extent through reading special texts that awaken the Surrounding Light, that sensation produces the recognition of evil.

People who begin to understand themselves more deeply will not become felons. They do find seemingly appalling attributes in themselves, but they regard them as obscene and wicked, and not as qualities they would like to realize. They are presented with obscenity within them as if on a screen before their eyes, but at the same time they understand that it is the Creator who plants these attributes there. Thus, they are presented with Creation as it is inside them.

Q: Is there not a paradox here? On the one hand, the Creator wants to give us delight and pleasure, but on the other He sends us pain!

A: Take Abraham, for example. We see that he did not want to go down to Egypt (symbolic of those of us who don't wish to occupy ourselves with spiritual development). He thinks: "What do I need it for? It is hard, unpleasant, and goes against my ego." A person can be pushed only by hunger, just as the famine forced Abraham to do down to Egypt. Spiritual famine, physical famine, and agony are the only things that compel one to act. That is what the Creator is waiting for.

It is said in the Torah that there is a path of Torah or a path of pain, meaning a good way or a bad way. In fact, the entire Torah and the entire wisdom of Kabbalah were given to us only so that we would advance in the good way. But if we do not follow the good way, the bad, meaning the natural way, will be our way to advance.

If we identify ourselves with the soul while in this life, then we belong to the Creator and connect to Him. If we do not identify with the soul, then we do not bond with our souls after death. If we haven't corrected even a single desire and made it equal in form with the Creator, then what makes us think that doing good or bad on earth entitles us to any spiritual ascent, just because we spent the last seventy years on earth?

Q: Is reality actually what we see around us?

A: We are captives in a picture of the universe that changes to match the changes in our inner properties. Our perception of the world changes only with the inner changes in us. But nothing really changes outside. There is only the Uniform, Simple Light around us, called The Creator. We discern only a tiny fraction of it with our senses, which we call "our world."

This means that this world is the smallest degree of the sensation of the Creator. If we intensify our senses, we will begin to feel the improved world alongside the sensation of this world, because the Creator would become more and more apparent.

These very words were repeated by Kabbalists who ascended high in the spiritual degrees, came near the Creator, and described their feelings and what they attained when they approached Him. The purpose is to enter that very Source; only then will we feel the actual reality!

Q: What is life for?

A: Life is a form of existence that has been joined with the lowest, most egoistic level of existence. It was given to us so we could try to rise from that lowly place to a state where our souls had been prior to their descent to our world. If we can attain the same state we were in before we entered our bodies, it is considered the highest and most perfect state.

Anyone who accomplishes this can be regarded as one who has fulfilled his or her role in the corporeal life. One comes to that state after quite a few lifetimes, during which some corrections had been made, with constant advances on an unconscious level. Only during the last one or two lives can spiritual progress be conscious.

We cannot tell what our role is in this world, what we should do, and within how much time. There is no fortune teller who can reveal this. Kabbalists, however, can do it, but are forbidden because that would halt one's spiritual progress. If one were to do so, that person would only go by personal calculations, which adhere to egoism. That is why Kabbalists refrain from such activities.

A spiritual path is a system of developing altruistic desires. Knowing what is going to happen in advance would be completely egoistic. That is why the term that defines spiritual progress is "faith above reason." This means that a Kabbalist can see and know everything. He can also do anything, but chooses not to, because that would ruin his progress as well as that of his students.

Do not experiment with prophecies and such; simply work on the development of altruism with faith above reason. Prophecy is forbidden precisely because it is possible (though, again, not for an ordinary person, only for a Kabbalist).

Q: Why is it that in the earlier phases of our development, when we are children, we fully realize our egoism, though our primary goal in life is to be rid of the egoism and become altruists like the Creator?

A: This is because the insatiable desires of a child for pleasure and the ability to satisfy them is like a model of the evolving human being. Egoism is a necessary phase in our evolution. It is a partial answer to the question, "Why do we need egoism if we must fight so hard to overcome it?"

Q: Why can't we feel the spiritual world just as we feel our own?

A: If we examine ourselves, we will find that we are locked in an internal scrutiny: our five sensory organs allow us to feel that there is "something" outside us. But if we had a different vision, for example, if we could see X-rays or ultra waves, we would see a completely different picture. If we were able to hear other frequencies, we would hear very different sounds. If our sense of smell and taste were different, we would feel different things.

What we feel is unquestionably a fraction of something that exists outside us, and that fraction is what we call "our world."

Contemporary science accepts the fact that our research of the world is limited by our sensations. Consequently, all our assumptions and measurements are subjective. The scientists themselves maintain that the results of their experiments depend on the experimenter, meaning they are subjective. Therefore, one cannot come to an absolute understanding of his or her environment, the reality in which that person lives.

Let us assume that there are other forms of life on other planets. And let us also assume that they have other sensory organs than our own. They would naturally feel their world in a completely different way than the way we would see it. They would define it according to their sensory organs.

REGRESSION

Q: Why must we descend to the lowest spiritual degree in order to be able to receive the attributes of the Creator? Can this process be avoided?

A: We creatures must have both the possibility and the strength to choose between two forces freely: our own egoism and the altruism of the Creator. One must be able to choose one's way independently and follow it.

In order to create that situation, the Creator must:

• Detach Himself completely from Creation, become disconnected.

• Create appropriate conditions for His Creations to discover and understand the universe.

• Allow Creation the freedom of choice.

The Creator set up these conditions in a gradual process. The problem is that as long as we have a sense of the Creator, we are not independent—we are completely subordinate to the Light. The Light influences Creation and passes on its own properties. In order for His Creations to become completely independent, the Creator must detach Himself completely from them.

In other words, only when we are devoid of any Light do we become independent of its every act. This operation, the departure of the Light from the vessel, is called "restriction."

The Torah begins with the word, *Bereshit* (In the beginning). It is the beginning of the process of the departure of the Creation from the Creator. The word, *Bereshit* stems from the word, *Bar* (outside), meaning the removal of Creation from the Creator so as to become a separate spiritual degree between Heaven and Earth.

"In the beginning, God created the heaven and the earth." Heaven is the *Sefira* of *Bina*, which consists of altruistic properties. Earth is the *Sefira* of *Malchut*, which consists of egoistic properties. Man's soul hangs between these two properties, which are the basis upon which the entire universe is built.

The Torah begins with the creation of Creation, the Upper World, and the creation of Man, the soul. But it does not speak of the end of Creation. The goal of the Torah is to guide us in this world, to show us how to ascend to the highest spiritual degree, to a state of eternal wholeness.

Q: How can mankind be so low and despicable, if God created it in His image?

A: Why did the Creator create man that small? The Creator did not create man small, but in His image. In order for mankind to attain that state through its own labor, and to equalize with the Creator, one receives a "point in the heart," the beginning of the spiritual vessel. One must then develop that point into a complete vessel through the study of Kabbalah, to the point where the vessel is able to receive the entire Light of the Creator and thus equalize with Him. Namely, our preliminary state is indeed microscopic compared to our ultimate goal, which is the equivalence with the Creator.

Q: Can one know if one is making spiritual progress?

A: Only when one begins to study Kabbalah, meaning spiritual development, do the low and egoistic desires actually appear. That is the proof that one has really begun to evolve.

Q: Can a person who has already climbed two or three degrees suddenly come to a halt, or even decline?

A: No, one cannot fall. One cannot even stop, and will continue to climb. Everything moves toward the final and best situation. It is either done by beatings from behind, meaning by nature, or in a positive way, when one is given a book and told that it is a means to accelerate one's progress. This is a way to outrun nature's beatings from behind. That is the entire difference between the path of Torah and the path of pain.

We want to use Kabbalah in such a way that the next blow will not catch us. If we succeed, then we will never fall again. We say that there are ups and downs, but those are actually only internal feelings. At one time we feel close to the Creator, and at another time we feel uncorrected and far from Him. For that reason, we define the first situation as an ascent, and the second as a descent.

However, it is only our own parts that we feel in each of the situations. Both situations belong to the same degree, the same *Partzuf*. We cannot climb a degree without tasting our situation and the lowness of our current state.

AIM

Q: What is the right aim?

A: The right aim is the single most important and most difficult thing that a person must do. It is very hard to attain the right aim, built under various influences of the Light of the Creator on one's ego.

The student gradually formulates the right aim, studies, corrects, and intensifies it. One constantly realizes that what seemed like the right aim yesterday now appears as disguised egoism. And tomorrow the student will again find that yesterday's aim was the wrong one, and so on.

Q: How do I know if my aim is right?

A: Indeed, how can we discern between wrong and right intentions? It can be done under the focused guidance of a group, a Kabbalistic teacher, and books. The group is the first and foremost power. Friends influence one another for better or for worse. The group should ultimately be comprised of people who are connected by spiritual laws from Above.

There are processes and movements in the group: apparent strangers can enter the group, and after some time they are no longer considered strangers. At the same time, people who were in the group might suddenly be pushed out, as though a centrifugal power threw them out without a reasonable explanation. They can be people who have already given everything they were supposed to give to the group. Each of us must fear being that person.

This melting pot gradually builds the condition by which any person who endures, despite the egoistic personal discomfort, will ultimately break through to the spiritual world. There is a lot of internal hard work needed here. But those who take that path begin to feel their inner changes and note how the understanding of their world changes daily. While they might recognize how they are becoming smarter than others, this is only a temporary reward.

However, there are times when the Surrounding Light leaves completely, and one cannot see the next day. The Surrounding Light should enter one's corrected vessel (one's feelings) when one corrects one's properties. That Light is what creates the sensation of tomorrow, even as it shines from afar, from the future.

A person can sometimes lose the sensation of the future altogether and become depressed, as one's mood is a result of the influence of the Light. If the Light begins to shine more brightly, then that person's face will reflect a happy grin. Kabbalists experience these feelings consciously. Their work is to try to carry on despite these situations. It is impossible to continue with their inner work when in such situations, and the only thing they can do then is to continue with a mechanical performance of whatever it is they were doing before that situation arose, such as attending classes and helping to disseminate Kabbalah.

In these situations, the brain is simply "turned off" and there is nothing one can do about it.

If these situations are a consequence of previous spiritual effort, then they are monitored by a superior *Partzuf* that a person cannot feel. That *Partzuf* is one's spiritual parent. Although we think we can do anything when we are in a good situation, or just explode when we are in a bad one, these states are all conducted from Above. They are given to us in order to show us how dependent we are on even the smallest amount of Light. That is enough for us to understand who we really are.

MISCELLANEOUS QUESTIONS & ANSWERS

Q: Can we influence the events of our lives?

A: We learn about the structure and the function of every system precisely so we can understand where and how we can intervene, and what can we change. We cannot influence our spiritual root directly; it is the Source from which we come, and we are at a lower degree, meaning our degree is derived from our root.

But through the correction, we attain equivalence of properties with our root, change how we feel about what we get from Above, and instead of feeling struck and tormented by fate, we begin to feel peace, serenity, calm, and completeness. We attain a collective understanding.

Q: What is Israel's role in the correction?

A: The Creator brought us to this world so that we, using the wisdom of Kabbalah, would discover the Upper World and lead our fate by ourselves. The people of Israel must pass the wisdom of Kabbalah to all the nations. If Israel does not bring the knowledge of the spiritual worlds to the rest of the world, the world cannot become a better and happier place.

The other peoples sense it unconsciously and express it in their hatred toward Israel. There is only one solution to all the problems: fulfill our task in this world, as this nation was chosen for precisely that purpose. We are chosen precisely in our duty to connect all the nations with the Creator. Until we do it, both sides—the Creator and the nations of the world—will continue to push us forcefully.

As time goes by, the moment of internal (spiritual) and external (physical) salvation approaches, as it is written in the *Introduction to the Book of Zohar* (items 66-71). Just as man cannot exist in our world without knowledge about it, so man's soul cannot exist in the Upper World without the necessary knowledge obtained through the wisdom of Kabbalah.

Q: We cannot talk about the thoughts of the Creator, but what makes the Creator choose one to turn towards Him?

A: It is certainly not one's virtue that brings one to this place. It is simply that the person got disconnected from the bottom part (*AHP*) of the collective soul called *Adam ha Rishon*. In such a person, there is a stronger expression of egoism, and the Light has a stronger effect, pushing the person more forcefully toward the purpose of Creation.

Q: How is the fact that one is chosen expressed?

A: One's "chosenness" is expressed in greater selfishness, and consequently, a greater sensitivity to the negative in the world. That is why, in large groups of people, there is also a great desire for the satisfaction of selfish desires, and consequently great pains.

Q: Why did the Creator create us incomplete?

A: We can claim that the Creator created us incomplete, inferior, and disabled. He lowered us into this terrible world, into horrendous circumstances in which every moment of our lives is sheer torment. But the question remains: "Why did He do it?" Kabbalah, on the other hand, poses a completely different question: "Could a perfect Creator create an imperfect Creation?"

Q: Does the Creator even know about our imperfection and the imperfection of the entire Creation?

A: We and the world we live in were created inferior for a purpose: so we could attain the degree of the Creator by ourselves, and would become like Him through our own efforts. All our intermediary states are necessary because they create in us the correct feelings to assess the perfection of the Creator, and the joy that awaits us at the end of correction.

Q: Are souls corrected in this world?

A: Every moment of our lives, whether knowingly or unknowingly, in the path of pain or in the path of Torah, our souls draw ever closer to the purpose of Creation, to the wholeness of the Creator. The worse the situation becomes, the faster we begin to understand and correct it.

Q: How can it be that the Creator created man in His image, but at the same time did not give him His primary characteristic—benevolence?

A: The contradiction between the desire of the Creator to give and that of the creature to receive in order to receive, which is Man's primary motivation for progress in our corporeal life, is one of the most difficult issues to resolve. In order to understand the Creator-creature relationship, we must understand, at least basically, the processes of creating a new life. These processes are elaborately described in the books of great Kabbalists.

If we want to delve deep into the heart of it, we can study them on our own, bit by bit, and open all the worlds, and even the logic of the Creator, that we say is missing. Naturally, the explanations that I can provide within such a limited framework are inadequate for such a complex system.

The purpose of our development is to consciously obtain the sensation of spiritual pleasure, instead of unconsciously, in various worldly forms. Only the search for transient delights, or those that shine from afar (but are much stronger), compel the spiritual body to seek perfection.

Therefore, in the case of a rapidly growing child, there are opportunities for pleasure everywhere, and the child can also continuously seek new ones. The simplest things bring joy. There is a good reason why we say that someone is "happy as a child."

Q: What is the connection between the generations and their intensity of egoism?

A: Each generation is characterized by a certain kind of soul. In earlier times, finer souls came down with only a minimal amount of egoism. But those people were virtually devoid of selfishness and hence had little incentive for development. Almost nothing happened for many centuries, but gradually, over a period of time in which the souls incarnated from one generation to the next, a process of accumulation of egoism was underway. With it came the growing desire to escape the suffering induced by it, and to feel only pleasures.

In our generation, everything is happening at a fantastic speed. We want everything this world has to offer! We no longer settle for controlling this world, we want to control the other worlds, too. But that control can only be obtained if we exit the boundaries of our world, and for that we must change our natural egoism, the engine that operates man, and invert it to altruism, thus equalizing with the Creator.

I have already said that for this we need no special talent, only an exceptionally strong desire. These strong desires fill the rougher and yet most developed souls that descend to the world in our time, and separate us from the previous generations.

Q: But the Creator created the creature in order to delight him, so why does He deny us pleasure?

A: No, it is not the Creator who denied us the pleasure. It is the creature who refused to receive it "for free." The creature was created perfect, like the Creator. The Creator cannot operate imperfectly. But the creature was so resistant to drawing far from the Creator that it refused to receive the pleasures that were offered to it.

Q: Why did the Creator give the creature the ability to refuse?

A: Because just as the Creator has freedom of choice, so He cannot deny it of the creature. In spirituality, the distance is measured not in meters, but in attributes (form). The very receiving of pleasure from the Creator without paying back creates an inevitable detachment.

Q: So who, in fact, is the creature, and what is the way to become man?

A: The creature can be defined as a sort of a collective soul, a global one. That soul refused the unilateral reception of the Light of the Creator. Because of its desire for equivalence of form, it performs a restriction (the First Restriction). It does that by creating a complete system of partitions that prevent the entrance of the Light into the spiritual vessels.

Later on, Kabbalah tells us that there was a breakage in the vessels and the Light was extinguished from the vessel. Kabbalah also tells us that after that, the collective soul was shattered, which brought it to its final state, the farthest possible one from the Creator.

In order for a person who obtains a certain part of that collective soul to start the process of correction, the Creator did the following:

1. He gave the soul an absolute will to receive, called "pride."

As a result, man stopped feeling the Creator.

2. He divided the creature into many little particles and placed them in the bodies of our world.

Q: Why are we to be corrected if, in the end, we return to the Creator, the same point from which we began?

A: The world that we perceive around us tells us more about purposelessness. In the end, the cause of every negative attribute in us and (as we think) in Him, is the Creator. But in order to understand at least something of the nature around and inside us, we must explain in detail the purpose of Creation, meaning its ultimate state. That is because the intermediary states can mislead. The Creator gave man the freedom of choice and the freedom of will to take this path to the final state, realize the purpose of Creation, and equalize with Him.

Q: What is the difference between corporeal and spiritual suffering?

A: Pain and pleasure in spirituality are a consequence of a *Zivug de Hakaa* (spiritual coupling) between the Light and the desire, using a screen. However, in our world, they are felt as the fulfillment or the absence of fulfillment of our egoistic desires. The sensation of the fulfillment or the absence of fulfillment is interpreted by us as pleasure or pain, or as good or bad.

That sensation is built into our five vessels that serve as sensors, providing a general picture of the world around us. It is that picture that determines how we relate to this world—whether good or bad, compared to what we have at our disposal.

Pain expresses the lack of pleasure at a certain degree, while at the same time it expresses a need to feel pleasure at a higher degree. For that reason, pain is a phase preceding the sensation of pleasure. In the spiritual worlds, however, there is no pain because there, this sensation is perceived as pleasure. The pain does not come as a result of a lack of pleasure, but as a result of great love. Consequently, pain is eternal and always good.

Q: If I reach a spiritual world, will I accept any pain or traumatic event as a joyful one?

A: The Torah directly tells us that anything that happens is done by the Creator, and not by anyone else. Only the Creator leads everything. It is the Creator who made all the tragedies and disasters. But why did He do it? However appalling it may sound, He did it for us. Only after we obtain spiritual attainment do we begin to understand the entire system of Creation and the calculation that brought the worst events that happened to us. We will then understand why tragedies are necessary for our existence and correction.

Unfortunately, it is the lack of understanding of the necessity for spiritual evolution that brings such tragedies upon us. This is spoken of openly in the *Zohar* and in the books of the Ari. If we do not start studying the books of Kabbalah, the wisdom that guides our spiritual evolution, we will not evolve to attain the purpose of Creation. Our people and the whole of mankind will be pushed ferociously to the realization of the necessity of spiritual development. There will be no way to escape it. That is why we place such emphasis on the circulation of the wisdom of Kabbalah, so that everyone will know and recognize its importance.

Part Two: Phases of Spiritual Evolution

CHAPTER 2.1
THE PURPOSE OF CREATION

There are five worlds between the Creator and our world: *Adam Kadmon*, *Atzilut*, *Beria*, *Yetzira* and *Assiya*. Beneath the world of *Assiya* there is the barrier and under the barrier there is our world. Our goal in this world is to attain the degree of the world of *Ein Sof* while our souls are still clothed in our corporeal bodies, thus attaining complete unification with the Creator. The properties of egoism change in every degree, according to the properties of the Creator, until finally egoism is completely replaced with altruism, and the attributes of our soul become identical to those of the Creator.

There are two properties of egoism in our world: "receiving in order to receive," and "giving (bestowing) in order to receive." The first assignment of a person who wishes to cross over to the other world is to restrict the use of one's own desires. That state is known as the "First Restriction." It means that one stops working with one's egoistic desires altogether.

We cannot change our will to receive, which is actually the only thing that the Creator created, but we can and should change the *aim* of our desire from receiving "for me" to receiving "for the Creator." Thus, the desire to feel pleasure does not change, only the aim.

For that reason, the method for changing the aim is called the "wisdom of Kabbalah," and because the aim is concealed from the eye, the wisdom of Kabbalah is also called the "wisdom of the hidden." It teaches how to receive by changing the aim. Consequently, the important thing is the aim behind every act, the purpose for which one does what one does. The 125 rungs of the ladder are degrees of gradual correction of the aim of the soul from "receiving for me" to "receiving for the Creator."

The five degrees of the will to receive, beginning with the weakest (*Keter*) and ending with the strongest (*Malchut*), are organized in descending order from the Creator to the creature, and constitute the five worlds.

When the Light of the Creator passes through the worlds, it weakens and becomes suitable for reception by weaker, altruistic desires. When the soul receives the Light of Correction from Above, it begins to change its aim from "receiving for me" to "receiving for the Creator," which is regarded as giving.

After the soul performs the First Restriction over all its desires, it reaches the "barrier." At that point, it refuses to perform any kind of work with egoism, though it is still unable to receive for the Creator.

When the soul corrects its aim to give in the degree of *Keter*, it means that it is now able to overcome its weakest egoism and can refrain from receiving anything for itself. At that point, it nullifies itself completely before the Upper Light. It is with this degree that the soul enters the world of *Assiya*, the first spiritual world above the barrier. If the soul can overcome its egoism when the Light of Wisdom shines in it, it rises to the world of *Yetzira*.

The greater the ability of the soul to resist its egoism, the higher it ascends in the spiritual degrees, until finally the soul comes to the world of *Ein Sof*. A soul is a spiritual entity that reveals its essence only past the barrier and the degrees above it.

The desires one works with in the spiritual world are bare, open; they are not clothed in the costumes of our world. A Kabbalist stops studying our world once in the spiritual world, and regards it as nothing more than a natural consequence, a branch of a spiritual root. Of more interest are studies of the reason, the root, and the beginning of every desire, not its consequences in the lowest and corrupted degree.

A person who rises to the spiritual world replaces corporeal desires with desires directed at the Creator. Just as the newly spiritual person wanted to enjoy every kind of pleasure in this world, now that person wants to enjoy the Creator in the same egoistic manner. That state is regarded as "suffering to sleep."

But through the illumination of the ever-Surrounding Light, there is a gradual increase in one's desire for spirituality, which eventually becomes greater than all other desires. Then, finally, with the help of that Light, one crosses the barrier and receives the aim to give, to bestow.

Only the Upper Light of the Creator can do such a thing to a person—answer every effort to attain spirituality and bring one to a state where the desire for spirituality becomes so intense, one cannot even sleep, overshadowing all other desires.

The process is the same for all the souls, but each soul has its own mission in this world. Each soul also has a different speed with which it makes its way to the Creator.

Every thought, every desire and every movement that we make in this world, regardless of who we are, comes with only one purpose: to bring us closer to spirituality. However, in most cases, this progress happens naturally, on the unconscious level, in the degrees of still, vegetative, and animate, in man.

Everything is planned in advance, according to the purpose of Creation. Our freedom of choice consists only of agreeing with whatever happens to us, with our understanding of where it all leads and the desire to become an active part in the events of our lives.

All the thoughts and desires of the world of *Ein Sof* pass through each and every one of us. But only those thoughts that correspond to our current degree are "captured."

Our degree of spirituality determines our range of influence and our outlook on the world we live in. As we evolve, our thoughts will grow deeper and we will find new connections between the objects and the phenomenon of reality. The level of our development defines how perceptive we can be of that part of the world of *Ein Sof* that we can feel.

There is no other way to want spirituality and awaken ourselves to the Surrounding Light except by studying in a group under the guidance of a Kabbalistic teacher. It is the only way to take part in the acting out of the design of Creation and shortening the process by which nature leads us to attain it. Only the Light can help us replace our egoistic attributes with altruistic ones. That is because our egoistic attributes stand as a barrier between the spiritual world and us.

The Surrounding Light replaces our desire to receive with a desire to give, thus carrying us across the barrier. We say that we want nothing of the physical, only of the spiritual, but if we had known how essential the change is across the barrier, that it is a transition from total concentration on personal gain to pure concern for others, we would have escaped the whole process.

Only after we cross the barrier do we encounter the "ocean of Light." The Light of the Creator shines only to the extent that we regard the Creator as more important than our egoistic desires. Once accomplished, we can slowly acquire the Light's property of bestowal.

The most important stage is the crossing of the barrier. Above the barrier, the soul knows the way by itself because it receives the Light, which teaches it the next steps and the needed operations like a tour guide, or a map. That is what the Kabbalists write about in their books.

How can a bad thought about the Creator be turned into a good one? We first need to understand that it is bad so we will think about its correction. It is true that evil can be seen only with the Light of the Creator, through His greatness. However, if the Light of the Creator does not shine, we cannot see. In the beginning, we all think our thoughts are good. But we are in this world, below the barrier, in the dark, in a place where the Light doesn't reach us.

When the Surrounding Light shines on us, we begin to see our real essence. It is a process called "the recognition of evil." But before the Light shines on us, we always try to justify ourselves. We think we are always right. But once under the Light of the Creator, we begin to see the evil in ourselves, which drives us to ask for help of the Creator, the Source of that illumination.

If our request is genuine, the Creator will change our natures. But the will to receive doesn't change, only the aim changes from "for me" to "for the Creator." That change is called "giving." Thus, one gradually changes one's properties to the properties of the Creator in each of the 125 degrees on the ladder.

Each degree consists of several processes:

- The recognition of evil. It is the realization of how much worse I am than the Creator in my left line.

- Examining what kind of help I actually need to receive from the Creator from the right line.

- Placing one line against the other, testing how much of the left line I can actually receive. This is considered coming to the middle line.

The result of these operations is that a part of my desires matches the Creator's, and I can ascend to the next degree. The process repeats itself in every degree until all my attributes equalize with those of the Creator.

Man's desires determine his acts. Consequently, it is impossible to do something without wanting it! For instance, if I know that I have to get up early tomorrow morning, then I go to sleep early the night before. Is that against my will? No! Nothing in this world can do anything without first wanting it, and without satisfying the desire with pleasure, which is the energy, the motivating force that enables any movement whatsoever.

We sometimes think that we are doing something against our will, but that is not the case. We simply calculate and decide that it is better to do something one way and not the other, even if we are doing something against our will. We will endure many things if our calculations justify them.

We make a certain desire close to our hearts and become able to carry it out by choosing it. But none of us can ever lift a finger without a motivating force, or without having a preliminary desire for it.

When we do something good for another, we think that it is really so, that we are actually doing something without seeking personal gain. But if we look deep into our thoughts, we will discover that it is all done for one purpose only: to please ourselves and only ourselves, and anything else is self-deceit.

When we begin to study Kabbalah, we begin to see how the system works, how everyone is a total egoist and thinks of no one but oneself, not even one's own children. At that point, you discover that your entire system of thought is built on illusions, and you think that you can actually do something for someone else.

It is only possible to give something to another if you receive something in return, if there is a profit for you. This is nothing to be ashamed of, it is our nature. We either receive for the purpose of enjoying, or give in order to gain something by it. It is no one's fault. The only thing that we should want is to change our attributes to those of the Creator.

Kabbalah teaches us to accept ourselves as we were created. We must not hate or even get upset when looking at our own or someone else's properties. It is hard for such a student of Kabbalah to be in contact with the outside world. Students have little patience when seeing egoism in the people they encounter. But each person is created with intention, and we should only try to help others change their properties to altruism.

Anything that is against our desire makes us suffer. It is written in the Talmud that if we want to take a certain coin out of a pocket, but bring out a different coin, we already suffer. Anything in life that does not match our desires perfectly causes us to suffer. Any bad mood, disease, or a lack of motivation to do this or that is interpreted by us as suffering.

But everything that happens actually happens in our favor. Everything promotes us one way or another toward the purpose of Creation. It is just that our distorted feelings portray the good as bad, and the sweet as bitter. Pure goodness can only be felt above the barrier, but for the time being everything is interpreted as pain. It happens because the Light still cannot fill the soul before the desire acquires an altruistic aim suitable for the Light, consequently leaving the Light outside.

Until we attain spirituality, the will to receive is our "angel of life." However, when we begin to study Kabbalah, we extend upon ourselves the Surrounding Light and slowly see how our will to receive is actually an obstacle between our egoistic nature and its transformation to altruism. We begin to see that this desire is the real enemy of our spiritual progress, thus turning the "angel of life" into the "angel of death."

We begin our process of recognition of evil from within our egoism. The sensation of the Light stands opposite the properties of the Light that we begin to feel. A huge desire appears in us to remove these cuffs from our hands at all costs. But because we cannot do it by ourselves, we desperately cry for the Creator's help. If our plea is earnest—it will be answered.

Those who want to attain spirituality must be like everyone else: they must raise families, work, and live normal lives. The important thing is what they do in their two or three free hours a day, the ones in which they are not committed to family or work. Those are the hours that they must examine themselves to see if they spend them in front of the television, in a restaurant, or laboring to attain a spiritual goal.

The difference between men and women in our world is a consequence of the relationship between the male part and the female part of the soul. As a result, men and women have different outlooks on life, different obligations and different objectives.

The male and female parts of every *Partzuf* in the spiritual world complement one another: the female part contributes its desires and the male part contributes its screens. In the end, it is their combination that brings spiritual attainment and perfection, which results in the revelation of the Light, the revelation of the Creator.

The correction of one of these parts does not come at the expense of the correction of the other, as occurs in egoistic relationships, where each pulls toward one's own side. In spirituality, everything exists in one *Partzuf*, one body, whereas in our world, we come in separate bodies. Every object in the spiritual world can exist only if it complements another object for a mutual goal.

It is therefore clear that according to Kabbalah, there can never be a "real" family, with a "real" relationship between the sexes unless it is between souls that want to be corrected spiritually. Then, to the extent that they are corrected, so will the egoistic relationships in the family transform into altruistic ones.

Spirituality is an intimate thing for every person. It must not be discussed with anyone and one's feelings toward the Creator should be kept to oneself to avoid spoiling someone else's individual progress. It is different for every person, and will become open to all only at the end of correction, since there will no longer be room for such obstructions as egoistic envy.

CHAPTER 2.2
PERSISTENCE

Naming a person is done in Kabbalah according to that person's will to receive. For example, if a certain individual has a desire to attain the Creator, feel Him and cling to Him, then that person is named Israel (from the words *Yashar El*—straight to God), even if still at the beginning of the journey, and unable to see the Creator or where this journey will lead. It is the desire that counts.

When one realizes the Creator's Will, that person will be called a "Kabbalist," someone who has attained a certain spiritual degree. For that reason, a Kabbalist is also called "One of Attainment."

Kabbalists gradually understand that there is no one but the attaining individual and the Creator. Strangers, acquaintances, parents, children and friends are, in fact, the Creator. He is the one standing behind these figures. One's discovery of the Creator is called "attainment."

The clearer the spiritual world becomes to us, the higher our spiritual degree is considered to be, until we finally realize that everything around us is the Creator. Then we acquire an even greater attainment—all our desires, thoughts, feelings, and aspirations are also the Creator.

So where is man here? Man is that within us that feels all this inside and reaches the ultimate conclusion that there is none else besides Him. The appearance of that feeling is called "adhesion with the Creator."

But what is the difference between understanding and feeling? We are born as feeling, not thinking, beings. Our minds evolve only enough to allow us to comprehend what we are feeling. Let us take a child as an example: childish desires are not great, and the child's mind is developed accordingly.

Another example is a person in the jungle who needs just enough wisdom to provide the necessities for survival. The more we want, the smarter we become, because the mind must get us what we want. The mind is but a consequence of the evolution of our desires. We seek and find all kinds of ways to get what we want. Thus, a strong will is the key to the development of the mind.

We needn't concern ourselves with developing the mind, only with developing desire. A person who studies the wisdom of Kabbalah needn't be smart. It is enough to want to feel the desire. It is impossible to see the spiritual world with our mind's eye' we can only feel it in our souls.

We should try to mingle with the suffering of the entire world, feel it, and experience it. Afterwards, we will be able to receive the Light of the entire world in the corrected vessel. Every time we learn about another person's pain, we should not regret that it is not us suffering. Rather, we should regret that people don't relate to suffering as a revelation of the Creator, because their vessels are still corrupted. People perceive the Providence of the Creator in the wrong way.

Do we have to justify the Creator's actions when we feel bad? The wisdom of Kabbalah is also called "the wisdom of truth." It is called this because a person who learns it learns to gradually feel the truth in an increasingly acute way. One cannot lie to oneself when standing before the Creator. It is then clear that the feeling in one's heart is the only truth there is.

But is the bad feeling not a testimony to man's accusation of the Creator? The good feeling in and of itself is already gratitude to the Creator. We speak to the Creator with our hearts; there is no need for words. Thus, in order to justify the Creator, we must always feel good.

When we hear that there is murder, oppression, and terrorism in the world, we must recognize that this is the best possible thing for our world, and it is only considered "bad" because of our corrupted souls. That is why our only option is to ascend spiritually and correct our vessels so that the evil we see and hear of will be perceived as good in our eyes.

Our only concern should be that in the process of the correction of the vessels and the spiritual degree, we will see how good He is to us and to the entire world.

Someone who is still climbing the degrees of the first spiritual world—the world of Assiya (called "all evil")—still feels events as bad. One who feels that the Creator's actions are bad is regarded as "evil" because he or she condemns the creator. (In Hebrew, the words "evil"—Rasha—and "condemn"—Marshia—come from the same root).

Later on, when entering the world of Yetzira (called "half bad and half good"), that person alternately feels what happens as either good or bad. It is as if the person is midway between each extreme, not knowing precisely how to define the situation.

The world of *Beria* is called "almost good." When we correct our vessels enough to ascend to the world of *Beria*, we feel with growing certainty that the Creator wants only what is best for us. Hence, when we have climbed to the world of *Yetzira*, we are called "incomplete righteous." When we ascend to the world of *Atzilut* (called "all good"), we see only good there, without a hint of evil. Consequently, if we have climbed to the world of *Atzilut*, we are called "complete righteous" (we justify the Creator and think that what He is doing is right).

Our feelings constitute our attitude toward the Creator in each and every situation. We cannot have a completely positive attitude toward the Creator and justify Him completely before we rise to the highest degrees, and that can only be in the world of *Atzilut*.

We should not stay in our current evil state, but should try and rise above it as fast as possible after we have examined and analyzed our situations. Then, we should try to reach a better state. But the truth is that we can never see our actual state while in it. Only when we move to a new level, when we are certain that we really did attain a new degree, can we examine and analyze our previous state.

For example, a ten-year-old child who is angry with his parents because they do not want to buy him a motorbike cannot assess his situation correctly. But what can he feel beside insulted? When he grows older he will be able to assess the event correctly. The most important thing is to try to move from accusing the Creator in favor of a higher state.

It has been said that the Creator created the world to delight His creatures. But that does not mean He wants to delight us because we suffered before. The Creator did it without any considerations and regardless of the amount of torment we had suffered. Staying immersed in pain never brought anyone happiness. Only self-correction brings one to the good. Humanity can go on suffering for thousands of years, but this will never bring any kind of correction; it will only increase man's desire for correction.

It is written in the *Introduction to the Book of Zohar* (item 6): "Our sages have instructed that the Creator created the world for no other reason but to delight His creatures. And here is where we must place our minds and hearts, for it is the ultimate aim of the act of the creation of the world. And we must bear in mind that since the thought of Creation is to bestow to His creatures, He had to create in the souls a great amount of desire to receive that which He had thought to give. For the measure of each pleasure and delight depends on the measure of the will to receive it. The greater the will to receive, the greater the pleasure, and the lesser the will, the lesser the pleasure from reception.

"So the thought of Creation itself dictates the creation of an excessive will to receive, to fit the immense pleasure that his Almightiness thought to bestow upon the souls. For the great delight and the great desire must go hand in hand."

If I want to eat a little, then I take little pleasure in the food. But if I am very hungry, then eating gives me great pleasure. Thus, because of His Desire to give the maximum amount of pleasure, He created in us this immense will to receive, to equal the amount of pleasure that He thought to give us. However, when we want something very much but cannot have it, then we suffer tremendously.

Increasing our desire for spirituality is a very complex question. We are incapable of feeling spirituality before we cross the barrier. We can only feel desires for self-indulgence. When we begin to realize this and understand that it is bad, we feel very bad about ourselves. Not only are we not nearing the Creator, but on the contrary, we find ourselves drifting away from Him. At first we didn't think we were that bad. Does that mean that we were closer to Him? And now, when we feel ourselves as evil, is it the Creator pushing us away and making us feel worse than before? It is the complete opposite! It is the Creator pulling us toward Him!

Our progress is measured by our negative feelings. That is because as long as we have not corrected our vessels, shame helps our correction more than anything. The only thing that enables humans to remain hu-

THE PATH OF KABBALAH

mane is shame. Unpleasant situations direct us more quickly in the right direction than pleasant situations, which normally corrupt even more.

To suffer from your egoism means to hate it, while clearly seeing that it is in you. Hatred serves to keep us away from the source of the agony. That, in turn, serves to build the right frame of mind for progress and a desire to approach the Creator.

We finally come to a state where we realize that we will not be able to resist committing a sin, even if we know about it in advance. Yet we still want it, or when we see it coming, we do nothing to distance ourselves from it, but simply stand and wait.

All this belongs to the part of correction. There is nothing that we can do by ourselves. All we can and should do is learn from every obstacle and failure along the way. Even if we sometimes think that we have overcome some situation, it will take no more than the next minute to realize we didn't overcome anything.

Sins and wrongdoing do not actually exist. They are all situations that we must go through in order to know the nature that was created by the Creator, so that we feel the necessity of correcting ourselves. If we can relate to everything that happens in this manner, then that is an act toward correction.

Let us take the sin of *Adam ha Rishon* as an example: the Creator created a soul and gave it an anti-egoism screen that could resist a certain amount of pleasure. After that, He placed before it a greater pleasure than it could resist. As a result, the soul could not resist the temptation and received the pleasure in order to receive, meaning it sinned. A sinful act is receiving in order to receive.

The soul consists of ten *Sefirot* divided into internal *Sefirot* and external *Sefirot*. The corrected part is considered internal, and the one that is as yet uncorrected, external. It is the external part that gives us the sensation of the world around us. This is where the feeling that there is something around us comes from. But in truth, everything I see around me is actually inside me. It is the uncorrected vessels that create a fictitious reality around me, and a person who enters the spiritual realm feels it at once.

We begin to need the Creator not only when He makes us suffer, but also when he lets us understand that it is He who stands behind the suffering. It is precisely then that we cry for help. In that state, our entire agony is concentrated in "the point in the heart" where the darkness is felt, and it is in that dark point that our connection with the Creator begins.

The questions will continue to trouble us until we cross the barrier. Although the questions will be asked by the same individual, they will always come with new vessels and new insights. Nothing ever regresses, only progresses, and we must experience all these situations.

CHAPTER 2.3
THE RECOGNITION OF EVIL

It is not enough to love the Creator and want to unite with Him. It is also necessary to hate the evil in you, meaning your own nature—the desire for self-indulgence from which you cannot escape by yourself. You should come to a state where you look inwardly, see the evil within you, and feel constantly tormented by it. You must know how much you are losing, and yet know that you will not be able to liberate yourself from the evil.

At the same time, we cannot come to terms with our state because we feel the loss that the evil inflicts on us, and the truth that we will never find the powers for salvation in ourselves because that trait has been imprinted in us by the Creator.

In order to exit our world and enter the spiritual world, we must experience a number of specific situations: First, we must feel that the situation we are in is intolerable. That can happen only when we feel, even if slightly, what spirituality is and how different it is from our own state. We must feel that all the good is there, that it is unending abundance, tranquility, eternity, and wholeness, and that everything is one Power that pulls us toward it.

In addition, there is the force in this world that rejects you from the situation that has now become intolerable to you. When these two forces—one drawing you towards spirituality and the other rejecting you from your current state—reach their peak, coupled with your awareness of total helplessness to liberate yourself from evil, that an explosion occurs and the Creator delivers you.

What you can and must do is to develop genuine hate towards the evil in yourself. Then, the Creator will deliver you from it. The Creator guards souls, proven by the fact that He saves them from evil. If one has even the slightest conscious connection with the Creator, that person is a fortunate individual.

All the situations that we experience in spirituality continue to exist and can be returned to at any stage, corrected, and used to continue our progress. Because the Creator gives, His creatures must try to want the same thing. The reverse is also true, as the Creator hates to be a receiver. He is complete to begin with and needs nothing; therefore, His creatures should hate reception, because that is the origin of all evil. It is only through hatred of evil that it can be corrected and become subordinate to the sanctity of the Creator.

If we encounter states of emptiness, indifference, and bad feeling, it means that our state already belongs to the next degree, which has not yet been corrected. Every situation begins in the dark. The day begins in the night; the vessels begin with the will to receive. Then they are corrected and receive the Light. Thus, every time we feel a new sensation of evil, we should be happy, because the next phase will be the reception of Light. There is no progress in the sensation of evil, because only the presence of two contradictory situations allows us to arrive at the middle line.

Baal HaSulam compared this movement to breathing: First, the lungs prepare themselves, empty themselves of air, and then fill themselves with new Light. In each and every place and in each and every thing there must first be a need or a lack. Only afterwards is the filling obtained.

Each person must eventually come to adhesion with the Creator. This long process was predetermined in the design of Creation, and began thousands of years ago. Souls now continue it in every incarnation. There is nothing in the gigantic computer of Creation that occurs without a reason. Everything is tied to other things with invisible wires. The world is one living body, and any change in even the smallest and most remote area affects the entire being.

The still, vegetative, and animate do not experience mood changes. But there is not a creature on earth that does not have a Godly spark. They all must come to the purpose of Creation, the end of correction. The still, vegetative, and animate degrees will follow in man's footsteps. Each has its own time, conditions, and place that they must be in. Being in this same place without understanding why, and taking all these steps and actions, brings everyone naturally to the purpose of Creation in one's own way.

This is the place to ask, "Why do some come to the wisdom of Kabbalah while others do not?" The answer is very simple: Those who come to the wisdom of Kabbalah have already accumulated enough agony to ask, "Who am I?" and "What am I living for?"

Those who lead ordinary lives never ask these questions. No one asks why they are happy, because if they are happy, they are convinced they deserve it. But if they suffer, then they don't understand what they have done to deserve it, and that question never brings peace of mind. Everyone must labor alone in order to draw nearer to the Creator, instead of waiting until the anguish brings them to action.

There is no difference between suffering in our world and suffering in the spiritual world. Both forms of suffering are ways for the Creator to control and guide us. If we could transfer physical pain to spiritual pain, we would correct some of our vessels and in that equalize our attributes with the Creator's, thus shortening our journey.

When a Kabbalist becomes physically ill, his body suffers. But because the physical body cannot attain spirituality, only one's inner sensation becomes spiritual, corrected, and awakens the Kabbalist, even as the body continues to suffer. While the soul of the Kabbalist continues to climb, physical health continues to deteriorate.

Why does the body not climb alongside the soul? Because the body cannot become spiritual! Spirituality is an inner ascent of the soul that has nothing to do with the outer part, meaning the biological body. The body is doomed to perish and be buried in the ground. That is the end of its correction. When a body expires, one gets a new body, just as we change a shirt when the one we wear needs washing.

Then again, there are souls like those of Rabbi Shimon Bar-Yochay, the Ari, or Rabbi Yehuda Ashlag, that have already corrected themselves and no longer need to descend to this world. They do it only to correct the world; they absorb agony from the entire world and thus suffer for it. That process is called the *Hitkalelut* (mixture/mingling) of the souls. Each soul becomes involved with other souls to help them correct.

We should relate to corporeal pain as a call to spirituality and contact with the Creator. When a person is attentive to that call, all torments are corrected and diminish. One who enters spirituality sees everything that the Creator allows. But a Kabbalist only wants to see that which will enhance spiritual progress; the rest is unimportant.

Every new situation is taken as a springboard for an even greater ascent; for that reason, the student takes the most positive aspects from the current degree, those that will help the student achieve the next degree.

In his *Introduction to the Study of the Ten Sefirot*, Baal HaSulam writes of four degrees: *Malchut, Zeir Anpin, Bina* and *Hochma*. Those are degrees of attainment of the Creator (*Keter*). When we attain the Creator, He reveals everything that occurred to us throughout the entire history of our souls. This includes the Creator's treatment of us every step of the way, how the Light left, what torments we underwent, and why these things happened.

Only now can we see that the Creator had always been good to us, and never had any other considerations. The fact that we regarded those events as bad was because of our corrupted senses, which perceived the approach of the Creator as negative. Everything we now see brings us greater love toward the Creator. Because of this, we must learn what happened in our newly corrected vessels.

In the next and final phase, the Creator demonstrates His attitude toward all the souls throughout the generations. Here is where we see how good the Creator has been to all His creatures. The result of such an attainment is eternal love for the Creator. The only thing that man cannot see is how each person will come to the Creator, whether naturally or with the help of the Creator, and when.

There is sufficient quantity and quality of desire in man to begin with. We must only learn to use it with the right intent: either we use our desires to satisfy ourselves and receive as much pleasure as possible with the least possible effort, or we only want to please the Creator by receiving for Him the maximum amount of pleasure. In other words, we receive in order to bring Him contentment.

We cannot change our aim by ourselves. Only the Creator can do that. If, while we employ our desires, the aim "in order to receive" makes us hate egoism, it is a sign that we have come to recognize the evil in us. At such a state, we will be rewarded with the alteration of the aim to bestowal. The passage from Lo Lishma (in order to receive) to Lishma (in order to bestow) is in fact, the crossing of the barrier between our world and the spiritual world. Such a state is called "birth," the acquisition of the screen; it is the crossing of the Red Sea that separates between Egypt and the Land of Israel.

Only the aim changes when we attain spirituality. The will to receive does not diminish as a result of it, but continues to grow and renew itself in every spiritual degree. We said earlier that everything has already been created and there are no innovations anymore. It is true that the entire will to receive has already been created, but before the attainment of spirituality I was only shown a small and negligent part of it. Now, however, I find greater and greater egoistic desires in each degree, but only to the extent that I am able to correct their aim.

If you should feel the evil within, be proud and grateful. This means that you have merited the revelation of your evil.

Our inner feelings are connected to the final goal of everything that happens, the final outcome, to that who gave us this situation and the reason for it. We must know that egoism is both opposite to the Creator, and of equal size. Furthermore, in each degree egoism becomes more and more aggressive.

It is forbidden to discuss what we feel with others, because the person you speak to may be in a similar situation to yours and cannot help you. Thus, you might force your corrupted state on your friend. You can speak about it to a Kabbalist-teacher, but it is best to talk to the Creator.

To attain spirituality, you must sort out your egoistic thoughts in this world. You must recognize the evil in them and your inability to attain spirituality because of them. You must face the agony that accompanies the sensation of the oppositeness between the Creator and you, and hate it as vehemently as possible. Then and only then will you discover spirituality.

The recognition of evil isn't merely an unpleasant mood due to an absence of some temporary thing that you want. Recognizing the evil requires the sensation of the Creator, the oppositeness of His altruistic nature to your own. You must feel your 100% egoism vs. His 100% altruism; you must feel that this situation is intolerable and have a burning desire to correct it.

Starting from the barrier and Above, when one already climbs the spiritual degrees, one feels the Creator. Now we must constantly correct our attitude toward the Creator, our aim. This is where the work of the recognition of evil is done. The shells surface opposite the Light, opposite the correction of the vessels of reception into vessels of bestowal.

CHAPTER 2.4

THE ATTRIBUTES OF THE LIGHT

The soul is the only thing that He created; it perceives the sensations of sight, sound, touch, smell and taste, through its filters. Behind the filters of the five senses are a "computer" and "software." The soul translates what it finds outside it into a language we can relate to: pleasure or pain. Thus, it is at the center of the soul in its innermost point where we feel if something is good or bad.

If the computer operates on the natural software, the program serves up the egoistic definitions of good and bad. If the computer has been reinstalled with an altruistic operating system, then the understanding of good and bad is no longer calculated with regard to the soul itself, but toward something that is outside it—the Creator.

There are two operating systems that the soul can use to evaluate reality:

1. The egoistic form for itself;

2. The altruistic form for the Creator;

There is no other reality but the Creator and the creature, the Light (bounty) and the desire (vessel).

At birth, we are naturally programmed to be egoistic. Because of that, in the "back of one's mind" is an egoistic picture called "this world."

A person feels nothing but the Light. The Light is processed egoistically and reflects inside us as "this world." If the egoistic processing did not influence us and insert its obstructions in us (as the program that attracts the good and rejects the bad, being concerned only with man's self-preservation), we would perceive a completely different picture. This would have been projected to the front of the soul, and would show us everything that really exists in spirituality; it would have displayed everything that exists outside us, namely, the Light, the Creator. Otherwise, the picture would have been subjective and would only reflect our internal content out of self-gratifying consideration.

The way to reprogram the computer from egoistic to altruistic is called "the wisdom of Kabbalah." We can use it to create the real picture of the world without a shred of egoism. We will be able to feel the actual Creation outside us, and come to "equivalence of form" and unification with the Light. It is a state where there are no partitions between the Light and the soul.

The sensation of the Light is somewhat like the sensation one feels in a state of clinical death. It is a state of partial detachment from the physical body (animate egoism). In that state there is desire to attain the Light.

However, attaining it is impossible until one rids the self of all egoism, both spiritual and physical. Hence, man's work is primarily in the physical body.

It is quite easy to get rid of spiritual egoism if we know which obstruction the egoism puts into our internal computers. All information enters through five filters, called "the five parts of *Malchut*," the five zones of the government of the egoism. These five channels transfer the data that comes in from the outside to a form of data the egoism can process, such as, "I feel good," or, "I feel bad." Every channel-filter that the signals go through has its own thickness (coarseness), which differs from person to person.

The more lifetimes the soul experiences, the greater its coarseness. It becomes not only coarser, but also more prepared for correction. However, people who are not developed egoistically do not need that much and settle for little. A greater egoist is one who is ready to be corrected, and feels the necessity for correction and to fill self with Light more intensely.

CORRECTING THE PROGRAM

When one's coarseness reaches its ultimate intensity, there appears a need to correct one's personal computer program. The coarseness increases over many lifetimes, not only of a person's life, but also of animal and vegetative, and even inanimate nature. Though nature itself rises, too, its ascent depends on man's situation and occurs only when man ascends.

When coarseness reaches its peak, the gap between man's inner picture and the Light also reaches its peak and an inner switch is turned on inside. This produces the feeling that one can no longer satisfy self with anything in the present or in the future.

This is the sign that one has stopped looking for something inside, in the back of one's soul, but now aspires to feel its surrounding reality. Hence, the quest for many forms of discipline and method until one finds Kabbalah, which is what one has been seeking.

Kabbalah is a system that can change these filters. While it will not remove them, it will change their focus from an egoistic intent to receive pleasures to an altruistic aim to delight. In fact, the only possibility that really exists is to receive in order to bestow, because when it comes to the Creator-creature relationship, the Creator gives and man receives. We have nothing to give the Creator except our willingness to receive pleasure from Him.

We can also use these filters for receiving in order to please the Light, the Creator. Then the data that comes from the outside will not be distorted or falsified, but will appear before us as it really is outside us. That concludes the design of Creation, which enables mankind to live without any disturbances from his selfish ego, and feel and live in the actual system of Creation. All the pleasures that humanity has experienced thus far and is destined to experience comprise only one part of 600,000 of the smallest pleasure in the smallest Light (*Nefesh*).

Even when only one soul completes its correction and receives the full amount of Light, it stands before all souls, looking over everything, before the data enters the system, before the pleasure penetrates all other souls.

One's coarseness is determined during one's first life in our world. But Kabbalah can develop and increase it dozens of times over and reduce the number of times one will have to reincarnate. It accelerates the process of one's ripening for the purpose of attaining the spiritual realm.

Human torments are an external expression of something that is missing. The torments do not vanish, but the Kabbalah replaces the animate-corporeal pains for spiritual pains that come from the absence of spiritual sensation. The qualitative change in suffering leads to a reconstruction of the internal vessel, the renewal of the soul. The sensation of the Light comes hand in hand with the growing desire to be like the Light, and processes that would have taken generations to complete are completed in only a few years.

CHAPTER 2.5
BUILDING AN INNER ATTITUDE

Studying the secrets of the spiritual world leads us to build an inner attitude towards it, which is also expressed in how we relate to our everyday lives. At the end of the process, our lives in this world should be subordinate to spiritual rules. This is the desire of the Creator. The more we are able to leave our egos, the better are our chances of feeling spirituality and liberating ourselves from our corporeal bodies.

The body is the root of our every problem. For example, the world of Atzilut serves as a model for building our society in this world. By doing that, we immediately fall under the influence of spiritual forces that guard, protect, and lead us. The bounty that each of us receives corresponds to our ability to sense these forces in corrected vessels.

The spiritual world and the corporeal world are parallel. Spiritual Light and power come down from Above, but cannot clothe our world because there is a different form of reception that prevails here. "For me" is the opposite of the spiritual form. If we organize even a very small community that lives according to laws of the world of *Atzilut*, then all the Upper Positive Forces will be able to clothe each of its members and raise them respectively to a high spiritual degree.

But building a spiritual frame of life demands serious preparation on our part. It is the best thing that one can do for oneself, for one's family, for the environment and for the entire world. The whole world will gradually feel better if even a small society lives by altruistic spiritual laws. We must aspire for that and the help will come from Above.

The Creator created a soul with a desire for pleasure. The number of desires is 600,000. If we divide the soul by 600,000, each part will be called a "human soul."

The difference between each soul is in the quantity and quality of the desire. I am created in such a way that I aspire to a certain pleasure, and someone else aspires to a different pleasure. Others have different desires, different pleasures, but the Light is one and the same. This means that the difference is only in our desires.

It is impossible to replace one desire with another. The soul consists of all the desires that were created by the Creator. Each desire is a certain kind of Light that comes as a unique pleasure and is felt by each person individually. We cannot feel any other pleasure than the one that fits our individual desire.

We are created differently to begin with—different in the kinds of desires we have and their intensity. Because of that, each person has unique incarnations in this world, as well as a unique path to attain the purpose of Creation.

However, we do have one thing that unites us all: the purpose of Creation, meaning the correction of egoism, the will to receive in order to receive that we have been given by the Creator, which we must change into a will to receive in order to bestow to the Creator. That change will enable us to unite with the Creator and cleave to Him. Consequently, we will acquire a great collective soul, eternal and endless, which will receive the perfect pleasure.

We are made of a very small egoistic vessel that can receive very limited delights in quality and quantity. We chase something, suffer because of its absence, seek it, and the minute we get it, we lose interest. Then come new pains chasing yet new pleasures, and so on until we end our lives in this world, having fulfilled none of our desires.

Now imagine that wanting something and receiving it are instantaneous! The minute you want something, you get it. What could be more perfect? We are not talking about tiny desires for animate pleasures, but about immeasurable desires to feel and attain endless spiritual delights that instantly fulfill every desire.

Anyone can increase the small egoistic desires, perpetuate them and receive fantastic bliss equal in power to the collective soul. This can be done by simply changing the aim from "for me" to "for the Creator." That process is called "equivalence of form with the Creator." Each soul must first mingle with all other souls, and according to its measure of mingling, its tiny desire is intensified to match the measurements of the collective soul.

One of the mottos of the socialist movement was, "From each person according to his ability, to each person according to his needs." In other words, "Give what you can and receive what you need."

That social rule is actually borrowed from spirituality and, in fact, applies only there. That is because the ability to receive only as much as you or I need depends on our spiritual degrees, on our screens. The more we want to receive, the more desires we will need to correct. Our desire to receive for ourselves does not let us receive what we actually need, and is in fact even more limiting.

Only by changing the aim from reception to bestowal, meaning crossing the barrier to spirituality, can we begin to understand the true meaning of the slogan, "Give what you can and receive what you need." That is the only way for complete and eternal fulfillment.

When we enter the spiritual world, we learn to give more and more and receive only the bare minimum to support ourselves. When we unite with the Creator, we become like Him, and then give everything without taking anything for ourselves. Precisely because of that, we are filled with everything. In the end, giving is itself the reward, which is why a life of giving is eternal, filled with Light that enters our vessels. This is also why the departure of the Light from the vessel is death.

CHAPTER 2.6
DISCOVERING SPIRITUAL PROPERTIES

In order to start perceiving the spiritual world, we must acquire spiritual attributes. But what does "acquiring spiritual attributes" actually mean? And how can we acquire them? People who have already discovered the spiritual world tell us that when they examine our world from the outside, they see its nature as a manifestation of pure, unadulterated egoism. This means that everything in our world is based on ego—the inanimate nature, the plants, animals, and people. In all the incidents and in every degree there is only one law—total pursuit of self-indulgence, according to the intensity of the egoism in each object or creature.

Because our every thought and act is based on a single resolution to receive as much personal pleasure as possible in any given situation, that and only that constitutes the essence of our nature. Hence, it is simply impossible to unite atoms into molecules, maintain an existing form, or develop physical bodies and a human consciousness without the pursuit of some egoistic goal.

Even if we think that the reason for one's action is to benefit one's fellow man, after we analyze the reasons behind it, we will find that there is nothing but a disguised egoistic ambition, a sophisticated form of egoistic exploitation. And because our nature is absolute egoism, we are only able to discover and feel external stimuli that correspond to our internal egoistic attributes.

The collective picture of the external stimuli that we feel with our egoistic attributes is called "our world." That is all we can feel with our egoistic attributes. In fact, it is not our sensory organs that are egoistic, but the heart that stands behind the senses, our ambition to derive the maximum pleasure from all these sensations. If there had been an altruistic heart behind these senses instead of an egoistic one, we would be able to retrieve completely different information with the exact same senses. That would have been the picture of the "next world," or the spiritual world.

But while being in the spiritual world, we would still be able to see the picture of our own world. This is because we do not stop living in this world and we do not leave to enter a different physical dimension, but simply add the collective picture to our perception of this world. We begin to understand the reasons and the consequences of everything that happens to us, and to distinguish the spiritual forces behind the physical bodies in our world.

One who is in the spiritual world begins to see the roots that influence reality and formulate the events of this world. Finally, the person begins to see and understand the reason and the purpose of existence.

Those who are still unable to feel or see this picture have only to believe that this possibility exists. A Kabbalist cannot describe or convey personal spiritual sensations to people who cannot see it for themselves. But if we take the counsel of a Kabbalist who has already passed this way, it can greatly help anyone seeking an outlet to the spiritual world.

CHAPTER 2.7
CORRECTING OUR DESIRES

Utilizing our desires in a different way is called "correction." This is a state where we are completely liberated from it, as though looking at it from the side, not governed by it.

For example, we can look at the will to receive as a will to bestow. If I know that you will enjoy my acceptance of your present, I will take it. By accepting your gift, I am converted from a taker to a giver of delight.

In order to return the pleasure to you, I must express great joy when I receive your gift. Thus, my desire doesn't change, only its direction.

Desires are always divided into light (fine) and hard (coarse), according to how they are used, the pleasure derived from them, and the possibility of transferring them from desires for reception into desires for bestowal. It is important to separate the desire from its clothing, to consider only the desire. Only then can I use all its parts—fine and coarse. But I must first restrict every new desire that surfaces and say, "Yes, this is indeed pleasure, but I can refrain from realizing it, I can resist it."

By doing this, I stretch a borderline between me and the pleasure and the giver of the pleasure. It is like a game—when a certain desire appears, I have to reject it, and afterwards receive only to the extent that I can do so for the host.

That is why our work is called *Zivug de Hakaa* (mating by rejecting), because we use the screen to detain and reject the pleasure, and only then accept it to the extent that we can use it in order to give to the benefactor. I must use every vessel at my disposal correctly, but I must first separate myself from the pleasure that reaches me.

When I think of the purpose of Creation, of the contact with the Creator, I aim my every act toward Him. That is what I should do with every desire, and that will intensify the pleasure I derive from them many times over. That way, I actually increase my vessels of bestowal.

We need only learn how to use our desires correctly and constantly analyze our situation. The essays and letters of Baal HaSulam and Rabbi Baruch Ashlag (Rabash) are very helpful for that.

We progress by understanding the situation. We are not the owners of our desires and pleasures. Only a constant study of each situation allows us to use our desires correctly. Our thoughts must be aimed at these questions: "Why was I sent this desire?" "How should I react to it, and why?"

We must observe things from the side, so to speak. These exercises teach us why the Creator does what He does. We sometimes have desires we cannot overpower, and sometimes we have some that we can. Sometimes we feel indifference, envy, hate, and so on. We must only keep things under guard.

Sometimes it is not what we do that is important, but the experience we gain by doing it. Because we cannot evaluate situations correctly, it is not important if we regard something as a sin or a misdoing. This is because such an incident can, regardless of which it is, be of great help to us. Every feeling is given to us by the Creator so we can acquire the necessary experience and knowledge.

In the end, we will understand that every time we try to do something and we do not connect with the Creator, we will be placing ourselves in a terrible state of acknowledging our evil to the point that we will want to relinquish our personal pleasure once and for all.

But the Creator wants us to enjoy ourselves; that is the design of Creation, and the joy must be genuine! Yet our intention must be to give that pleasure to the Creator and not remain on a beastly (animate), egoistic level. What should change is the principle of reception, the approach to pleasure.

The entire Creation consists of a will to receive; there is a feminine root in how we relate to the Creator (in the sense that we are receivers). The desire to bestow is our masculine root (in the sense that we want to give). Consequently, Creation itself is divided into a feminine side and a masculine side. If Creation adapts itself to the Light and becomes like it, then it is considered the masculine part. If it remains outside the Light as a receiver, then it is considered its feminine part.

Everything that happens in this world is a consequence of the dividing of the soul of *Adam ha Rishon* into 600,000 spiritual souls. These parts are at varying levels of correction and should fulfill masculine and feminine parts interchangeably, meaning they should sometimes follow the right line (bestowal, masculine part) and at other times they should follow the left line (reception, feminine part).

All the names in the Torah are names of spiritual attainments on the spiritual ladder. But in order to attain a certain name, you must play both the masculine and the feminine parts, meaning the right and left lines. For example, in the degrees of Pharaoh, Moses, Israel, and a Gentile, there is both a feminine and a masculine part. But each name can only be attained once and in a certain degree.

Man and woman are a union of Zeir *Anpin* and *Malchut* of the world of *Atzilut*. Its essence and degree create different names and a higher spiritual degree. The male and female states are set in each of the 125 degrees. If that is the case, then how should men and women behave in this world? Each should behave according to the possibilities that he/she has been given within a specific sex.

Although we are egoistic and seek nothing but personal profit, we must be grateful to the Creator for having allowed us to see ourselves as we really are, as unpleasant as it may be. We should try to learn to react to things moderately as we observe ourselves from the side.

That is, in fact, our entire work—to become owners of our situations and to control our emotions. We may sometimes lose our tempers, but we must examine why things happen and what should be done from now on. That teaches us to separate the mind from the heart, and emotions from reason. *Introduction to the Book of Zohar* (item 11): "And the worlds concatenated onto the reality of this corporeal world, meaning to a place where there is a body, a soul, a time of corruption and a time of correction."

The body is called "the will to receive for myself." It expands from the root of the thought of Creation through the entire system of the impure worlds, and becomes increasingly coarser. This period of time, when it is under the control of the will to receive for myself, is called "the time of corruption."

Later on, through the practice and the study of Kabbalah, which aim to give to the Creator, the body (will to receive) begins to purify itself from the will to receive that is initially imprinted in it, and gradually acquires a will to bestow. That gives it a possibility to receive the Light of the Creator, the soul that extends from the root of the design of Creation. The soul passes through the system of pure worlds and clothes a body. This period is called "the time of correction."

In that state, one faces the ladder of the spiritual degrees, which expands according to the thought of Creation from the world of *Ein Sof*. This helps continue in the acquisition of the aim to give to the Creator, until one's every act to bestow (even the reception) will only be in order to give to the Creator, and take nothing for self.

Reception in order to bestow is considered complete bestowal. Thus, by attaining that, one attains equivalence of one's properties with the Creator's, namely adhesion with Him. When that happens, one receives the complete eternal abundance that the Creator had intended to bestow when He designed Creation.

It is impossible to turn the will to receive into a will to bestow. Why? Because receiving is our essence and remains with us. It must therefore be clothed with an aim to bestow, meaning the direction of received bounty should be changed. In that situation, one's body (desires) will commence its process of correction, or cleansing.

If, for example, ten grams of the body are cleansed, then ten grams of the body can now be filled with Light. When the Light descends, it also restricts itself to ten grams to fit the corrected part of the body and clothe it. The two world systems—pure and impure—act synchronously and help one another in the correction process. Each newly obtained spiritual degree helps us ascend to the next, until we finally reach the last degree, the attainment of eternity, perfection, and wholeness, the ability to view life and death from a new perspective.

PART TWO: PHASES OF SPIRITUAL EVOLUTION

CHAPTER 2.8
THE RIGHT WAY TO ADVANCE

The society we live in is flooded with the perpetual pursuit of beastly (corporeal) pleasures such as money, glory, and sex. It is impossible to sin in such a state, and it is just as impossible to keep *Mitzvot*. This is simply not spirituality.

However, there is hope in that situation, provided we are willing to restrict the use of these desires, or to better phrase it, direct our desires for spirituality. When that happens, we are admitted into the first degree in the spiritual world, where there is a Light many times stronger than the one shining in our world.

We ask for a screen in order to resist animate pleasures and refrain from receiving them for ourselves, but only with the intent "for the Creator." We obtain a screen and thus correct our first degree. After that we ascend to the next degree, in which we are faced with an even greater will to receive and consequently a greater Light. By acquiring a screen with a greater anti-egoistic power, we correct that degree as well, and continue to climb.

Let's picture our world as a horizontal line of zero value. The first egoistic will to receive in the scale of degrees will be considered as -1 (minus one) and will be felt as a decline, or a fall. The screen and the Light that is received with the intent for the Creator will be worth +1 and will be considered an ascent. The distance between -1 and +1 is equal to the size and height of the *Partzuf*.

When one completes the first degree, one is then given -2 worth of egoism. That necessitates a +2 worth of screen. This is how the ascent to the next degree occurs. The higher one climbs, the lower one falls, but only in order to rise even higher.

Malchut of the world of *Ein Sof* broke after having failed to receive the Light "for the Creator" in the world of *Nekudim*. That was the breaking of the vessels. As a result, the vessels of bestowal and the vessels of reception were mixed, and every egoistic desire absorbed sparks of

THE PATH OF KABBALAH

the Creator's altruistic desires, which enable the egoistic desires to bond with the Creator and with spirituality.

The greater the task one is destined to carry out, the higher the level of vessels one is equipped with, and the deeper and higher are one's descents and ascents. Because of that, we must never judge others by their acts, because we cannot know what corrections others are currently going through.

The best thing to do is have the following picture before us: the soil and the earth are the egoistic level, where we are. The sky is where the Light comes from. If the Light has no contact with us, we cannot detach ourselves from the ground. Such are our traits.

If the Light does shine for us, then we seemingly detach ourselves from the ground and rise above our egoistic will to receive. The minute the Light stops shining, we fall to the ground, as though we'd never been off it. We have no powers of our own to rise above it. Only the Light of the Creator can lift us.

The higher one's place is in the spiritual world, the greater the distance between the ups and downs. Thus, the fall in the world of *Atzilut* can reach almost as low as this world. That is why the great Kabbalist, Rabbi Shimon Bar-Yochay, when he was one degree before the last, suddenly felt himself (and called himself accordingly) as "Shimon from the market." All the knowledge and the corrected properties, everything disappeared and he became completely ignorant. That is how he described his situation in the book of *Zohar*.

It happens to everyone, even to a person who has just begun the spiritual ascent. How does one rise after one falls and get back on track? One does it by participating in the group, even without a shred of desire. In that state, one must continue to act mechanically or automatically, because when in descent, it is impossible to even read a book. Sometimes, the only way out is sleep, detachment from everything, and just letting time do its work.

The most dangerous state is when we are at the highest spiritual point and begin to enjoy the pleasure we receive, the security, the stability, and the clarity, all the pleasure that comes with eternity.

That very moment can be the cause of our fall. It is very important to remember that this state was given to us precisely so we can continue focusing on delighting the Creator precisely in that situation.

It is impossible to prevent ourselves from falling altogether. The falls are necessary for progress, because if it weren't for them, we would have no other way to acquire additional desires to receive, with which to rise again.

The term *Partzuf* describes our attitude toward others, which reflects the degree of our development. It is impossible to receive the Light before we obtain a desire for it. It is impossible to obtain good without first obtaining evil. For example, when we rise in spirituality by fifteen degrees, and we fall on the 16th, it is because our actual attributes have been disclosed in their worst shape, since in the ascent we are exposed to a greater Light, and that enables us to see ourselves compared to the corrected properties of a higher degree.

The spiritual degrees we go through continue to live in us. We can only see evil when we ascend to a higher spiritual degree. The greater the Light that shines, the worse we see ourselves compared to it. That is how it goes until the last degree, the end of correction.

Rabash (Rabbi Baruch Ashlag) writes in a letter to his disciples (letter No. 2): "The truth is that there is another reason for it: Baal HaSulam explains in his book, *The Study of the Ten Sefirot*, that the Ari describes why *Melech HaDaat* (King of *Daat*) in the world of *Nekudim*, who was the degree of *Keter* and the highest *Melech* (king), fell lower than all other kings when the breaking occurred. That is because those of the greatest coarseness are also the highest when in possession of a screen. But when they lose their screens, they become the worst, and consequently fall lower than all other kings.

"His words can also be interpreted to describe those who follow the ways of the Lord: those people have a desire for both corporeality and spirituality, as it is said, that those who were close to Baal HaSulam had a screen and *Aviut* (coarseness), but now that he was gone, they had no one to submit to, and were left with coarseness but no screen, and were only looking to become rabbis and 'pretty Jews.' Therefore, I (Rabash) suspect everything that comes out of their hands, for there is no one to restrain them.

"I am speaking briefly here, for I do not want them in my thoughts, for you know the rule that "One is where one's thoughts are," but because I know your fondness for the truth, I am compelled to bring to my mind the coarseness that hasn't a screen, which are broken vessels that are as yet not on the path of correction, and may God have mercy.

"Let me give you a short example so that you understand the above: it is known that each and every degree has a middle part that consists of both. Between the still and the vegetative there is the coral; between the vegetative and the animate there are the stones of the field, which are animals that are connected to the earth by their navels and receive their nourishment from it, and between the animate and the speaking there is the ape. That raises the question: what is between true and false, which is the point which consists of both.

"Before I clarify this, I will add one known rule, that something small is hard to see, whereas a large object is easier to see. Consequently, when one lies only a little, one is unable to see the truth that he is on a false path, but thinks that he is going in a truthful path. However, there is no greater lie than that because he hasn't enough lies to see his actual state.

But in one who has acquired a great deal of lies, the falsehood has increased within to such an extent that if this person wants to see his actual state, he can now do it. Thus, now that he can see the falsehood, meaning that he is on a false path, he sees his real state, meaning he sees in his heart the truth of how to get on the right track..."

An observer who hasn't any connection to the wisdom of Kabbalah will always think that he or she is doing nothing wrong, and is just like everyone else. This person believes that he or she is taking the right path because of the very small amount of recognition of evil that he has obtained. But once a substantial amount of falsehood has been accumulated, the person will be able to see the truth of the situation (provided this is the person's true desire).

At that time, it will be recognized that the person has been on the wrong path all along. This will allow the person to change to the right path—the path of truth. When we recognize the fact that our current state is intolerable, and that we have come to the end of our rope, then we will ask for the Creator's help.

"...It turns out that this point—which is the truthful point that he is taking a false path—is the middle between true and false. It is the bridge that connects between truth and falsehood. This point is the end of the lie, and from here on begins the path of truth. We can similarly understand what Baal HaSulam wrote, that in order to obtain *Lishma* we must first obtain the greatest *Lo Lishma*, and then we can come to *Lishma*.

"In the same manner, we can interpret the above, that *Lo Lishma* is considered falsehood and *Lishma* is considered truth. When the lie is small, meaning when the Mitzvot and the good deeds are few, then one has a small *Lo Lishma* and is unable to see that truth. Therefore in that state one says that one is on a good and truthful way, meaning working *Lishma*.

"However, when one engages in Torah and Mitzvot day in and day out in a state of *Lo Lishma*, one can then see the truth, because the multiplicity of lying magnifies it. Thus, one can see that in fact, one is on a false path, and at that time begin to correct one's actions. It means that in that state one feels that everything one does is only *Lo Lishma*.

"From this point on one moves to the path of truth, meaning *Lishma*. Only at this point begins the transition from *Lo Lishma* to *Lishma*. How could one change one's situation previously, while arguing that one was working *Lishma*? Thus, if one is idle in the work it is impossible to see the truth of being immersed in falsehood. Nevertheless, by accumulating Torah and *Mitzvot* in order to bring contentment to The Maker, we can see the truth that we are on a false path, called *Lo Lishma*, and this is the middle point between true and false." (Rabbi Baruch Shalom Ashlag, *Shamati, Igrot,* letter No. 2).

The Creator operates in any situation we are in, whether good or bad. One does not and cannot make any decisions. One can accelerate one's development, but certainly cannot change it. If we look at this path through the eyes of egoism, we will be terrorized and terrified. But if we perceive the egoism as an evil thing that must be destroyed, if we look at it from the outside, we will immediately want to uproot it and replace it with altruism.

CHAPTER 2.9
SPIRITUAL REWARD

People want to be rewarded for anything they do. Even when working to attain spirituality, we want to be rewarded because we are made of pure egoism and cannot operate any other way. Behind every act, there is always an aim; otherwise our egoism would not permit us to make even a single step!

We begin our spiritual work from zero, as if the Creator had shone on us from afar with the illumination of Surrounding Light. This illumination compels us to act and we decide to give up all the beauties of this world in favor of a spiritual sensation.

We do not even know what exactly is it we want to receive, because the Light shines on us from a distance without clothing our vessels. At this point, the Light merely gives us the sensation of the future pleasure we will find in spirituality, which we cannot find in the world around us. The Surrounding Light operates on us and attracts us to spirituality, turning us into our own undertakers.

First, we want to use the spiritual world the same way we use this world. We believe that acquiring spiritual forces will give us the ability to predict the future, control it, perhaps even fly. But little by little, we come to realize that instead of all that, we must give all our strength and devote our every goal to the Creator. We must nullify ourselves and relinquish our control over ourselves in favor of the Creator's control over us. This is how we truly grow.

There is a question: "What is the connection between a Jew by birth, and a 'spiritual Jew'? The answer is: In someone who was born Jewish, there is a tendency to become a Jew in the spiritual sense. The Creator matches souls with bodies in a way that the "genetic" Jews, as well as all those who join them, must correct themselves first. That is not an indication that Jews are higher quality than others. In fact, Jews today are greater egoists than are members of any other nation. In a corrected state, Israel is a corrected desire directed at the Creator. Israel is the name given to altruistic desires, meaning desires for bestowal (GE–Galgalta ve Eynaim). The name "Gentiles," or "nations of the world," is given to egoistic desires, or desires to receive (AHP–Awzen, Hotem, Peh). That is why it is said that Israel, meaning GE, will be a minority. When the rest of the nations are corrected, the Light of Hochma will appear in each and every soul, as well as in the collective vessel of mankind.

The nations of the world subconsciously feel their dependency on Israel. They are given that feeling by the Creator to press on the Jews and set them in motion towards correction. It is difficult for us to imagine what this means in terms of spiritual growth, when one group has to wait for another and is completely dependent on another for one's own correction.

The state of Israel is a gift from the Creator and has a right to exist only to the extent that it gives altruism the right to exist. This is the idea of nearing the Creator that is spreading throughout the world. The Creator's Will to render delight is not enough. It takes movement on the part of man, too, from below, to want to receive this precise pleasure.

We still don't feel this desire and are therefore slowly losing what we were given, without even being aware of it. We are still not ready to receive the spiritual Land of Israel. Furthermore, we are even willing to give our land away because we are not spiritually connected with the gift that we've been given.

The word *Eretz* (land) means *Malchut*, or *Ratzon* (desire). The word *Ysrael* (Israel) comes from the words, *Yashar El* (straight to God), meaning the land of Israel is a state where one's every desire is directed toward the Creator. When a person is in that state, we say about him that "he is in the land of Israel," or that he has returned to it.

That is why it is said that there is nothing more important than being in the land of Israel. It is also said that all the *Mitzvot* are valid when performed in the land of Israel, and performing them outside of Israel is merely a reminder until such time that one arrives at the land of Israel.

That is why we are not only unable to receive the present of the land of Israel, but we are even willing to be rid of it. We do not feel the Giver of the present, and that makes us unable to appreciate its importance.

As long as we are not cleansed from the shells, they will continue to pressure us. That is why, today, we are dependent on the Arabs. They will continue to run our lives for us until we replace our egoistic vessels with altruistic ones. Everything that happens in this land is defined by spiritual roots. These roots can be affected through our desires.

We have no other alternative except to be worthy of the land of Israel, either through the path of Kabbalah or the path of pain.

When we try to make contact with the Creator, discovering and feeling Him, we perform our work under one of two conditions: "single concealment" or "double concealment." One is completely blind while in double concealment, and the Creator is completely hidden. Such a person exists only in this world.

However, in single concealment, we begin to understand that it is the Creator who influences our work, though we are yet to feel the

Creator explicitly. However, from time to time the feeling of connection with Him disappears and we sink entirely into our world once more. These states constantly change in such a person.

This struggle of a person with self is expressed in one's free choice. Free choice is only possible in a state of complete concealment of the Creator. Therefore, one should appreciate this state, for it is the only state that can bear fruit and produce shoots that in due time will bear spiritual fruit.

This spiritual fruit is attained precisely in a state of concealment, when we advance without knowing or understanding anything, in total darkness, against every reasonable conception. When we attain the revelation of the Creator we reminisce over our dark past, for now when we see the Creator and feel Him, we seemingly lose our freedom of choice.

There are two kinds of providence: general and private. General providence is executed through the Surrounding Light and acts on mankind and nature as a whole. It is this providence that leads the entire world by a predetermined plan toward the end of correction. It leads to the realization of the fact that technological "progress" is leading humanity to a dead end. It may render superficial sensations of satiation and abundance, but it produces an inner void, a complete emptiness.

Private Providence, on the other hand, works on each and every person individually, through Inner Light. A person who begins to seek connection with the Creator in our world is affected by the Private Providence of the Creator.

The contact with the spiritual world is created when there is a screen that rides over the egoistic desires. When we change our egoistic properties and turn them into altruistic ones, we receive the Light of the Creator in our corrected vessels, corrected properties.

The process of spiritual ascent is a long and strenuous journey. One must be reborn in every single degree until finally resembling the Creator, and then blending with Him completely.

CHAPTER 2.10
THE SENSATION OF THE LIGHT

The Creator influences us through various things in our environ-ment. It is our duty to understand that everything that happens to us is nothing but the Creator approaching us. If we react correctly to this influence, we will begin to understand and feel what it is that the Creator actually wants from us, to the point where we will begin to feel Him.

The Creator influences us not only through certain people, but also through the entire reality. The world is built the way it is precisely because it is the best way for the Creator to influence and promote us to the purpose of Creation.

When we encounter various situations in our everyday lives, we do not feel the influence of the Creator behind them. That is because our properties are completely opposite from His. But as soon as we begin to equalize with the Creator, even if just a tiny bit, we immediately begin to feel Him.

In response to every strike of fate, we should ask the right ques-tion: "Why was it given to me?" not, "What have I done to deserve this punishment?" or, "Why is the Creator doing this to me?" There are no punishments, though we find many depictions of them in the Torah. There are only inducements to move mankind toward the perfect state.

Our minds are but tools of extra support that aid us in correctly perceiving what we sense. We should relate to our lives as one big class-room where the Creator is our teacher. Only He has all the knowledge and gives only as much as we are able to perceive at any given moment. With this attitude, slowly but surely the sensation of the Creator will come to our every newborn spiritual sense.

However, for the time being we keep turning our backs on the Source. We will be able to face it and approach Him only if we make a conscious effort. That is why the Creator sends us books and group mates, so we can make spiritual progress.

The student is in the corporeal world and the teacher is in the spiritual world. Because of ego, the student cannot understand or appreciate the teacher.

However, if students can "erase" their own minds, their reasoning, and their opinions, and operate with the mind of their teacher, who is already in the spiritual world, they can thus connect themselves with spirituality, even if on an unconscious level.

We do not see or feel the Creator in this world. For that reason, our egos cannot act for the Creator. However, students can see their teachers, talk to them, and learn from them. They trust and respect their teachers. Because of that, they can do things for their teachers.

It is much like the process where the AHP of the superior (the teacher) lowers itself into the GAR of the inferior (the student). Reaching the AHP of the teacher means to accept every act, thought, and advice given. If the student "unites" with the AHP of the teacher, the teacher can raise the student temporarily and reveal what spirituality is.

When we read such books that were written by righteous men such as Baal HaSulam, Rabbi Shimon Bar-Yochay, and Rabbi Baruch Ashlag, we connect with them through the Surrounding Light that purifies our desires, meaning our vessels.

Therefore, when we read these books, we must always remember the writer's spiritual degree. That enables us to not only connect with the ideas and direction, but also forms a bridge that could help us in our progress as we bond with the author. It is not important if the author is alive or not; we can bond in our feelings while studying the author's books.

At the age of 18, the eldest son of Baal HaSulam, Baruch Ashlag, finished his studies at the Yeshiva (school for orthodox Jews) and started to work as a construction worker. He would rise before dawn, eat a kilogram of bread and onion, drink a little water, and go to work. Bread and onion was also his supper. On holidays he would add a little herring or something else that would make his meal more festive.

Rabbi Baruch Ashlag lived a very hard life. He was among the workers who built the Hebron-Jerusalem road. The workers lived in tents and would move from place to place while doing each section of the road.

The cook permitted Baruch Ashlag to study in the kitchen from 3 a.m. In return, Baruch would fill and warm the pots so the cook wouldn't have to rise so early in the morning.

He continued this way of life even after he got married. His wife and children lived in Jerusalem, and when he arrived there, he would attend his father's lessons, which meant walking from the old city of Jerusalem to Givat Shaul (the neighborhood where Baal HaSulam lived), over an hour's walk each way. In those days, there was also the possibility of meeting a jackal on the way.

In the house of Baal HaSulam was poverty and shortages to the point of hunger. But there were things that were a must for him, such as paper, ink and coffee. He wrote constantly, for writing was his life.

When Baal HaSulam died, Rabash stopped working and began to build a group of students. However, things went slowly and with great difficulty. His students began their studies at the ages of 14-15, and when they grew and got married, their ambition to study diminished significantly. Instead of coming daily, they would come only once a week or even once a month.

Every person is given unique problems to solve. Sometimes, the smallest obstacle can become an impassable wall.

Later, in 1984, I brought my teacher dozens of new students, and Rabash began to write articles for daily group lessons. But even before that he would always write about the spiritual worlds that he discovered. I recorded all my lessons with my rabbi.

Today, there are several books based on that material, much of which was written on small scraps of paper. These now constitute an important addition to the writing of Baal HaSulam.

Baal HaSulam spoke of many things, but there was one thing he described very clearly: we must not forget that there is a Leader to the world, and sometimes, when the need arises, He sends His messengers. Other times He lets us advance by ourselves.

There are many ways to connect with the Creator, and many supporting operations for which He is responsible. Thus, we can regard any obstacle on our path of study, including the departure of our teacher from this world, as a change in our own private providence.

The Creator changes His Providence, but always for the best, meaning every such change brings us closer to the end of correction. Although our egoism dictates its conditions to us and says that the former situation was better, easier, more pleasant, we must still try and see the Guidance of the Creator vividly in every situation and event.

Even when the Kabbalist dies and his many students are left without a teacher, it is a qualitative change in their work, since providence has become faster and tougher.

When we come closer to spirituality, we begin to feel much like a parachutist being thrown into the air for the first time. We know that there is a parachute behind us, but in the first seconds that we are in midair, we pray and ask ourselves, "What did I need this for?"

Then the parachute opens above us and we feel complete certainty. But that does not last very long because we will soon have to land on the ground. We forget that the parachute protects us, and use our own abilities to land safely. However, our fear is really subjective because it is actually the parachute that holds us and takes us slowly to the ground.

Rabbi Baruch Ashlag used to say about one of his students that when the student was given a new office, he was summoned to the minister's office. But the same night there was a banquet at the Rabbi's. He did not go to see the minister and did not get the job; he chose which was most important for him—meeting the rabbi.

Rabbi Ashlag did not leave behind any articles that were ready for print, because he did not want to publish his articles after his father, his great teacher. However, time passes and the demand for Kabbalistic texts changes. Today's students can no longer absorb the material the way it was presented to us.

We can say that Rabash was the last of the great Kabbalists of the past. Contained within him was the entire history of Judaism. His knowledge of the history of Judaism and the great rabbis of the last generations was very impressive, and he would tell their stories as though they were a part of his own life.

We can clearly see from his stories that in the beginning of the 20th century there was a spiritual decline that reached so low that the gates to the spiritual world began to close, and a time of spiritual darkness began.

If a person in previous centuries had been offered the opportunity to devote an entire life in return for spiritual attainment, that person would instantly agree. Today, however, we are so immersed in our daily nonsense that we cannot break free from it.

Students today must aspire for a very close connection with their teachers because they represent a very high degree of spiritual development, and the attainment of that degree is the goal of every student.

When Rabash's students were next to him, they felt an immense source of spiritual power. It was very difficult to think like him, much less understand his actions and motives. It was also difficult for the Rabbi to relate to his students, as he had to reduce himself to their level and conceal his attainment in order to give his students the freedom of choice.

Any understanding is given according to one's own spiritual progress. That keeps one safe from breaking. It is very difficult to understand a person who lives a corporeal and spiritual life at the same time; it is always bewildering to determine why some things are important and others are ignored by such a person. Sometimes it is completely incomprehensible before you reach a minimal spiritual degree.

Rabash was very interested in natural sciences such as physics and chemistry. He immediately connected everything he learned with Kabbalah and saw what had been revealed and what had not.

The desire to take a spiritual path is given to us by the Creator, but man must make the effort that this course demands. Students of Kabbalah must ask themselves constantly what their purpose is in such studies. Are they studying Kabbalah to take the knowledge into their egos, or to feel the Creator and correct themselves?

Any person who marches on the path to spirituality and learns about the way to ascend to it circulates the books and the media that contain Kabbalah lessons. By doing so, it is like adhering to the Will of the Creator and spreading His ideas in the world, thus becoming a partner of the Creator in this world, approaching Him in actions and thoughts.

The revelation of the Creator to the creature is a moment when the creature equalizes its own properties with the Light that extends from the Creator. That is to say, the Creator appears in the specific property that has been equalized with Him.

We must complete the equivalence of our attributes with Him on the entire spiritual ladder while we are in this world and within one lifetime. All our past lives are but preparation to climb the rungs of the ladder until we reach the world's Maker.

CHAPTER 2.11
LINKING THE WORLDS

Reality consists of a Creator, or the will to bestow and give pleasure, and a creature, or the will to receive pleasure. There is nothing else in our reality except these two components.

When the will to enjoy is corrected through a spiritual screen that acts against egoism, it is called a *Partzuf*, which is a spiritual object. When the *Partzuf* receives pleasure in order to please the Creator, performing

Zivug de Hakaa, this act is called a *Mitzva*, and the Light that enters the *Partzuf* is called "Torah."

If a person can receive the Light of the Torah into one's corrected egoism while performing a physical *Mitzva*, then the physical world and the spiritual world are now combined within that person.

In order to do this, one must first learn what one wishes to attain from this act. Simply performing *Mitzvot* (plural for *Mitzva*) gives no spiritual attainment, but only places one in a degree of "spiritual still." Only one's aim—its power and direction—can bring one into the spiritual world and determine the spiritual degree and extent of sensation of the Upper Light (attainment of the Creator) that will be achieved.

It is said that a "*Mitzva* without an aim is like a body without a soul." This means that a *Mitzva* without an aim is "dead" in the spiritual sense. It is in a degree called "still."

The purpose of Kabbalah is to teach us how to aim correctly. That is the reason that Kabbalah is called "the wisdom of the hidden." Only the individual can know what he or she aims for, and sometimes even that is unclear to the person involved.

Therefore, Kabbalah teaches us to examine our exact intentions so we will eventually begin to feel our egoism and our real essence—the desire to enjoy without any reservations or consideration of the needs of others.

In the beginning of our spiritual quest, we cannot quite understand why we become so engrossed in Kabbalah, and engage so heavily in the study. We do those things without any awareness of our motives. Only afterwards, when we discover the Creator, do we begin to see and feel how we've been led from Above, and then it all falls into place.

All the worlds have been prepared in advance within us. They do not exist without the perceiving person. One perceives only this or that section of the uniform and eternal Light that extends from the worlds. We refer to it as "our world" and give these sections names. These names are spiritual discriminations that we make through which we begin to gradually attain the outside world, the world that is outside our own.

If we want to accelerate our progress, we must receive additional desire for spiritual elevation from one another, meaning we must cling to others' desires for spiritual elevation. However, we come in contact with many people who are not related to Kabbalah, and may thus pick up their thoughts and wishes. If we bring these external desires into the group, we may unconsciously "infect" our friends and obstruct their spiritual progress. That will turn against us in a form of weakness and lack of motivation for the study. Hence, all of us must be very hesitant in our choices of environment and moderate our connection with it.

Our mission is to clean ourselves entirely from external issues, whether good or bad, according to our current opinions. We must live only our pure selves, through which we will be able to feel the Creator. We can advance using our own vessels (desires), or we can use vessels that come from a superior *Partzuf*, meaning the vessels of our teacher.

Rabash had many students who would get together once a week to stimulate feelings about the importance of their work. This would help create a collective vessel. Every Kabbalist since the time of Rabbi Shimon Bar-Yochay held weekly assemblies of friends for this purpose. The Ari and Rabbi Moshe Chaim Lutzato (Ramchal) wrote about such assemblies, as well as other Kabbalists in Russia, among which are some of the greatest teachers of the previous generations.

The influence of the outer society awakens our beastly desires, which become a serious obstacle for spiritual progress. We must avoid the company of people who try to influence us, either consciously or unconsciously. Even speaking to such a person can result in a loss of spiritual achievements that took months to attain.

I do not wish to encourage isolation from society, but a beginning student must be extra careful regarding the knowledge that he or she absorbs. After all, our only free choice consists of choosing the right environment, meaning the society that we join and whose influence we are subject to.

We are but egoistic points that should ripen to spiritual work. This "point in our heart" that opens and ripens is the root and the beginning

THE PATH OF KABBALAH

of everything. All other activities are but consequences and results of that point. The only thing that was created is a will to receive pleasure, meaning a desire to enjoy for one's own gratification at varying degrees of evolution.

The desire for self-indulgence is called a "shell." It covers us until we develop enough to ask to be rid of it in order to reach the fruit itself, the corrected shell itself.

The corrected shell *and* the fruit are a desire to bestow, to give and receive pleasure, like the Creator. A shell is a spiritual concept; its spiritual body consists of (like the body of a pure *Partzuf*) a *Rosh* (head) and a *Guf* (body). The *Rosh* of the shell is called *Daat* (wisdom) and the *Guf* of the shell is called "reception." The pure *Rosh* is called "faith above reason" and the *Guf* itself is called "bestowal."

Only a group of friends united by their desire can bring others out of the situations they fall into, where they are unable to control or criticize themselves. If one meets with friends on a day-to-day basis, it helps purify one's thoughts and gives a thrust forward in the right direction.

CHAPTER 2.12
THE BODY AT THE END OF CORRECTION

Will we retain our physical bodies after the end of correction? Kabbalah never speaks of the physical body because it is simply not a part that needs correction. There are no changes in the body except for its aging. Only the will to receive pleasure needs to be corrected. Our bodies are only flesh; they need sleep, physical pleasures, food, and rest.

They have nothing in common with the internal, spiritual correction. That is why the body doesn't change when the soul changes. Even our characters remain the same. My rabbi was still running around at the age of eighty. He just didn't know how to take things slowly. That was his character and it never changed.

In our current state, we are unable to imagine what the world will be like when our souls are corrected. Our bodies will lose their meaning.

Will there still be a universe and everything around us? Will we bear children? Will we live and die?

Today our lives are filled with agony and pain. We cannot begin to imagine how the physical lives we live today can be filled with spirit at the end of correction.

Diseases are a consequence of inner corrections and should vanish once the corrections are done. It is the correction until the end of the 6,000 years that we are talking about. We cannot discuss or explain the seventh, eighth, ninth, and tenth millennia, just as we cannot explain what it means to remain without a physical body when our life in this world is through. It is also impossible to explain how the body does remain after the end of correction, because all our situations are branches that exist because of their spiritual roots, and once correction occurs, that connection is nonexistent.

We do not correct the will to receive in and of itself, or the egoism. We correct only those parts of the desires that have connected and mingled with altruistic desires during the breaking of the vessels. That is why we cannot see the full picture of suitability and equivalence of form at the end of correction. If we would actually feel it, we would be completely healthy every *Shabbat* (Saturday) and no one would die on that day. It is impossible for us to picture a perfect state.

We do not get the answers to our prayers and requests from Above at the time we make them, or even near it. It can happen months later. A Kabbalist can feel spiritual states of *Shabbat* or a holiday on weekdays too.

For example, if my soul connects with someone else's, then the question I had will present itself in that person's emotions, while for me the question might have already been replaced by another. These perpetual changes are called "reincarnations of the souls." We cannot understand how these jumps occur or why, but there is a certain degree of spiritual attainment that once there, reveals how souls bond and separate. It can be compared to a welling forth, a continuous flow, transition from place to place and from one soul to another. But there is no accurate definition for it.

There is a collective and an individual part in every one of us. The collective part remains unchanged, while the individual can and does change. As soon as one wants to receive something from the Creator, and that someone is in a state of seeing the Creator's face, that person's soul is ready to receive the Light of the Creator, and instantaneously and naturally receives it. The spiritual world is different from our own because every desire is immediately answered.

Baal HaSulam writes that the attribute of *Malchut* that is clothed in the worlds is called the "self." That attribute expands down to the world of *Assiya*, where it is felt as an independent entity. The self always remains, but its form is corrected. When one corrects one's self, one immediately begins to feel the Creator.

The breaking of the vessels played a major and positive role in continuing the process of correcting the desires. Without it, we would always remain in the still, vegetative, and animate degree and would never be able to make even the slightest connection with the Creator.

Our bodies experience a variety of sensations. The spiritual body contains no emotions. Instead, there are *Sefirot*, which are completely different from emotions. I cannot say that my vision is a consequence of my spiritual vision, called "wisdom," that reflects the sensation of a certain Light that is clothed in the appropriate spiritual vessel.

For example, using the screen, I can feel the Light of *Haya* in a vessel that has *Aviut Aleph* (first degree coarseness). There is a field of waves around us, and each sense perceives waves of different wavelength. The same thing happens in spirituality; there is a special kind of Light that enters its appropriate vessel. However, there is no connection whatsoever between the animate emotional system and the spiritual sensation of the Light.

We correct our left line through the right line, thus building a middle line from the both of them. The middle line renders a possibility to equalize with the Creator to the extent that we have corrected ourselves. That completes the job of that specific degree.

Afterwards, we reenter the left line and must again correct it with the right, thus building the middle line, and again we receive a certain portion of the Light of the Creator, which in turn makes us just a little more like Him.

The process repeats itself when that degree is also completed. It might seem dull from the outside, but that is the way to climb the spiritual ladder. It is a perpetual process of intermittently acquiring desires and fulfilling them. This is life, and it is a magical feeling indeed! It is like a very intense hunger and satiation experienced simultaneously.

The maximum intensity of using the right aim over our desires in each degree is also the bridge through which we pass on to the next.

Our time in history is a transition period toward spiritual evolution. Every soul can absorb only as much as its own level of development makes possible. We must not pressure people to study Kabbalah, because if they are not interested, it means that their time has not yet come.

CHAPTER 2.13
QUESTIONS & ANSWERS

WHAT IS THE MEANING OF OUR LIVES?

Q: People asked about the meaning of their lives in previous generations, but in our generation everyone can study Kabbalah. Is that because of our virtues or because of our sins?

A: Yes, it's true that such questions are not new. But in our generation, the question about the meaning of our lives is being asked more acutely. The souls that return to our world are riper now, better prepared. In the past, people were less interested in finding the meaning of their lives, and more interested in science, social science, culture, literature, and so on.

THE PATH OF KABBALAH

But nowadays we have become disillusioned with everything: there is less talk about the ability of science to provide peace of mind and confidence; people often seek answers to the most basic questions about the anguish they experience, and they are finally beginning to understand that the source of all this trouble is the concealment of the Creator and our dissimilarity from Him. People are beginning to feel a yearning to connect with Him, and that ultimately leads them to Kabbalah.

Humanity is approaching a state of searching for the meaning of life, but not at the level of our world, as they realize that there is no happiness in high technology, or the development of our culture and ethics. Drugs and other accessories for pleasure produce a desire to avoid such questions as the desire to understand the meaning of life, but nonetheless, it remains as vital.

KABBALAH & ME

Q: Has everything been preordained?

A: The starting point and final point are determined by the Creator. But the way from the starting to the final points depends on us. We have the ability to choose which way to reach the purpose of Creation. But even at the starting point we operate under the pressure of our absolute egoism. We are its slaves and are motivated only by egoistic desires.

When we change our nature from egoism to altruism, we also become slaves, but this time to an altruistic nature. The freedom of desire is only in the choice of whom to serve: Pharaoh or Moses. Therefore, the entire Torah is a guide to attain the purpose of Creation. As it is said, "I have created the evil inclination, I have created for it the Torah as a spice" (Gomorrah *Masechet Kidushin* p. 30;2), meaning, "I have created egoism and I have given the Torah/Kabbalah in order to correct it."

All the parts in the Torah were given to us to match our attributes with those of the Creator. But each generation must focus on a certain part of the Torah.

A Kabbalist named Moses rose to the spiritual world through his spiritual understanding, meaning he was able to feel spiritual degrees, and he described them in a book he called "the Torah."

The Torah strictly forbids depicting spiritual phenomena as physical entities. It is forbidden to picture a distinguished old man named Moses climbing down Mt. Sinai with a book of Torah in his hand. Torah means "the Light of the Creator." Every word in the Torah is a name of the Creator. The names of the Creator are one's sensations of Him, while He Himself has no name.

It is the attaining individual who gives names to the Creator according to one's perception of Him: "Kind," "Merciful," "Mighty," "Fearful," and so on. The Torah describes everything Moses discovered and understood of the spiritual worlds, everything that the Creator revealed before him and commanded him to convey to us so that we perform it.

The purpose of the creation of this world by the Creator is spiritual unification with Him, the correction of man's properties, or in other words: spiritual ascent. There are 620 spiritual degrees from our point, which is the lowest possible, to the Creator. Each of those degrees is called a Mitzva.

When we correct ourselves through a certain altruistic act, we perform a certain Mitzva and consequently ascend to the corresponding degree. This means that there are 620 further corrections of adoptions of altruistic desires that we must perform after we rise above the egoistic nature of our world.

At the last and highest spiritual degree, we unite with the Creator completely. Our properties and desires become completely identical to those of the Creator. We must attain that state of complete sameness of attributes with those of the Creator while living physically in our world.

Thus, the completion of the entire Creation is attained, and the gap between the highest and the lowest points of Creation is breached. In that state, everything returns to the Creator, to His Attributes, to the Source and to a state of infinite altruistic bliss. It is only at that spiritual degree that the soul is liberated from the necessity of going through the degrees of "this world" again.

But as long as there are corrections to perform, we must return here over and over again. Only when we complete our correction through the study of the wisdom of Kabbalah is this cycle finished.

Why do people interpret and relate so differently to the text of the Torah? After all, the Kabbalists themselves described the spiritual world for us and gave us this book. They called it "Torah" to indicate that it relates to the words, *Ohr* (light) and *Hora'a* (instruction).

Kabbalists can sense the Upper Worlds and depict these sensations in their books in a unique language. But those who can not yet see and feel the spiritual worlds cannot understand the explanations of Kabbalists. After all, there are no physical bodies like our own in the spiritual world, and there are no names that you can use to name the objects there. It is, in fact, impossible to convey these feelings in a language that humans understand.

But because everything that exists in our world stems from the Upper Worlds, and every physical object has a spiritual root above, Kabbalists decided to name every spiritual entity according to its worldly branch, which seemingly passes from Above downward, from a spiritual root to a corresponding material body in our world. The spiritual root is the cause and the worldly branch is the projection, the consequence.

The entire Torah was written in this descriptive language. It speaks only of spiritual forces, as do all the other holy books. The books can be divided into those that use a legal tongue, such as the Talmud, or a historic tale tongue, such as the Pentateuch. But all these books describe nothing but the spiritual worlds. They have no intention whatsoever of referring to our world.

Confusion is created only when we read these books and automatically interpret the words according to our understanding, which knows only terms of our world. As a result, we begin to think that it speaks of things that happen in our world. But a Kabbalist who reads the same text understands precisely what the author meant in each section of the book. It is a lot like a musician who can sing the music by merely looking at the notes.

Q: We don't feel the Creator and consequently we don't believe that He exists. We cannot see the Upper World; we don't know and don't understand a thing about it. None of the existing sciences enables us to influence the future, so on what grounds do you claim that it is possible to influence it?

A: The wisdom of Kabbalah does not study the phenomena of this world, but its spiritual roots in the Upper World. These roots affect everything that happens in our world and produce the events of our lives. A person who studies Kabbalah begins to see and understand the Upper World.

By seeing the Upper World, we begin to feel the Creator and understand how He created the spiritual world. The wisdom of Kabbalah refers to this act as the "first day of Creation." In the acts that follow, meaning in the next days, the Creator created the nature of the Upper World and the forces that manage it. The last act of the Creator, on the sixth day, was the Creation of *Adam ha Rishon*.

Because *Adam ha Rishon* was the consequence of the last act of the Creator, he also constitutes the purpose of the entire Creation. Everything that was created before him was created for him. So judging by the program of the Creator, what should become of man? He must attain spiritual unity with the Creator, become like Him in every aspect, equalize with Him, and learn to manage his own destiny.

Furthermore, man must attain the highest spiritual degree of total completeness alone. That means that he must first be at the lowest spiritual degree, completely opposite to the attributes of the Creator, and then rise to the spiritual degree of the Creator through his own spiritual efforts.

The wisdom of Kabbalah can be used to observe both the spiritual world and our world, and the reciprocation between them. Knowledge that constantly descends from the Upper World to ours and materializes before our very eyes. Our reactions to this information rise to the Upper World as knowledge and determine whether we feel our tomorrows as positive or negative.

Therefore, the Creator, who is at the highest spiritual degree, formed this Creation from an egoistic attribute, which is the complete opposite of Him, and filled it to the brim with Light. He then emptied it and lowered it to the degree of "our world." A creature that ascends the spiritual ladder receives a much more intense pleasure than prior to its decline to this world.

Q: If there is an Upper Force that governs us and every little insect in our world, then how are we different from robots?

A: If we use Kabbalah to change our inner properties, we also change the external influence that operates on us. Because this entire world is built to guide us to perfection, our process of individual correction also changes a bit of the outside world as well, and uncovers its better side toward us. It is then easier for both the individual and for all mankind to progress to the ultimate goal. The beginning and the end points are preordained, but the road there can be a path of Kabbalah or a path of pain. Which path we take is up to us.

Q: Will Kabbalah help my professional progress?

A: Kabbalah not only enhances one's sensation and attainment of Upper Worlds, it also deepens, expands, and refines other emotions. We improve our connections with our environment and the events around us, and learn to regard science as a trivial thing that is used only for mankind's general sustenance and adaptation to the world around us, and nothing more.

When we first begin to study Kabbalah, we are normally quite confused with all the new terms and emotions. Later on, we begin to relate to science from a superior point of view, seeing it as something incidental. That helps us avoid bowing before science, and relate to it in a truer and more profound manner. Kabbalah enables scientists to progress and obtain a more complete attainment even on the level of our limited world.

Q: You mentioned that there is general providence that leads mankind in general, and that one who begins to study Kabbalah can change one's life and fate. Can a person who studies Kabbalah some-how change the collective current of life in his environment, not only for himself, but for others, too?

A: It can be done, but only by circulating Kabbalah to other people, gently and without being a missionary. We can discretely inform people around us that there is such a thing as Kabbalah and interest them in reading books that were written by Kabbalists. That is enough to put one in a completely different state regarding the Creator, where there is already a different kind of Providence on Him from Above.

I have no other answer: books, audio and video files, our Internet site (www.kabbalah.info). We do everything to provide people with what-ever means they choose to change their fates. In any event, people will come to it in just a few years' time as they realize that mascots, charms, and blessings are not the solution to how to change their lives. We must all determine our own fates, and not discharge ourselves from this re-sponsibility. Changing our lives cannot be bought for money or any other currency.

THE SPIRITUAL WORLD

Q: What is a spiritual birth? Is it anything like a physical birth?

A: Everything that happens in our world matches perfectly what happens in a spiritual birth. When one is completely liberated from ego-ism, this state corresponds to that of a fetus in its mother's womb. The fetus then goes through nine months of spiritual development that correspond to a state of conception, until it is born as an independent, though small being. Then there are two years of infancy and feeding at the "breast" of the superior. Then, the infant continues to grow (at the expense of the superior *Partzuf*, but in a separated form) until the age of thirteen, and from that age begins the state of *Gadlut* (adulthood). This is how every person's soul develops.

Everything the Kabbalah books describe, everything that happens in our world and everything the Torah speaks of are processes of ascent on the spiritual ladder. There is nothing but a human being and the Creator, and our entire way is meant to bring us closer to Him.

Q: How can one know one has attained a connection with the spiritual world?

A: Everything we can imagine comes as a consequence of our experiences in the physical body. Therefore, all the "flying" experiences and other such "spiritual events" are completely disconnected from the actual spiritual world.

The sensation of spirituality can be obtained only by means of a screen, an anti-egoistic trait that can be acquired only through the system of Kabbalah. This necessitates group work, the right teacher, and a number of years of intensive study with the right books. Sometimes a person can get a feeling of the spiritual world without any preparation. However, it is a passive feeling because one is unable to correct the self when receiving it as a gift from Above without prior efforts to create the screen.

This has nothing to do with the evolution of an ordinary soul in the path of correction; it is just something that the Creator needed to do according to His own program of development of unification and separation of souls. That is why He did it. If we could see the entire picture of the reincarnation of souls we would understand why the Creator acts this or that way with a certain soul. No part of our collective soul can attain the goal, the spiritual degree of the Creator, before it has been corrected.

The Creator will allow no one, under any conditions, into the spiritual world without a spiritual effort. If He did, one would be unable to create a vessel, the desire necessary to feel the perfection of the Creator.

Q: What would happen if the Creator appeared before us right now?

A: In that case, we would take the pleasure for ourselves and would never be able to exit this egoistic pleasure, though it is so small it is practically nonexistent compared to spiritual pleasures—those sensed with the aim toward the Creator. The Creator hides from us to allow us to build a screen, which is the aim towards the Creator. Only afterwards will He reveal Himself to us. Only then will the pleasure be infinite and lasting, because that is the nature of altruistic desires.

Q: But you keep saying that all we need in order to enter the spiritual world is the revelation of the Creator?

A: What I mean in this case is not the pleasures that come from the Creator, but the revelation of His Godliness. When that happens, we will nullify ourselves before the Creator and be able to cancel our egoistic desires and obtain a screen. Only afterwards will the Creator reveal Himself as the Source of all pleasures.

Q: How do you differentiate between "good" and "evil"?

A: Our perception of good and evil is very different from how they are perceived in spirituality. Good and bad in our world are based on subjective, egoistic feelings, meaning something is good if it is good for me, and bad if it is bad for me. Only when one transcends egoism does one grasp what good and evil really are.

Everything is done by the Creator, but we are unable to justify His Actions. Global disasters, wars, and annihilation of entire nations, horrendous torments, and trouble everywhere are called good by those who attain the collective picture of the universe and the worlds.

Q: What is the "freedom of desire"?

A: When one attains the spiritual world, one attains everything that descends to our world—the roots and where and how they concatenate to our world. Every earthly event begins in the spiritual world. Everything that happened and that will happen to us stems from there.

The system of Kabbalah means having faith above reason, and the Kabbalist never exploits knowledge for self-gratification. That is why the knowledge of self or others is of no significance because the Kabbalist will never use it in the ordinary way people want.

Many people ask me about the future, but I tell them to go see a fortune teller. What I can do is advise about what one should do, but it is forbidden to open the picture to others because you are denying them freedom of choice and freedom of desire. That will result in the loss of their desire for living, because if everything is known before it even happens, then why bother living? Our lives are only pleasant when we have a little bit of freedom of desire. That is what separates us from all other creatures in Creation and we must utilize that freedom.

Q: When one attains the spiritual world, what does one find there?

A: One finds absolute harmony within. One finds that everything is conducted by an Upper Force that brings all Creations to a single goal. One finds one's own goal and stops making mistakes. One understands why illness occurs, and the purpose of the troubles in life. One begins to understand the good or harm that actions bring and how to behave with others. There is no longer a need to learn anything from anyone because this person becomes a part of Creation. There are no needs to satisfy within; it is toward this state that the Creator is leading us.

There are only two choices we have: the first is the one all of mankind is presently taking. It entails suffering and running from pain to pain without any ability to find any reason for living. This state may continue until the pain accumulates and brings one to a spiritual degree. It is impossible to know or feel the previous amount of pain that has been accumulated, but every soul keeps its own account and needs a different amount of suffering to bring it to spirituality. This is the first path, the path of pain. It is a very long and agonizing road.

However, the Creator gives every person a way out of the anguish that befalls us and offers the spiritual world through a second path—the path of Kabbalah (Torah). The Hebrew word, "Torah," means "instruction." There are clear instructions in the Torah/Kabbalah that teach us how to attain spiritual attainment, while combining it with family life, study and work. It tells us how to discover our inner spiritual worlds, as well as the outer physical world.

DESIRE

Q: If we are only a desire, like all other Creations, then what is our deepest desire?

A: Our deepest desire is to cleave to the Creator. That is everyone's unconscious desire. It has been imprinted in us to begin with and it is the only desire that we are actually eager to satisfy. But that desire only becomes clear to us to the extent that we are willing to accept and realize it. Until that point, the Creator continues to push and tempt us with new desires, meaning the primary desire is clothed with other desires.

Q: What if, as a spiritual seeker, I suddenly have an urge to steal something?

A: There will not be such a desire. There can be a desire to steal, but there will be a thought that follows it, because that is the Creator's way of showing us how despicable and dirty we are.

Along with the desire will be the sensation of repulsion at such a desire appearing in us. That is why the "recognition of evil" exists. An ordinary person does not regard such desires as evil, but rationalizes, "Well, I'm no different than anybody else."

It is written that God said to Abraham, "Look now towards heaven" and promised him that his seed and his people would be like the stars in the sky—innumerable. Stars are sparks of returning Light that broke from the collective soul. One collects these sparks, corrects them, and thus ascends. For that reason, the sparks, which are souls that rise upward, are called "stars." The Creator promised Abraham that if he followed this path, the entire heavens would be his.

DEATH

Q: Does a part of the soul pass on from parent to child?

A: A human is a two-legged animal. It has a vital force called the "animate soul." When a person dies, the soul leaves the body, just like that of any other animal. But Kabbalah speaks of a different kind of soul, one that is the Light of the Creator.

A soul has a certain amount of Light that enters only when that person acquires specific altruistic attributes. It has nothing to do with the identity of one's parents.

Q: Most people find death distressing, but what is the death of the body really like?

A: Our problem with death begins with what we tie our egos to—do we associate the ego with our bodies, or with our souls, our internal part? If one lives inside the properties and desires of the soul, then one remains with it and connects with it. For such a person, death is not tragic, but just a transition to a different state. It is as though certain obstructions that the body had are removed so one can pass to a more perfect and complete state, with an improved ability for spiritual progress.

It turns out that death is something in which one can only be happy. Death indicates that you are on the right path for spiritual progress and have already completed a certain portion of the journey. Now that that part is completed, you are free to continue without the weight of the physical body.

Q: What happens to a person who experiences clinical death?

A: People who experience clinical death experience a detachment from the ego because they enter a post-mortem state. Though not yet spiritual, that state is no longer animate because clinical death separates one from one's ego. One is incapable of feeling what spirituality is like before acquiring a screen, because one lacks the sensation tool called "Returning Light," the aim for the Creator.

However, one can still feel the fineness of spirituality because of the pain that was suffered. Agony neutralizes egoism because it brings the ego to a situation where it is willing to become nullified if only to stop the pain.

A rabbi was once sent to an imprisoned man in Russia. He was in a very poor mental state, without any knowledge of Hebrew, but he wrote poems in Hebrew about sublime spiritual states only a Kabbalist could experience. Of course, he did not use Kabbalistic terms, but he experienced states of disconnection from our world. Those experiencing clinical death also feel a higher spiritual state because they have gone through such extreme torments that the ego inflicted, they are enough to repel one from one's egoism.

These torments make us start looking at ourselves "from the side," and we begin to feel some spiritual sensation. However, that is not the way the Kabbalah advises us to take because we have the Kabbalah as a cure. In the path of torment, people feel these things in the worst possible situations, but that is not the way we should go.

Torments do not come directly from the Creator. When the animate soul dies, we feel a little more Light from Above, but it is billions of times smaller than the lowest spiritual state we acquire as a result of our own labor!

Q: Do we pass to the spiritual world when we die?

A: The soul is man's spiritual vehicle, man's inner self. It is in a certain spiritual state before it enters this world. Because the purpose of Creation is to raise the soul from its lowest to its highest possible state, the soul receives additional egoism, additional negative properties that hide the spiritual self from us.

The self had a certain spiritual foundation; it was above this world before it received additional egoism, which caused it to descend into this world. Egoism is added in the form of the desires of an animate body; this is how we begin to feel our birth and existence in the corporeal world. However, if we remove our additional egoism, we will immediately return to the place from which we descended into this world, meaning at our soul's original degree in the spiritual world.

Now we relate to the world as does everyone else. What we must do is to use our egoism to rise in spirituality. This way, we ascend by 620 degrees higher than the degrees from which we began.

When we rise from our world and reach the end of correction, we rise to the world of *Ein Sof* and feel 620 times more complete then our preliminary state. Our animate bodies die because we take away their egoistic satisfaction. The meaning of death is that the spiritual force that gives us the desire to live and absorb the force of life is taken away.

MISCELLANEOUS QUESTIONS & ANSWERS

Q: Why do all the meetings with the Creator occur on mountains (Mt. Olives, Mt. Moriah) etc.?

A: The word, Moriah comes from the word, *Mora* (fear); the word, *Har* (mountain) comes from the word, *Hirhurim* (contemplations) of *Mora*, which is a screen for the *Gar* of every degree. Sinai comes from the word, *Sina'a* (hatred), because there is concealment of the Light of Mercy.

Mt. Olives is *Malchut*, the point of this world, the end of all the worlds. Every place where *Malchut* ends without touching the point of "this world" is called Mt. Olives.

Q: Is there any connection between the spiritual Mt. Olives and the physical one?

A: There is no connection between the spiritual Mt. Olives and the physical one. That is why any person can call the mountain by that name, and not only one who has attained the spiritual Mt. Olives.

Q: How can we, as ordinary people, name anything according to its spiritual root if we haven't attained it and don't even know that it exists?

A: Any person, even a non-Jew, can name any place on earth according to one's spiritual roots, even without attaining these roots. That is because all people are messengers of the Creator, just as is the entire Creation and the whole of nature. Just as an ordinary person chooses that a mountain should be called Mt. Olives for some earthly reason, so a Kabbalist determines that this mountain should be named that way because of a spiritual root.

This teaches us that the difference between the attainment of an ordinary person and that of a Kabbalist is only in the depth of the attainment. The former sees only the external layer, and the latter sees the entire depth down to the primary reason. That is why Kabbalah is also a science. The only difference is that Kabbalah studies the full depth of the matter to its innermost layer, meaning the desire that was created by the Creator, which is robed by all other properties. For this reason, a Kabbalist and an ordinary person can both give something the same name because the olive trees grow on the same mountain.

The ordinary person has his or her own reason for calling something by its right name. Furthermore, the internal property with which the Creator created a spiritual object will appear in any language with the same meaning.

Q: What is a dream?

A: During sleep we are disconnected from spirituality. There are only electric currents that run through our minds and nothing more. If we disconnect the brain from the body during this time, there will not be any dreams. We can disconnect the ego from the body so that the body will sleep separated from the ego.

The state of slumber has nothing to do with spirituality. It exists in every living creature. The state of *Dormita* (slumber) in Kabbalah is the name given to the time when the Light leaves the *Partzuf* to a higher *Partzuf*. All that the *Partzuf* is left with is called *Kista de Hayuta* (a small pocket of life force), which is a uniting and strengthening force. That is the spiritual meaning of slumber. If one thinks of an idea during sleep, it is because the lessened connection with the physical body allows for clearer sight. As a result, the mind and imagination operate on a higher level, but that has nothing to do with spirituality.

Q: How and when does one attain spiritual understanding?

A: One comes by spiritual understanding only by making the spiritual effort of studying the wisdom of Kabbalah, as well as persistently struggling with the egoistic desires. The precise moment of understanding is untraceable. One cannot know when that time will come, because the spiritual efforts must be directed not toward understanding, but toward giving to the Creator. However, we must always believe that "God's salvation is as the wink of an eye."

Let me clarify attainment for you: I feel the consequences of my attainment within. I feel the delights I will receive ahead of time. If I can taste them, then the consequence will be experienced inside me. For example, I cannot say that there is any pleasure in a salad; the pleasure is in me to begin with, and the salad is just a means to bring out the delight in order to satisfy my desire. We can weigh or otherwise measure the salad any way we like, but we will not find any pleasure in it.

This means that the sense of pleasure exists inside us, including the sensation of the Creator. Generally speaking, we feel everything inside us. That is what I meant by saying that we feel "the giver behind the salad." The question is not how much salad, or how good was the salad we ate, but what kind of pleasure we experience at the time, because the pleasure is felt in the spiritual part of us.

Why did the Creator make it so that we would only be able to reach an altruistic vessel from an egoistic one? Even our ability to find the pleasure center in the brain and stimulate it will only be an external expression of these spiritual vessels.

Again, why did the Creator create an egoistic vessel from which we would rise to an altruistic one? Let's say that we rely on a small egoistic vessel that can contain ten grams, but we receive these ten grams from the Almighty Creator, and we use them to please the Creator. In that state, our pleasure depends on how great the Creator is, not on how great the ten grams are.

The ten grams are only an axis with which we can turn everything inside us and come to a reality where the pleasure is infinite. Then, time disappears and a state of perfection is created because of the connection with *Ein Sof*.

Q: Let us say that Israel, the Creator, and Divinity are one. What then is Divinity?

A: There is nothing but the Creator and the creature. The Creator created a creature, which is the will to receive pleasure from the Creator. The only thing that this desire can do is receive. It names what it feels, meaning it names the reflection of the Creator in its feelings. It all depends on our sensations, meaning how we are influenced by the Creator. These feelings are a consequence of two elements: the Creator Himself and our own sensations.

If we change those, we will feel the Creator differently. We will never know what the Creator is when not perceived through our senses. That is why we never speak of the Creator Himself, but only of how we feel Him inside us, in our senses. That feeling in our senses is called "Divinity."

Q: Can we know when we deserve to be punished or rewarded?

A: Let's say that a person was standing on a high porch. A part of it suddenly collapses and the person falls off and dies. Or perhaps a natural catastrophe suddenly happens. Whom do we blame?

When children break something we can punish them, but we will be doing so from within our animate understanding of reward and punishment. In that manner, we teach the child our own understanding and approach.

That is how it used to be in Russia. If I did not accept communism, they could punish me and even kill me. They set their own rules and their own justice, meaning their own understanding of good and evil. In fact, there must be an honest and objective system of reward and punishment, but not one that favors the initiators of the system, but the wellbeing of those who keep it.

It is impossible to provide an accurate and concise explanation of the concepts of reward and punishment. If the system is correct, it should teach us something and not merely exist. However, we cannot be objective; we don't know what hides behind our actions, which contradict the purpose of Creation because of our corrupted vessels. There is no reward or punishment from the Creator's perspective. He has no desire for man to do this or that.

There is only one assignment with regard to the Creator—to bring mankind to a special inner state, such that will enable us to receive the bounty and delight that is intended for us after we attain the purpose of Creation. The Creator has no desire to punish or reward anyone for any activity. He always leads us toward the purpose of Creation.

If that is the case, then to whom do these concepts of reward and punishment relate? A child? An adult? At which degree, which level of understanding does reward or punishment begin? A person who grows up in this world becomes subjugated to its rules. If we could know someone as well as the Creator does, we could predict that person's every move in every situation. That brings up the question: "Where is our freedom of choice, and what exactly are we liberated from?"

Is it freedom from the natural properties that the Creator inserted in us, or freedom from the influences of our environment? Where is that juncture where we can become free from both our own nature and our surroundings? If we knew for certain where we could choose freely, we could also speak of reward or punishment, because the steps we would take would be steps made through choices free of our own nature and other external influences.

We should know that with every move we make and every step we take, it is the Creator teaching us, fine-tuning our senses and directing us toward the purpose of Creation. If we could see it that way, then reward and punishment would take on a completely different meaning, depending on our goals.

In that case, everything that we would go through—the good and the bad—would be regarded as a reward. The bad would not be regarded as painful or tormenting, but as tutoring. Thus, we could interpret everything positively. It would mean that the division between reward and punishment simply did not exist, because we would find only positive aspects in how the Creator treats His creatures.

However, we do not come by such a feeling in only one experience, but after all sorts of concealments by the Creator. In the beginning, there is double concealment, then single concealment. After that comes the revelation of the Creator, and finally the attainment of eternity, completion, and love towards Him who has always loved us, and has always wanted to give each and every one of us nothing but the greatest possible pleasure.

Part Three: The Structure of the Upper Worlds

CHAPTER 3.1
ALTRUISM

All holy books describe spiritual states that one should attain. They all deal with one thing only: choosing the spiritual over the physical, choosing the greatness of the Creator. The Creator doesn't need our respect because He is completely devoid of egoism. The one thing He does need is to bring us pleasure, to the extent that we prefer Him over the corporeal world and become like Him.

Recognizing the greatness of the Creator testifies to one's degree of correction. Our pleasure upon unifying with the Creator can be infinite, eternal and complete, but only when it is not limited by egoism.

Altruism is a special characteristic that can be called forth to correct the vessel. Egoism brings nothing good—just consider the high percentage of wealthy people who commit suicide. Even if we give people everything and fill their cups of desire to the brim, they will still not feel that there is a meaning to their lives. In fact, receiving pleasure eliminates the desire for it. It is possible to feel the reasoning, the taste, only on the border between pleasure and pain.

The Creator set the demand to correct the vessel by turning it to altruism instead of egoism in our favor, not in His. Our current status is called "this world." Our next state is called "the next world." A "world" is what we feel at this minute; the next sensation is "a new world."

Any person who begins to learn something new and leaves it after some time still gets something out of it. It remains alive within. Each and every one of us unconsciously feels what is most important in life.

There are many different kinds of people. Some are shrewd and clever; they succeed easily and become rich and influential. Others are born lazy and evolve slowly. They are what we call "good-for-nothing." They might, in fact, be working harder then the clever ones, but they attain less. Some of them may find it difficult to get up in the morning, but we can never accurately assess their efforts, because they depend on so many inner qualities. We haven't any tools for measuring one's properties and internal efforts. I do not mean a physical effort, but an internal, mental effort.

Baal HaSulam wrote that 10% of the population is altruistic. Such people derive pleasure when they give to others. Just as an egoist can kill if he does not get what he wants, so can an altruist kill if he cannot give what he wants. Giving is a means for pleasure for him.

Such people are still egoistic because underneath they still aim to receive something from the giving, though it is concealed. Naturally, they, too, must be corrected. In fact, they have a longer way to go to become conscious of their egoism.

The fact that they are not really altruists requires a longer period of self-recognition, at the end of which they will be compelled to face their own egoism. The coarser and more egoistic one is, the closer one is to spirituality. In that state, egoism is immense and ripe and can begin its path toward the spiritual world. All that remains now is to realize that egoism is harmful, and to ask the Creator to change one's intention from "receiving for self" to "receiving for the Creator."

Shame appears in *Malchut* of *Ein Sof* when it understands the meaning of *Behinat Shoresh*, of *Keter*. It is a state where there is a sensation of absolute contrast between man and the Light of the Creator. *Malchut* itself cannot feel the Light itself, only the properties the Light evokes. The Light itself has no properties; it is abstract. *Malchut* discerns properties because of the influence of the Light on its own attributes.

All our reactions are compulsory and useful. This includes the spiritual reactions of our souls as well as our animate, physical reactions. It is a common concept that every disease is a result of the body's attempts to maintain its balance.

For example, let's say that a person has a certain illness. In response, the body deliberately raises the temperature in order to fight the bacteria and defend itself. A disease is regarded not as a state of sickness, but as an external expression of something that happens in the body, a breach of the inner balance. That is why it is not good to suppress a symptom of a disease, which might actually suppress the body's ability to defend itself.

Our egos are highly sophisticated. If we feel a desire that we cannot satisfy, the ego immediately suppresses it to prevent unnecessary anguish. But the minute the conditions ripen to attain that pleasure, the relevant desires awaken. That applies as well to an old or sick person. Such people have no other desire but to go on living. Our bodies suppress unattainable desires.

The wisdom of Kabbalah completely denies the theory of evolution. The creature evolved according to the four phases of Direct Light, when *Behina Aleph* became *Behina Bet*, which turned into *Behina Gimel* etc. But when *Malchut* of *Ein Sof* was created, it absorbed all the desires of the upper ten *Sefirot* (four *Behinot*). They are now in it and cannot be changed in any way.

The appearance of the worlds and the *Partzufim* do not testify to a change in desires, but to a change in intent. Desires are activated according to one's aim. The desires themselves remain unchanged, and do not create anything new. The same principle applies to thoughts we think today that we did not think yesterday. It is simply that they were concealed from us, but they were always within us. The thoughts appear gradually, but they are not new.

It is impossible to turn one degree of existence into another, such as breathing life into an inanimate object, or turning a plant into an animal. There are intermediary degrees between inanimate objects and vegetative states, such as corals. Then, between the vegetative and the animate there is a form of life that feeds directly off the ground called

"Field Dog." The ape exists between the animate and those creatures that can speak.

The only thing that could happen would be a Godly spark pulling one toward the spiritual, thus creating in one a desire to attain something greater than this world. At that point, one would become the "Son of Man."

Science and technology have been developed only to lead us to a dead end, to the understanding that technology is not the way to go. But before we look for the new way, we must first reach that dead end.

All the Kabbalists had students. It is strictly forbidden to classify students as better or not so good, or those who want spirituality more, or want it less. All of us were born with certain desires, and none of us can say why we were created this or that way, or why our desires are the way they are. The classification and sorting processes happen naturally in the group and produce a stable and strong group.

The Ari formulated a new system. But even his disciples did not quite comprehend his system, except for Chaim Vital. There were great Kabbalists in the Ari's group, but none of them received his entire knowledge, except Chaim Vital. The method that the teacher uses depends on the kinds of souls that descend to this world. There were other forms of study before the Ari, but from the discovery of his method, it became possible for everyone to study, provided they had a strong enough desire.

Baal HaSulam did not make any fundamental changes in the Ari's method, but only enhanced and deepened it. He wrote a detailed commentary to the books of the Ari and to the *Zohar*. Thanks to this commentary, anyone who wants to study the wisdom of Kabbalah and enter the spiritual world can comprehend the inner meaning of the text and find the true meaning of the books of the Torah.

Souls that came down to this world before the Ari, received their spirituality on a superficial level. After the demise of the Ari, the souls that descended to the world studied and analyzed themselves and the spiritual world in a spiritual-scientific method. For that reason, the books that were written before the Ari are written as tales, whereas books that were written after his time are written in the style of *The Study of the Ten Sefirot*, in a language of *Behinot*, *Sefirot* and worlds. It is an engineered psychology, a scientific approach to the soul.

Kabbalists do not need to practice this or that science or make experiments. They can provide all the explanations from the perspective of the Kabbalah, the origin of all sciences. Each science has its own language. If Kabbalists are not scientists they will find it difficult to describe this or that phenomenon in the professional terms of that science.

Kabbalists feel the actual laws of the universe that are the origin of the material and spiritual essence. But what language should they use to describe the reciprocation between various phenomena? How should they describe the spiritual force that constitutes the foundation of this world, and what are the reciprocal relationships between spiritual objects?

There is no single formula in our world that can define these things. Kabbalists can convey these feelings to one another, but they cannot convey them to those who have not yet entered the spiritual world. Even if there were some way to convey a certain feeling, it would still be impossible to use it in our world before one changes oneself. If people changed their qualities, we would be able to communicate in a spiritual language and perform spiritual acts.

We all receive and suffer according to the level we are on. Turning anguish into something spiritual requires a screen. This cannot be given at whim. Such a demand creates a barrier, a separation. That is why the wisdom of Kabbalah is also called "the wisdom of the hidden" (for those who have not attained it).

In the *Preface to the Book of Zohar*, Baal HaSulam depicts four levels of recognition: matter, form clothed in matter, abstract form, and essence. Our science can only deal with what concerns the matter and the form clothed in the matter. A form without matter is a completely abstract concept that cannot be clearly analyzed. The essence, the thing that brings life to objects, or creates responses, is completely incomprehensible.

The same thing happens in the spiritual world. A Kabbalist who learns something in spirituality, attains the matter and the form that is dressed in the matter, but a form that is not clothed in matter is unattainable. This means that the spiritual world also has its limitations in understanding and perception of the universe. But when Kabbalists reach a certain level, they receive a gift from Above that opens up all the secrets of the universe.

CHAPTER 3.2
WHAT DOES KABBALAH DEAL WITH?

Scientists have discovered that plants react differently when different people approach them. For example, if a certain person harms a certain plant, the plant will remember it, and if that person approaches it again, the plant will react with intensive internal "waves." Fish and animals also feel others in various ways. Much like plants, when the Creator is revealed to us, we can feel our surroundings, feel the "other." That revelation occurs in the same senses in which we feel other people as ordinary people. That external sensation is absent in the inanimate nature, and exists only a little in plants.

The science of Kabbalah deals with man's revelation of the Creator. The Creator is outside us, as is everything that is around us. He is external, alien. He is even farther and more concealed than everything we see around us. He is behind our reality.

Our ability to feel our surroundings, as well as our other abilities and properties, depends on the measurement of egoism in every creature. It is that property, the measurement of the desire for pleasure, that develops the needs that each creature must satisfy and the creature's properties and abilities.

Thus, all the properties in animate nature, such as the ability to move and understand, exceed the abilities of inanimate nature. The same ratio exists between the animate and the human nature. The least egoism can be found in inanimate nature. It only appears in statistic, physical laws that will preserve the properties.

Such a low level of egoism creates only minimal needs that do not require internal changes, which would express vitality and create the need for movement.

Coral is an intermediary state between the still and the vegetative because it has a greater amount of egoism, which renders it an attribute of growth.

Greater egoism begets the vegetative nature and the need to change, swallow and defecate, grow, react to external conditions, and even develop a memory. An even greater egoism produces many more types of living organisms, which are equipped with an ability to learn, remember, adapt, and move about freely, depending on their degree of egoism.

The characteristics of every species are a direct consequence of the amount of their egoistic desire. That is the only factor that emanates from the appearance of this or that property or ability. Everything that characterizes any object stems from a single origin: its amount of egoism.

Thus, the ability of an object to feel outside itself exists even more intensively in mankind, for its goal is to sense the Creator. But you can also say the opposite: because people can feel outside themselves, we can conclude that the purpose of the creation of mankind is to be in contact with the Creator.

However, in addition to this property, it is vitally important that we use our minds to enhance our sensitivity to others many times over. Through this sensitivity, we become capable of feeling the joy and agony of others like us.

The mind helps us develop our ability to sense others more clearly. It confirms the idea that man is the only creature for whom the revelation of the Creator has been prepared. To perceive the Creator, one must develop a full capacity to feel the surrounding environment the way it really is. One must be able to feel outside oneself, meaning regardless of one's personal egoistic interests.

We are constantly faced with our inability to understand one another. Our egoistic interests do not allow us to feel outside ourselves. They do not let us come close to nature and to those who are like us, but rather drive us farther away from each other. Therefore, if we want to make the most of our lives here, we must develop our ability to sense those who are like us and be able to understand them.

However, if we want to sense the Creator, we must develop more than just the ability to sense those who are like us, but also our own minds. Our enhanced intellectual ability will enable us to intensify that sensation many times over, relate to people around us impartially, and even ignore our egoism altogether in our attitudes to others.

With this perception, we can feel the Creator as much as we can feel others instead of ourselves. The more we can feel compared to those still in vegetative and animate degrees, the harder it will be for us to describe the intense emotions we feel, to the point that it will become virtually impossible.

Moses independently developed the ability to feel "outside himself." It was that ability that led him to attain the highest spiritual degree, and it is that ability that enabled him to speak face to face with the Creator.

The purpose of Creation is to be able to sense the Creator, and the way to do it is formulated in the verse, "Love thy neighbor as thyself."

The degrees of our evolution, meaning our ability to feel and draw near Him, are called "degrees of spiritual growth." Every individual, and the whole of mankind, treads the gradual path leading to the purpose the Creator preordained.

The Creator pushes us along that path by inflicting pain on us, so as to force us to question the origin of the anguish. By examining the origin of the pain, we should eventually understand that the best thing for us is the connection with the Creator, the connection with the strongest, eternal Power that controls our lives. That connection accompanies us in this world and in the next.

Kabbalah should help us become more capable of objective perception of reality. It must lead mankind to acutely analyze and recognize the correct "good" and "evil" and realize that evil is our very nature. It is our nature that prevents us from seeing "past our own noses." We are compelled to think only with our "gut feeling."

Kabbalah maintains that the Mitzvot (commandments) should not be kept as a goal in and of themselves, but that there is a completely different purpose for them. Our sages clearly say that the Creator cares not if we slaughter from the throat or from the back of the neck, meaning He does not care about the simple observing of the laws. That is not what He expects of man and that is not why He gave us the Mitzvot.

Those who turn the means for correction into the end, and choose to settle for it as a way of life, teach others to stay away from Kabbalah, which states that the rules are only a means to an end, while the goal we should strive for is to feel Him through a correct performance of His Will and His Counsel.

Man's purification is the Torah's real goal, and the observing of Mitzvot is only a means to attain it. If the performance of Mitzvot is not directed toward this aim, but is out of habit that has become a need, then it will not bear the right fruit.

It is as though one who operates without this intent simply does not exist! The Zohar writes that a Mitzva without an aim or purpose is like a dead body (a body without a soul). Therefore, one must obtain the desired aim. Only then can one understand why one exists.

The intention to attain the purpose of existence, to sense the Creator, and to unite with Him must be authentic. It is the only reason for doing anything. Anything one does with this aim in mind is considered a Mitzva.

In other words, if we perform a Mitzva while thinking only of an egoistic purpose, it is as though we did nothing! That is how we should relate to every Mitzva. It is the only approach where the act helps us purify ourselves from our egoism.

It is not enough to learn how to mechanically perform rules. It is a lot more important to learn what will produce the right aim and obtain faith, meaning the sensing of the Creator. That study should precede the mechanical operation of rules. When we acquire the correct intention, then by keeping these statutes, which are in fact the desires of the Creator, we will actually become closer to the Creator.

We must emphasize that Kabbalah does not negate the physical performance of *Mitzvot*, except when the mechanical performance substitutes the internal. Mechanically performing *Mitzvot* is only a preparation, and will bear fruit only if one actually acquires a spiritual intention in the act.

Before performing *Mitzvot*, one should learn anything that will help to acquire the right aim. That is what Kabbalah books teach and nothing else!

CHAPTER 3.3
THE STRUCTURE OF THE UPPER WORLDS

FOREWORD

This course is based on the article, *Preface to the Wisdom of Kabbalah*, written by Rabbi Yehuda Ashlag. Rabbi Ashlag wrote this article as one of his introductions to the *Sulam* commentary that he wrote on the *Zohar*. According to the method of the Kabbalah, one learns about the extension of existence from Above downward, from the Creator down to this world.

Consequently, students acquire the means for spiritual elevation from below upward, exactly like those degrees of progression from Above downward that they learn about. This is in accordance with the definition of Kabbalah: "This wisdom is no more and no less than a sequence of roots that hang down by way of cause and consequence, with fixed, determined rules interweaving to a single, exalted goal described as the revelation of His Godliness to His creatures in this world" (Rabbi Y. Ashlag, *The Essence of the Wisdom of Kabbalah*).

THE NECESSITY FOR LEARNING KABBALAH

"It is also evident that it is impossible for the whole of Israel to attain this great purity, except by the study of the wisdom of Kabbalah, the easiest way suitable for those without knowledge as well. But through the study of the literal Torah alone, it is impossible to attain purity but for singled out individuals, and with great efforts, but not for the majority of the people." (Rabbi Yehuda Ashlag, *Introduction to Talmud Eser Sefirot*).

"The attainment begins from the hidden Torah, and only afterwards does one attain the remaining portions of the Torah, and only in the end does one attain the revealed Torah." (The Vilna Gaon, *The Siddur*).

"I have seen it written that the prohibition from Above to refrain from open study in the wisdom of truth was only for a limited period, until the end of 1490, but from then on the prohibition has been lifted and permission was granted to study the *Zohar*. Since 1540 it has been a great *Mitzva* (commandment) for the masses to study in public, old and young... and that is because the Messiah will come because of that and not because of any other reason. Therefore, we must not be negligent." (Rabbi Azulai, *Introduction to Ohr Hochma*).

"Woe unto them who make the spirit of Messiah vanish from the world, so as never to return, make the Torah dry, without the moistness of mind and knowledge, for they confine themselves to the practical part of the Torah, and do not wish to try to understand the wisdom of the Kabbalah, to know and educate themselves in the secrets and the reason behind the Torah and the *Mitzvot* (commandments). Alas, they cause by their deeds the poverty, the ruin and the robbery, the looting, the killings and destruction in the world." (*Tikkunei Zohar*, Tikkun 30).

"The Study of the book of *Zohar* is preferable and above all other studies." (The Chidah).

"Redemption depends primarily on the study of the Kabbalah." (The Vilna Gaon, *Even Shlema* 11,13).

"On the learning of the *Zohar* there are no restrictions..." (The Hafetz Chaim).

"If my generation had listened to my voice, they would have started to study the book of *Zohar* at the age of nine." (Rabbi Isaac from Kamarna, *Notzer Hesed*).

"When one as much as reads the words... what is it like? It is like a sick person who drinks a therapeutic potion that helps, although one is not proficient in the wisdom of medicine." (*Remez*, part 3, page 2).

"In the future only with the help of the book of *Zohar* will the children of Israel go out from the exile." (The Book of *Zohar*, Parashat Naso).

CHAPTER 3.4
FUNDAMENTALS

It is written in the *Book of Zohar* that all of the worlds, both Upper and lower, are found within man. Our entire reality was created for us alone. However, while we feel that we are inside reality, we do not feel that reality is inside us. Why is this world alone not sufficient for us? Do we need the other worlds, the Upper ones, and what they contain?

In order to understand this, we would need to learn the entire wisdom of Kabbalah. The reason this reality was created was the Creator's Will to benefit His creations. Therefore, the Creator made His creatures with a desire to receive that which the Creator wanted to give—and this desire is the creature's nature.

The Creator is Above and transcends space and time. His Thought works like an act itself. Therefore, when it came before His Will and Thought to make creatures and fill them with enjoyments, so it happened that instantly, all the worlds were created. These were filled with all the creatures and all were filled with the delights that they received from the Creator.

If so, then why did the Creator also create from His Essence all the worlds down to this world, and lower the creature down to our low degree? The Ari (Rabbi Yitzchak Luria) answers this question in his book, Etz Chaim (The Tree of Life): "In order to reveal the perfection of His deeds."

However, the creation of the worlds and the descent of the creatures reveal instead the imperfection of the Works of the Creator! But the answer is: this was done in order that the creatures would perfect themselves, that they would reach the degree of the Creator on their own, which is the only perfection.

Hence, the Creator created the ladder of the worlds. Through this ladder souls descend unto the lowest rung, in which they are clothed in bodies (in desire to receive) of this world. By means of learning Kabbalah, the souls begin to ascend on that ladder until they all return to the Creator.

The Soul consists of Light and vessel. The Light of the soul comes from the Creator, from His Essence. The vessel of the soul; i.e., the desire to receive Light and benefit from Him, is created by means of this Light. Hence, the vessel is a perfect fit for the Light that comes to fill it. The essence of the soul is the vessel, because the Light is a portion of the Creator.

Consequently only the vessel is considered a creature. It is created out of nothing; that is to say, this will did not exist before the Creator decided to create it.

Since the Creator wanted to benefit His vessel in a complete manner, as is fit for Him, He created this extremely large vessel (that is to say this desire to receive), according to the greatness of the Light (enjoyment) that He wanted to give.

This creation is an innovation that never existed before. It is called "Existence out of Absence." However, if the Creator is complete, how can there be anything that is not included in Him? According to what we have already said, it is clear that that which was not in the Creator prior to the Creation is the desire to receive.

The Creator cannot have a desire to receive because He is complete. But if He is complete, shouldn't He also have the desire to receive? The answer is *no*. If He had the desire to receive, that would mean that He wanted something He did not have; which would mean that He lacked something.

It is impossible to say this because He is complete, and hence lacks nothing. That which He needed to Create is only the desire to receive from Him, because He wants to give. Consequently, He only created the desire to receive, for everything else is already present in the Creator.

Connection in the spiritual realm occurs as a result of the equivalence of characteristics (desires or wills). Separation in the spiritual realm occurs as a result of a difference in characteristics (desires or wills). If two spiritual entities have one form, have the same desires (or wills), the same goal, then they are attached and are one, not two. The reason for this is that in the spiritual realm there are no bodies. The spiritual world is a world of "raw" powers and desires that are not clothed in any sort of substance. But the "desire to receive for self" is called "substance" and "body."

Therefore, if all the desires of two spiritual entities are equal, then the entities are one. They are one because there is not a thing that separates them from one another. It is possible to distinguish that there are two, and not just one, if they are different in form.

They are only separated from one another to the degree that there is a difference in form between them. If everything in one is equal to the other, then they are one. If everything in one is opposite to the other, then they are as far from one another as east from west. If among all their desires they have but one in common, then they touch one another via this common will. If their wills resemble each other's more or less, then according to the equivalence or change of form, they are close or far apart.

We have no conception of the Creator Himself. Therefore we cannot say even a single word about Him. But the actions that we experience from Him enable us to understand Him and name Him.

We learn from the wisdom of the Kabbalists that the Creator has only a will to bestow. (A Kabbalist is a *Mekubal* in Hebrew, from the word "receive," because they receive from the Creator). He created everything in order to bestow His Goodness upon us. Therefore, He created us with the desire to receive that which He wants to give to us. This desire to receive is our entire nature.

However, this causes us to end up being in an opposite form to the Creator's. The reason is that He is totally and exclusively aimed at bestowing, and has no desire to receive. We, on the other hand, are made exclusively of the desire to receive for ourselves, as thus we were created by Him. But if we remained only with this desire to receive for ourselves, we would remain forever distant from the Creator.

People who live in this world, and also live and experience the reality of the Upper Spiritual Realms, are called Kabbalists. We have the opportunity to hear about the Creator from them as they share what we ourselves have not yet experienced. And the Kabbalists tell us that the Creator is the Absolute Good, and created everything in order to give us good. The Kabbalists tell us further that the Creator is perfect and complete, and therefore His Actions as well are both perfect and complete.

But how is it possible that from this complete and perfect Worker an imperfect and incomplete work emerges to begin with? How is it that His Works must still be mended? Creation is only the desire to receive, and from this aspect it is imperfect and incomplete, since this will is opposite to that of the Emanator. Hence, these desires are in a state of separation. However, it is specifically the desire to receive that makes it possible for the creature to carry out the Will of the Creator, to receive everything that the Creator wishes to give.

However, when the Creator gives and the creature receives from Him, they are separated. This is because the manner of their actions diverges. And if the creature would remain a receiver, then he would not be perfect or complete. Consequently, the Creator would also not be able to be called "perfect and complete" because from a perfect and complete worker come forth only perfect and complete works.

Therefore, the Creator restricted His Light and created this world restriction-by-restriction, until this world, the most darkened place, finally emerged. In this world the creature has the desire to receive for self alone. Therefore the Light in it is so slight that the Source of life is not even sensed.

However, by proper use of "Torah and Mitzvot" (this will be explained later), we can obtain the completeness and perfection that we have lacked since the time of Creation.

What is this completeness and perfection? It is that of obtaining equivalence of form with the Creator. That the creature, too, gives, like the Creator. And then the creature is worthy of receiving all of the good and the enjoyment included in the thought of Creation. At this point, both creature and Creator are in a state of adhesion in equivalence of form, having identical desires and thoughts.

There is a *Segula* (a special property, a remedy) in the correct practice of "Torah and Mitzvot": a person receives a spiritual power that leads to an equalizing of wills with the Creator. However, this power will only be revealed in one who practices "Torah and Mitzvot" not to receive a personal reward, but to bestow contentment upon the Creator.

There are five degrees in the equivalence of form with the Creator: *Nefesh, Ruach, Neshama, Haya, Yechida* (NRNHY). These five degrees are attained from the five worlds—*Adam Kadmon, Atzilut, Beria, Yetzira,* and *Assiya.* Each degree has its own five inner degrees as well. Thus, there are in total 125 degrees from this world to the top of the ladder.

By practicing Torah and Mitzvot in order to bring contentment to the Creator, a person slowly merits and attains (degree by degree) the vessels of the will to bestow. This way a person climbs these degrees one by one until reaching complete equivalence of form. Thus, the Thought of Creation is carried out in man, who will receive all the enjoyment and perfection that the Creator prepared for him. And man's greatest benefit is that he attains true adhesion by attaining the desire to bestow, as the Creator does.

See what is written: "All of the worlds, Upper and lower, and everything within them, were not created but for man." All these degrees and worlds only serve to complete the will of man, in order to help him acquire equivalence of form with the Creator, which he lacks by the nature of Creation.

In the beginning, successive worlds and degrees went through a progressive process of restrictions and developments, up until our own material world, in order to come to a body of this world, which is a desire only to receive and not to bestow. At this degree, a man is like an animal or a beast, which is the complete desire to receive, denied of any bestowal. In such a state man is the complete opposite to the Creator, between whom there is no greater separation.

When we study Kabbalah, we invoke the Surrounding Light to shine upon us from afar. This Light is found outside our vessels (our will) and waits until we fix our vessels and shape them into a form of bestowal upon the Creator, and then the Light enters it. Therefore, this Surrounding Light is called the Light of *Neshama*. When we learn Kabbalah, this Light clothes itself in our will and helps us attain the form of bestowal.

Man only attains this desire to bestow gradually, from below upward, by the same route the degrees descended during the time of development from Above downward. All the degrees are measures of desire to bestow. The higher the degree, the farther it is from the desire to receive, and closer to the desire to bestow.

A person gradually acquires all the degrees until reaching the point of merit to become "entirely for bestowal," or not receiving anything for personal pleasure. Then a person has reached completion, with a true adhesion. This is the goal of Creation, and is the only reason for which man was created.

Once we know all this, we are permitted to study the wisdom of Kabbalah without any fear of anthropomorphism. This is because studying Kabbalah without proper guidance confuses the student. On the one hand, all the *Sefirot* and *Partzufim* (spiritual objects) from the world of *Atzilut* to the world of *Assiya* are complete Godliness and are united with the Creator.

Yet, how is it possible that this should be of Godliness: that all of the worlds are innovations, coming after the restriction, that they have all different types of changes, numbers, above, below, ascents, descents, couplings?

From the aforesaid, it is clear that all of these changes—ascents, descents, restrictions, and numbers—are seen from the perspective of the souls that receive them.

Reality can be divided into two divisions: potential and actual. It is much like a man who builds a house. In his thought he already has a house. However, the "substance" of that house cannot be compared to the "substance" of one actually built. This is because in theory, the house is composed of a substance of thought, and is a potential house. Yet, when the house begins to turn from thought to action, it takes on a different substance - that of trees and stones.

Thus, it is possible to distinguish potential and actual in the souls as well: the emanating of the souls from the Creator actually begins only at the world of *Beria*. All the changes that occur before the world of *Beria* are considered potential, without any tangible distinction from the Creator.

It is said that all the souls are already included in *Malchut* of *Ein Sof* (infinite), in the middle point of the entire existence. This is because this point in a state of potentiality includes the vessels of the souls, which are to emerge in "fact" from the world of *Beria* and under. The First Restriction was made in the middle point only in the aspect of "potential" with respect to the future souls.

All the vessels and the worlds from the First Restriction up, until the world of *Beria*, emerged and developed from the middle point, and they are only "potential" worlds, with respect to the souls. Only when souls actually begin to emerge from the world of *Beria* and below, do the changes in the degrees of these worlds begin to influence them.

It is much like a person who hides under clothes and concealments in order to not be seen or sensed. The person certainly remains unchanged. Similarly, the ten Sefirot (*Keter, Hochma, Bina, Hesed, Gevura, Tifferet, Netzah, Hod, Yesod, Malchut*) are only ten concealments, inside which the *Ein Sof* conceals and hides itself from the souls.

The Light of *Ein Sof* is in a state of absolute rest, and so it is when it shines from within the concealments. However, since the souls receive the Light of *Ein Sof* through the concealments, they feel as if changes occur in the Light. Therefore the souls that receive the Light are divided into ten degrees, in accordance with the divisions in the concealments.

All these concealments are only from the world of *Beria* and below, because only there do the souls that receive from the ten *Sefirot* via the concealments exist. In the worlds of *Adam Kadmon* and *Atzilut*, the souls do not yet exist, because there they are only in "potential."

The ten concealments in the ten *Sefirot* rule only in the worlds of *Beria, Yetzira* and *Assiya*. Nevertheless, the ten *Sefirot* are considered Godliness just as before the First Restriction.

The only difference in the vessels of the ten *Sefirot* is that in the worlds of *Adam Kadmon* and *Atzilut*, they are potential vessels, whereas from BYA (*Beria, Yetzira, Assiya*) the vessels of the ten *Sefirot* begin to manifest their covering power and concealment. However, the Light in them remains unchanged as a result of the concealments.

If in the worlds of *Adam Kadmon* and *Atzilut* the souls (who are the receivers) are not revealed yet, then what is the purpose of these vessels of *Adam Kadmon* and *Atzilut*, and from whom are they hiding and concealing themselves? The answer is that in the future, when the worlds of BYA, together with the souls in them, ascend there, they will receive according to the degree of the ten *Sefirot* in *Atzilut*, or *Adam Kadmon*.

As we have mentioned above, the worlds, the innovations, the changes, and the degrees, all refer only to the vessels. These bestow to the souls and measure out to them, so that they might receive from the Light of *Ein Sof*.

However, when the souls ascend in the degrees, they do not make any changes in the Light of *Ein Sof* itself, because the concealments do not affect the one who is concealed, but only the one who wants to perceive the one who is concealed, and receive from it.

One can distinguish three aspects in the *Sefirot* and *Partzufim* (spiritual objects) wherever they are found: the Creator's Essence, vessels, and Lights. The receivers have no thought and perception of the Essence of the Creator.

There are always two contradictory aspects in the vessels: concealment and disclosure. In the beginning, the vessel hides the Essence of the Creator so that the ten vessels in the ten *Sefirot* are ten degrees of concealment. However, after the souls receive these vessels with all the conditions in them, these concealments are changed into revelations for the attainment of the souls.

These two contradictory aspects in the vessel become as one, because the measure of revelation in the vessel precisely matches the amount of concealment in the vessel. The coarser the vessel, the more it conceals His Essence and reveals the larger stature of the Creator.

The Lights in the *Sefirot* are the same stature, worthy of appearing for the attainment of the souls. While everything extends from the Creator's Essence, the reception of the Light is nonetheless only according to the characteristics of the vessel. Therefore, there must be ten Lights and ten vessels, that is to say, ten degrees of revelation to the receivers, according to the characteristics of those vessels.

Thus, there cannot be a difference between the Light and the Creator's Essence, but only in what reaches us from the Creator, through its clothing in the vessels of the ten Sefirot. Therefore, anything attained we name "Light."

CHAPTER 3.5
THE FOUR PHASES IN THE EVOLUTION OF THE VESSEL

Kabbalists attained spirituality and wrote about it in their books. They perceived that the root of the entire reality is a Supreme Power, which they named "His Essence," because they could not attain the power itself. However, they did perceive that there is a thought, an aim, to create creatures in order to delight them, which comes from His Essence. They named that thought and aim "The Thought of Creation," or "Upper Light." It turns out that from the creature's perspective, the Light is the Creator, because it cannot attain His Essence. Hence the Creator-creature contact is maintained through the Upper Light.

In short, there is a Light that stems from His Essence. The Light wants to create a creature and delight it by filling it with pleasure. That is, the purpose of the Light is to create a creature that would feel the Light as pleasure.

The Kabbalists therefore called the creature a "vessel," and call the Light, "filling." The Light that stems from His Essence in order to create the creature is called *Behinat Shoresh* (Root Phase), because it is the root of the entire reality. That Light then creates a desire to take pleasure in the Light. The desire for pleasure is also called "Will to Receive" (Light).

The intensity of the pleasure depends only on the intensity of the desire to receive it, just as in our world one may have an empty stomach, but no desire to eat. Hence, the desire is the vessel for the filling, and without it there is no pleasure. There is no coercion in spirituality and the filling is only equal to the desire.

The Light that stems from His Essence creates a vessel and fills it. The pleasure that the creature feels when it receives the Light is called

Ohr Hochma (Light of Wisdom). The desire created by the Light that fills it is called *Behina Aleph* (First Phase). It is called by that name because it is the first *Behina* (appearance/manifestation) of the future vessel. But that desire is not yet an independent one, as it is created directly by the Light.

The actual creature is the one whose desire to enjoy the Creator's full Light for its own delight. This desire and the decision to enjoy it for self arise from within. Such desire needs not be imprinted in it by the Creator.

In order to receive Light, the creature must know how intense the pleasure from the Light is before it receives it. Then, it must be filled with Light, and then feel what it is like to be without the Light. Only then is the real desire for the Light created.

In much the same way it happens in our own lives, when a person is given a new fruit to taste there is no preliminary desire for it. But if one tastes it and feels the pleasure in it, and the fruit is then taken away, the person begins to crave it and wishes to bring back the pleasure. It is precisely that desire, the new desire born in man, that is what man feels as an independent will.

Hence, it is impossible to build the vessel all at once. In order for the desire to know what to delight in, and recognize its own desire to enjoy, the desire must go through the entire chain of events. That condition is presented as a law in Kabbalah: "The expansion of the Light and its departure, make the vessel worthy of its task," which is to receive Light and enjoy it. The phases of the evolution of this desire are called *Behinot* (phases/discernments/observations) because they are phases in the building of discernments/observations in the will to receive.

Thus, along with the pleasure, the Light renders the vessel with the attribute of bestowal. And the vessel suddenly discovers while enjoying the Light that it wants to give, just like the nature of the Light that fills it. This is because the Creator purposely rendered the Light with the ability to convey its own attributes along with the desire to bestow. Once the Light fills up the vessel in the first phase, the vessel feels that it wants to be like the Creator. And because this is an entirely new desire, it is an entirely new observation, named *Behina Bet* (Second Phase).

Behina Bet is a desire to give. The pleasure it feels at resembling the Creator is called "the Light of Mercy." Thus we see that *Behina Aleph* is opposite to *Behina Bet* because the desire of *Behina Aleph* is the will to receive, whereas that of *Behina Bet* is the will to bestow. The Light in *Behina Aleph* is a "Light of Wisdom," and that of *Behina Bet* is a "Light of Mercy."

When the will to receive in *Behina Aleph* begins to enjoy the Light that fills it, it immediately feels that the Light is the giver of the pleasure and that the will to receive is the receiver of the pleasure, and thus begins to want to be like the Light itself. Rather than receive the pleasure, there is a desire to give it, like the Light.

Hence, the original will to receive leaves, and the vessel remains empty of the Light of Wisdom, because pleasure can be felt only when there is a desire for it.

The will to receive cannot remain without the Light of Wisdom, because the Light of Wisdom is its livelihood. Therefore, this will to receive must take in a little bit of the Light of Wisdom. Thus, this new desire, called *Behina Gimel* (Third Phase) consists of two desires:

- A desire to resemble the Light.
- A desire to receive a small amount of Light of Wisdom.

The vessel now feels two Lights: the Light of Mercy in the will to bestow, and the Light of Wisdom in the will to receive.

When *Behina Gimel* receives Light, it finds that between the Light of Wisdom and the Light of Life, the former is more consistent with its nature. It then decides to receive this Light fully. Thus an independent desire to receive the Light of Wisdom, and the very desire with which the Creator wants to fill the creature is now created.

We see that the Light that emanates from His Essence creates a vessel in four steps. That is why that final desire, named *Behina Dalet* (Fourth Phase), is in fact the only creature. All the phases that preceded it were only phases in its evolution. In fact, the entire Creation is comprised of that fourth phase. Everything that exists, except for the Creator, is that *Behina Dalet*. This *Behina Dalet* is named *Malchut* (Kingship), because the will to receive governs it.

FOUR PHASES

The fourth phase is the only creature. It is divided into outer parts and inner parts. The outer consists of *Sefirot*, *Partzufim*, worlds, and our world, and the still, vegetative, and animate. The inner part consists of the human souls. The difference between those parts is only in the magnitude of their will to receive.

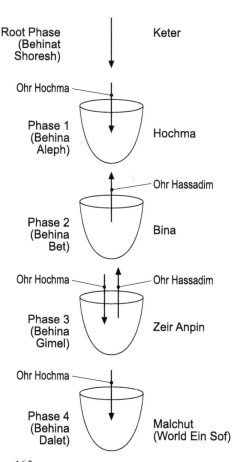

When the fourth phase is entirely filled with the Light of Wisdom, it is called *Olam Ein Sof* (World Without End), because its desire doesn't limit the reception of the Light. The fourth phase receives through the four prior phases: Root, First, Second, and Third. It turns out that the fourth phase is divided into five parts (including its own phase) of will to receive.

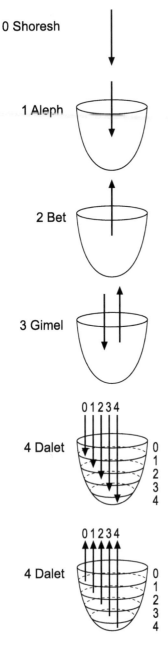

0 Shoresh

1 Aleph

2 Bet

3 Gimel

0 1 2 3 4

4 Dalet

0
1
2
3
4

0 1 2 3 4

4 Dalet

0
1
2
3
4

SUMMARY

Light comes from the Creator, or the Root Phase. The Light then creates a creature, the fourth phase, in four phases. The essence of the creature is the desire to receive pleasure. The pleasure is the sensation of the Light within the desire. The fourth phase is then divided into four inner parts, which receive Light from the four preliminary phases. The fourth phase, filled with Light of Wisdom, is called the "World of *Ein Sof*" (no end). The parts of the fourth phase are called "souls" and "worlds." The worlds contain *Partzufim*, *Sefirot* and everything that is not souls.

CHAPTER 3.6
THE FIRST RESTRICTION, SCREEN, PARTZUF

When the Light of Wisdom fills up the will to receive in the first phase, it also gives it its nature—that of bestowal. That is why in the end, after having felt the nature of the Light that fills it, the first phase changes its desire from that of reception to that of bestowal.

The Light works the same way in the fourth phase once it exits the third phase after having filled itself with the Light of Wisdom. Then it, too, begins to want to give, like the nature of the Light inside it. As a result, the desire to receive disappears from the fourth phase.

The Light gives the vessel its desire to bestow when it fills up the vessel because the vessel feels not only the pleasure from the Light, but the desire of the giver as well. The Creator could have created a vessel that would not feel Him as a giver, but only the pleasure at reception. That's how those with an undeveloped will to receive and children feel in our world, as well as insensitive and mentally unstable individuals.

Once we grow from children to adults, we become ashamed to receive. That sensation is so developed in us that we would choose any pain in the world over the pain of shame. This attribute was created by the Creator so that we would be able to use it to rise above our nature, which is the will to receive.

In order to be ashamed to receive, we must feel that we are receiving. That is possible only if there is a giver and we feel His Existence. If I don't feel the Host, I will not be ashamed. But if He's standing right in front of me, then I will be ashamed. I cannot receive directly; because I have to relate to Him, give Him something in return for what I receive, which turns it into a tradeoff rather than mere reception. Then I, too, become a giver, because he, too, receives from me.

The sensation of the Creator awakens in *Malchut* such intense pain when it is received that it decides never again to use its will to receive pleasure for itself. This decision is called "Restriction." The name "First Restriction" indicates that this is the first time something like this happens.

THE PROGRESSION OF LIGHT LEADING TO THE RESTRICTION

By not receiving Light, *Malchut* stops being the receiver, but she still gives nothing to the Creator; she still does not attain her desire to be like the Light, the giver of the pleasure. By not receiving pleasure from the Creator, *Malchut* does not attain the equivalence of form. Thus we see that the First Restriction is not an end, but a means to acquire the ability to give.

The purpose of the Creator in Creation was that *Malchut*, the creature, would receive pleasure. That thought of Creation is unchanging. Because of that, the Creator continues to pressure *Malchut* to receive it. *Malchut* feels that the restriction is not enough to attain the status of

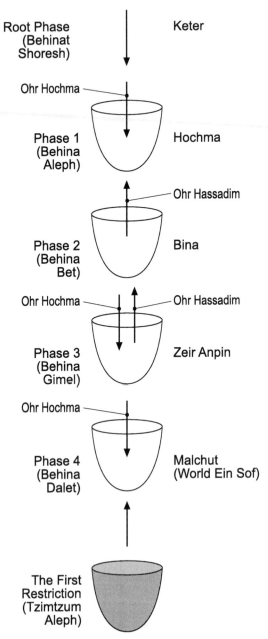

The Giver, but how can the creature, whose only attribute is that of reception, give anything to the Creator?

By feeling its Upper Nine attributes (the attributes of the Creator that *Malchut* feels within), which comprise the way the Creator relates to *Malchut*, it begins to understand how it can give back to the Creator. It decides that if it would receive the Light and enjoy it because the Creator enjoys its delight, then that would make its reception tantamount to bestowal.

The reception of pleasure by the receiver in order to please the giver turns an act of reception into one of bestowal. If *Malchut* receives the entire Light (pleasure) that the Creator had prepared for it, then it will give the Creator just as much as He is giving *Malchut*.

For example, there is a guest and a host. The host treats his guest with delicacies the guest would love to have. (The desire is a perfect fit with the Light in both quantity and quality, because the pleasure-Light created the vessel-desire this way). But although the guest is very hungry, the presence of the host makes him feel ashamed, and that stops him from eating. The shame stems from the fact that he feels himself as a receiver, and the host as a giver. The shame is so strong that he can no longer eat.

But the constant pleas of the host, who has prepared it all for him, finally persuade him that the host will enjoy it if he eats. Then the guest thinks that if now, after having rejected the pleasure several times, he will agree to eat, it will be considered a favor to the host. In this way, he will become the giver, and the host, the receiver.

The hunger and the desire to receive delight and pleasure are referred to in Kabbalah as a "vessel." The pleasure emanating from the Creator is called Direct Light, and the power to reject it is called a "screen." The Light that is rejected from the screen is then referred to as Returning Light. With the power of the screen; i.e., the force to reject enjoying for self and taking pleasure only for the Creator, the vessel can face its own will to receive. One might understand that the vessel rejects the Light, but it would be more accurate to say that the vessel rejects the use of the desire in order to please itself.

THE SCREEN REJECTING THE LIGHT

The vessel cannot return Light to the Creator, but can only change the intention. The intention to delight the Creator, what we call "the Returning Light," is only a synonym for pleasure. Direct Light is tantamount to the pleasure that the Creator wants to render the creature. Returning Light is the pleasure that the creature wants to give the Creator.

Once the vessel (guest) is certain that it will not receive for itself, it examines the magnitude of the Light it returns (how much pleasure the vessel wants to give the Creator). It then decides to receive from

the abundance before it; i.e., the Direct Light, which holds the delicacies and pleasures the Host has prepared for the guest. However, it will take only as much as the guest can eat in order to please (delight) the Creator; i.e., the Host.

Kabbalists are people who feel the Light that comes from the Creator and every action He performs, but when they write about spirituality, they convey their feelings in technical terms. Therefore, if the reader has the screen and the strength the books describe, he or she can translate the words into feelings by repeating the same actions described in their books.

The Light stems directly from the Creator, hence the name, "Direct Light," and wants to dress the vessel, but then it collides with the screen. When the screen rejects the Light, refusing to receive it in order to receive, the vessel asserts the limitation of the First Restriction, which is to not receive for itself. Once the vessel is certain it will not receive for itself, it calculates how much it can receive in order to bestow (delight the Creator). Sensing the Light and calculating how much of it to receive is done prior to actually receiving it. The part that decides and plans this is called *Rosh* (Head), and the place where the screen is located is called *Peh* (mouth).

After the decision in the *Rosh* has been made, the vessel receives the Light into the part called *Toch* (inside, interior). This is the part

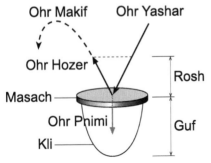

of the vessel where the reception is actually made (the sensation of the pleasure inside the will to receive). The Light of Wisdom (the pleasure) is then received with the intention to delight the Creator. That intent is called *Ohr Hassadim* (Light of Mercy).

In Kabbalistic terms it would sound like this: Direct Light clothes the Returning Light, and the Light of Wisdom clothes the Light of Mercy.

The vessel can receive only a small portion of the Light that stems from the Creator because the screen doesn't have sufficient strength to receive all of it. That is why a part in it is filled with pleasure and a part remains empty. The part that remains empty is called *Sof* (End). We can now see that the creature is comprised of three parts: *Rosh, Toch, Sof*. Together they comprise what we call a *Partzuf* (Face). The *Guf* (Body) of the *Partzuf* (all its desires) is divided into *Toch*, which receives Light, and *Sof*, which remains empty.

The border inside the *Guf* (Body) of the *Partzuf*, where the Light stops, is called *Tabur* (Navel). The Light that is received inside the *Partzuf* is called "Inner Light."

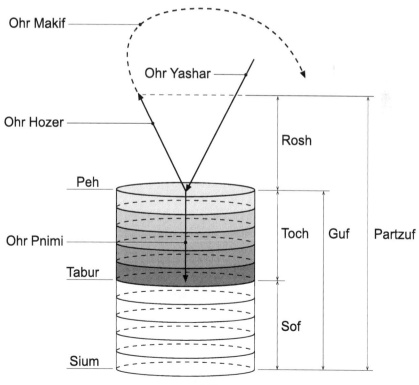

The part that remains outside the *Partzuf* is called "Surrounding Light."

Direct Light is divided by the screen into Inner and Surrounding Lights.

Malchut consists of five phases. The screen decides how much to receive in each phase. Each phase is then divided into a part that receives and a part that does not, which is why there are five phases in the *Toch* and five in the *Sof*.

Summary: When the Light corrects the vessel, it gives it the Will of the Creator. That is actually what we need for the Light to come (the very same Surrounding Light that we awaken during the study if we want to attain the purpose of Creation) and correct us to want to emulate the Creator in everything we do, meaning to bestow. That is the uniqueness of the Kabbalah, and that is its importance. The study awakens the Surrounding Light that corrects man.

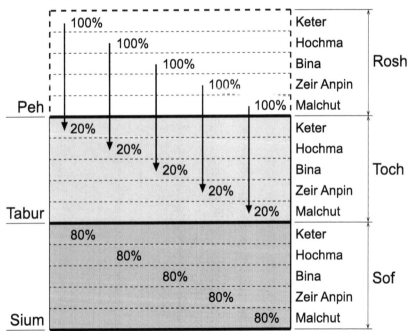

CHAPTER 3.7
EXPANSION AND WITHDRAWAL OF LIGHT

Once *Malchut* (who is considered a female *Partzuf*) decides to receive some of the Direct Light into her *Toch*, she stops receiving. *Malchut* always calculates in the *Rosh* (head) what is the maximum amount of Light she can receive in order to bestow. She always receives only a small part of the Direct Light, as receiving in order to benefit the Creator is against her nature.

As previously mentioned, the part of Direct Light that remains outside the vessel is called "Surrounding Light." It continues to pressure the vessel, which limits its expansion in the *Partzuf* and wants to break through the screen and fill up the entire vessel, including the *Sof* (end) of the *Partzuf*, just as it was prior to the restriction.

The *Partzuf* understands that if it only receives a part of the Light, meaning if it only fills itself as far as the *Tabur* (navel) and remains in that situation, the thought of Creation would not be carried out. In order for it to be carried out, the entire Light must fill *Malchut* as it did prior to the restriction, except with the aim to bestow. But if the *Partzuf* receives more Light, meaning below the *Tabur*, that would be reception in order to receive, because it doesn't have a screen with which to activate these vessels in order to bestow.

Thus, the *Partzuf* decides to not receive altogether and returns to the situation from before the reception. That decision is taken in the *Rosh* of the *Partzuf*, as do all decisions. Once the decision has been made, the screen that dropped from the *Peh* (mouth) to *Tabur* begins to rise back up to the *Peh*. The ascent of the screen makes the Lights exit the *Partzuf* through the *Peh* to the *Rosh*.

The decision to stop receiving the Light was made because there is a pressure on the screen that stands at the *Tabur* by the Surrounding Light. This lets it into the *Partzuf* to become Inner Light as well, while the Inner Light also keeps pushing down. These two Lights want to cancel the screen, which serves as a border that doesn't let the Lights through.

The pressure the Lights activate on the screen is called *Bitush* (Beating) of Inner Light and Surrounding Light.

These two Lights press on the screen that stands at the *Tabur* and limit the reception of Light into the *Partzuf*. They want the screen to drop from the *Tabur* so that all the Surrounding Light can enter the *Partzuf*.

That situation is much like a person who receives some of the food given to him by his host and feels great pleasure at the reception. However, this weakens him, because he feels what great pleasures there are in the delicacies that he did not receive.

As a result, the screen returns from the *Tabur* to the *Peh* and the *Partzuf* empties itself of any Light. Just as the Light entered the *Partzuf* through the *Peh*, so it now leaves. The expansion of the Light from Above downward, from the *Peh* to the *Tabur*, is called *Taamim* (flavors).

The withdrawal of the Light from the *Partzuf* is called *Nekudot* (points). Once the Light withdraws from the *Partzuf*, all that's left is a reminder (*Reshimo*) of the Light, called *Tagin*. The *Reshimo* from the Light of *Nekudot* is called *Otiot* (letters).

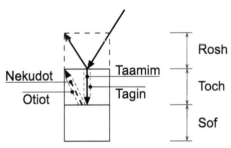

The expansion of the Light and its withdrawal makes the vessel fit for its task, because only after the vessel feels the pleasure, which is then withdrawn, does it create a real desire for that pleasure. Once the Light is gone, there remains a *Reshimo* in the vessel. It is a *Reshimo* of the past pleasure, meaning the *Nekudot*. When the vessel is emptied of the Light, the *Reshimo* determines the desire and the yearning in the vessel. The *Reshimo* from the withdrawal of the Light is called *Otiot*, or vessel.

Prior to the restriction, the fourth phase received Lights from all four phases. The Light came to her from His Essence through the root, first, second, third and fourth phases. That is why there are five phases in the fourth phase itself. Each phase of the five phases in *Behina Dalet* (the fourth phase) gets its Light from the corresponding phase:

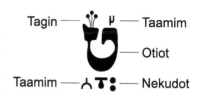

- *Behinat Shoresh* (the root phase) in *Behina Dalet* gets Light of *Yechida* (the Highest Light) from *Behinat Shoresh*.

- *Behina Aleph* (first phases) in *Behina Dalet* gets Light of *Haya* from *Behina Aleph*.

- *Behina Bet* (second phases) in *Behina Dalet* gets Light of *Neshama* from *Behina Bet*.

- *Behina Gimel* (third phase) in *Behina Dalet* gets Light of *Ruach* from *Behina Gimel*.

- *Behina Dalet* (fourth phase) in *Behina Dalet* gets Light of *Nefesh* from *Behina Dalet*.

Only *Behina Dalet* in *Behina Dalet* feels that her will to receive pleasure is really hers. Therefore, only this *Behina* is regarded as a creature. The other preceding phases in *Behina Dalet* are desires that *Behina Dalet* gets from *Behinot Shoresh, Aleph, Bet,* and *Gimel*. The desires in her preceding phases, though they are desires to receive, stem from the Creator, not from *Behina Dalet* herself.

Behina Dalet consists of five *Behinot* (phases). That structure is unchanging. These *Behinot* can be divided, filled, or joined in order to receive Light, but their structure nonetheless remains the same. It is named "the tip of the *Yod* (·), *Yod* (י), *Hey* (ה), *Vav* (ו), *Hey* (ה)."

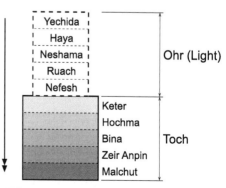

The worlds and everything in them, except people, stem from the phases that precede *Behina Dalet* of *Behina Dalet*, and do not possess their own independent will. They are activated by the desires imprinted in them by the Creator, and are therefore not defined as creatures. Only human souls stem from *Behina Dalet* in *Dalet*, where the will to receive is really hers. Hence, only human souls are regarded as creatures.

The real desire to receive for herself is created only in *Behina Dalet* of *Dalet*. She is the only one that feels as a receiver; therefore she is also the only one that decides to restrict the reception of the Light. But the Light leaves the other *Behinot* in *Behina Dalet* as well; because only the *Dalet* of *Dalet* actually receives, and the preceding *Behinot* only develop her will to receive. When she stops receiving, the Light withdraws from all of them, because all five *Behinot* (plural for *Behina*) are in fact one vessel, the tip of the *Yod* (·), *Yod* (י), *Hey* (ה), *Vav* (ו), *Hey* (ה).

After the restriction, when *Malchut* receives the five Lights through the screen, they still go inside the same five parts of *Malchut*. The order of the entrance of the Lights into the *Partzuf* runs from the smallest to the greatest—*Nefesh, Ruach, Neshama, Haya, Yechida*—hence the name NRNHY (pronounced NaRaNHaY).

CHAPTER 3.8
ENTRANCE AND EXIT OF LIGHTS IN THE PARTZUF

The five parts of *Malchut* are called *Behinot Shoresh, Aleph, Bet, Gimel, Dalet*. After the restriction, when those parts receive Lights through the screen, they are called *Sefirot*, because the Light shines in them (*Sapir* means illumination in Hebrew). Therefore, from that stage on they are referred to as *Sefirot*.

Shoresh – Keter.
Aleph – Hochma.
Bet – Bina.
Gimel – ZA (Zeir Anpin).
Dalet – Malchut.

174

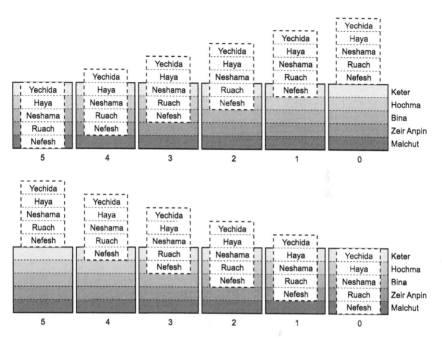

The *Reshimot* (plural for *Reshimo*) from the Withdrawing Lights are called *Otiot*. Once the five Lights—*Nefesh, Ruach, Neshama, Haya, Yechida*—have withdrawn from the five *Sefirot*—*Keter, Hochma, Bina, ZA, Malchut*, there remain five *Reshimot*, or *Otiot*: tip of the *Yod* (·), *Yod* (י), *Hey* (ה), *Vav* (ו), *Hey* (ה).

Later on, we will learn how Kabbalists denote spiritual forces in writing, how they build letters, names and words from lines and dots, which is how all the holy books are written. It turns out that writing is information about spiritual acts and forces. When Kabbalists read books, they can perform the actions according to the instructions received from the letters.

When we read in those holy books, we think they are about past events, but the Torah specifically states: "The entire Torah is the names of the Creator." All the words in the Torah tell us either about the vessels or their operations. This means that the entire Torah is the very same wisdom of Kabbalah we are studying now, just written in a different language.

As a rule, there are four languages: the language of the Torah, the language of the *Agada* (legends), that of the Talmud, and the language of Kabbalah. All of them were devised by Kabbalists who attained spirituality in order to tell us how to attain the purpose of Creation.

GENERAL OUTLOOK

The Will of the Creator is to benefit (delight) the creatures. The creatures are the ones that are meant to acquire and attain the benevolence of the Creator on their own. For that purpose, the Creator created an independent being that is completely detached from Him. The creature doesn't feel the Creator because Light is higher than the vessel, and when it fills the vessel, it controls it and determines what the vessel will now want.

Therefore, in order to maintain its independence, the creature must be made in concealment from the Light, without feeling the presence of the Creator and spirituality. It is born in the farthest point from the Creator, a degree called "This World." However, when the creature is independent of the influence of the Upper Light; i.e., the Creator, it is also denied the ability to understand reality in general and the purpose of life. The Creator must prepare such an environment for the creature that would be fitting for it to be born and evolve.

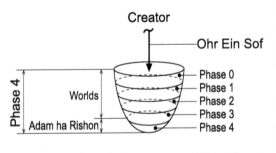

Such an environment would be:

A. To restrict the Light to the minimum possible, step by step. This is how the degrees were built, starting with the closest to the Creator—*Ein Sof*—and ending with the degree of

"This World," the farthest from the Creator. This recurrence is called "the expansion of the worlds and the *Partzufim*" (plural for *Partzuf*).

B. Once the starting point has been made ready for the creature, he must also be given a possibility to rise above that situation and attain the degree of the Creator. How can that be done? Our problem is that after the First Restriction, no Light comes to the creature, which is in the degree of "This World." Therefore, the Creator prepared a *Segula* (remedy) for people in this world–the Surrounding Light, which shines even into the restricted vessels.

Rabbi Yehuda Ashlag writes about this *Segula* in item 155 of his *Introduction to the Study of the Ten Sefirot*:

"Therefore we must ask: why then, did the Kabbalists obligate each person to delve in the wisdom of Kabbalah? Indeed, there is a weighty thing here, worthy of being publicized: that there is a magnificent, invaluable remedy for those who delve in the wisdom of Kabbalah: that although they do not understand what they are learning, but through the yearning and the great desire to understand what they are learning, they awaken upon themselves the Lights that surround their souls.

"Meaning, everyone from Israel is guaranteed finally attaining all these wonderful attainments that God has resolved in the Thought of Creation to grant each creature. But he who has not attained it in this life will attain it in the next and so on, until he has completed that which He preliminarily thought of. And while man has not attained perfection, these Lights that are destined to come to him are deemed "Surrounding Lights." That means that they stand ready for him, awaiting his attainment of the vessels of reception. Then they will be dressed within the able vessels.

"Thus, even when the vessels are absent, when one delves in this wisdom, mentioning the names of the Lights and the vessels related to his soul, they immediately illuminate him to a certain degree. However, they illuminate him without dressing in the internality of his soul, since he doesn't have the vessels needed to receive them. Indeed, the illumination one receives time and again when studying, draws upon him grace from Above, imparting him with a bounty of sanctity and purity, which greatly furthers one toward one's perfection."

In item 156, Rabbi Ashlag adds: "But there is a strict condition in the practice of this wisdom, that they will not materialize matters in corporeal and fictitious forms, for by that they breach the commandment, 'Thou shalt not make unto thee a graven image, nor any manner of likeness,' for then they are harmed instead of helped."

It follows that only the correct study of Kabbalah can bring one to the purpose of one's life. That is what the Kabbalists maintain, and who knows reality better?

The Surrounding Light is the *Segula* with which anyone can begin the ascent from this world to the spiritual world. Without this Surrounding Light, we would have no possibility of overcoming our situation. The vessel can only be corrected by means of the Light, and the Upper Light cannot descend to this world, hence the necessity for the Surrounding Light.

When Kabbalists attain spirituality, they cannot describe it in words because spirituality contains only feelings. Therefore, the books of Kabbalah are written in the Language of the Branches, when words of this world are used to discuss spiritual subjects.

The spiritual world is an abstract, "virtual" place. There are only forces and emotions there, no bodies. The spiritual terms must constantly be renewed because we cannot understand a word of what the Kabbalistic books speak of before we have an emotional connection with spirituality.

The primary mistake people make is believing that there are "Kabbalists" who teach that there is a connection between the human body and the spiritual vessel. They imply that the spiritual vessel somehow clothes the body, with each corporeal organ having a spiritual counterpart. According to that perception, if a person makes a physical gesture, *any* physical gesture, there is some spiritual content to it. They think that by doing so, one actually performs a spiritual act.

Their mistake stems from the fact that Kabbalists wrote their books in the language of the branches, and used corporeal words to define spiritual concepts. That is why there is such a strict prohibition in the Torah that states, "Thou shalt not make unto thee a graven image, nor any manner of likeness." This means that it is forbidden to picture spirituality in physical images, not because it can inflict some harm on the Upper World, but because false imaginings would stop one from understanding how the Creator works and thus interfere with the attaining of one's goal.

Therefore, the student must repeatedly study the primary concepts of the wisdom of Kabbalah, such as Place, Time, Motion, Absence, Body, Body Parts or Organs, Mating, Kissing, Embracing, etc. until every term is correctly understood.

This is what Baal HaSulam writes about in his *Introduction to The Study of the Ten Sefirot*. A person who wishes to study Kabbalah correctly will do well to stay away from all other books on the subject except for the *Zohar*, the writings of the Ari, Baal HaSulam, and Rabbi Baruch Ashlag.

The interpretation of the Torah as historic episodes contradicts the statement that the entire Torah is the names of the Creator, that it is a Torah of the world of *Atzilut*, and that every word in it is a holy name. It is important to remember that it does not speak of this corporeal world and corporeal people.

All the names in the Torah are holy names, even names such as Pharaoh, Balaam, and Balak. The *Zohar* explains that each name indicates a certain spiritual degree: Pharaoh stands for *Malchut*, Laban stands for *Partzuf Hochma*, and so on.

RESHIMOT

In order to ensure correct action, there must be clear understanding of what it is the vessel wants to achieve, how to achieve it, and how strong the desire is to achieve it.

There is only one creature beside the Creator, and that is the will to receive. Therefore, reality consists only of a Light and a vessel, pleasure

THE PATH OF KABBALAH

and desire, or in Kabbalistic terms, *Hitlabshut* (clothing) and *Aviut* (thickness, coarseness).

After any spiritual act, when the Light withdraws from the vessel and the vessel becomes empty after having being filled with Light, there remain two "memories" of the previous situation:

A. *Reshimo de Hitlabshut*, an imprint of the Light that was present in the vessel but that has now departed.

B. *Reshimo de Aviut*, an imprint of the vessel on the screen that remains in use.

(The prefix, *de* means "of" in Aramaic, thus *Reshimo de Aviut* means "Reminiscence of *Aviut*")

These two *Reshimot* are considered as one *Reshimo*. If this *Reshimo* does not remain in the vessel, it will not know what to want or how to get it. The entire process of the creation of reality from its beginning in *Malchut de Ein Sof* to its end in this world, is a sequence of situations of *Malchut de Ein Sof*. She experiences these situations by means of the Light that surrounds her. It awakens the *Reshimot* in her, which remain after every situation she experiences.

The state where *Behina Dalet* is filled with Light is called *Malchut de Ein Sof*. After *Behina Dalet* feels that she is receiving, she decides to restrict the reception of the Light. The Light then withdraws, and what remains in *Malchut* is a *Reshimo* of the Light that was in her. Even after the restriction, Light continues to shine in order to fill up *Malchut*. But now she calculates and decides to receive only as much as she can in order to bestow to the Creator.

The data needed for the calculation is:

A. *Reshimo* of the clothing of the Light in the previous situation
B. will to receive in order to bestow.

Once *Malchut* makes these calculations in her *Rosh* (head), she then receives in the *Guf* (body) what she has decided to receive.

World/*Partzuf* Name	Reshimo de Hitlabshut/Aviut		World/*Partzuf* Name	Reshimo de Hitlabshut/Aviut	
The world of Adam Kadmon:			**The world of Beria:**		
Partzuf Keter	Galgalta	4/4	*Partzuf Keter*	Atik	4/4
Partzuf Hochma	AB	4/3	*Partzuf Hochma*	AA	4/3
Partzuf Bina	SG	3/2	*Partzuf Bina*	AVI	3/2
Partzuf ZA	MA	2/1	*Partzuf ZA*	ZA	2/1
Partzuf Malchut	BON	1/0	*Partzuf Malchut*	Nukva	1/0
Partzuf Nekudot de SAG:			**The world of Yetzira:**		
Partzuf Nekudot de SAG		2/2	*Partzuf Keter*	Atik	4/4
			Partzuf Hochma	AA	4/3
The world of Nekudim:			*Partzuf Bina*	AVI	3/2
Partzuf Katnut		2/1	*Partzuf ZA*	ZA	2/1
Partzuf Gadlut		4/3	*Partzuf Malchut*	Nukva	1/0
The world of Atzilut:			**The world of Assiya:**		
Partzuf Keter	Atik	4/4	*Partzuf Keter*	Atik	4/4
Partzuf Hochma	AA	4/3	*Partzuf Hochma*	AA	4/3
Partzuf Bina	AVI	3/2	*Partzuf Bina*	AVI	3/2
Partzuf ZA	ZA	2/1	*Partzuf ZA*	ZA	2/1
Partzuf Malchut	Nukva	1/0	*Partzuf Malchut*	Nukva	1/0

When the vessel completes the reception of that part of the Light that it decided to receive, the Surrounding Light beats on the screen and forces it to return to the *Peh* (mouth). The result is that the entire *Partzuf* is emptied of Light.

When the screen ascends from the *Tabur de Galgalta* to the *Peh*, the Inner Light exits *Galgalta*, leaving a *Reshimo* of the Light that was in there, a *Reshimo de Hitlabshut*. But the *Reshimo* from the strength of the screen that received the Light is not left, because the screen decided to stop receiving the Light and disqualified itself from working with its own strength. Hence the *Reshimo* of the screen disappears.

The screen now rises from *Tabur* and is once more at the *Peh*. Because of that, it feels the Upper Light in the *Rosh*, which demands to be accepted. That creates in *Malchut* a will to receive the Light in order to bestow once more. At this point begins the birth of a new *Partzuf* on the *Reshimot* that remained from the previous situation.

Summary: A *Reshimo* of Light is a part of the Light that is left when the Light has withdrawn. It is the nucleus and the root of the creation of the new *Partzuf*. The *Reshimo* from the screen is then lost and a *Zivug* (spiritual mating) is made on a new *Reshimo*.

RESHIMOT THAT CREATE PARTZUFIM

Reshimot from the *Aviut* of the Screen of the Worlds:

World of *Keter*	World of AK	*Aviut* 4 (*Dalet*)
World of *Hochma*	World of *Atzilut*	*Aviut* 3 (*Gimel*)
World of *Bina*	World of *Beria*	*Aviut* 2 (*Bet*)
World of ZA	World of *Yetzira*	*Aviut* 1 (*Aleph*)
World of *Malchut*	World of *Assiya*	*Aviut* 0 (*Shoresh*)

When the entire reality expands until there is not a single *Reshimo* left in the screen, it is the end of the world of *Assiya*.

Malchut of the world of *Atzilut* creates yet another *Partzuf*, called *Adam ha Rishon* (the First Man). That *Partzuf* was broken and divided into many parts that fell below the world of *Assiya*, to a place called "This World."

The smallest *Reshimo* in the broken vessel is called the "Point in the Heart." That is what we feel as desire for spirituality when we are awakened from Above. These *Reshimot* are clothed in certain individuals in our world and do not let go of them until they correct them with a screen and fill them with Light.

If a person feels this *Reshimo*, he is worthy of attaining spirituality, feeling the Upper World, and coming to know the true reality. He will find the guidance to get there in the books of Kabbalah. Each generation has books that are right for the specific type of souls that descend in that generation.

The books that are intended to guide our generation into spirituality are the books of Rabbi Yehuda Ashlag (Baal HaSulam), and Rabbi Baruch Ashlag (Rabash). Besides these books, the other prerequisite that must be met for correct learning is studying in a group whose purpose is to attain the purpose of Creation, headed by a Kabbalist teacher.

The evolution of reality from Above downward created a ladder that man can climb upward. A person who reaches a certain degree discovers in it *Reshimot* from an even higher degree, which enables a continued ascent up the ladder. *Reshimot* from higher degrees also exist in us. They are *Reshimot* of our own adjacent degree. By working on those *Reshimot* we can exit our world and enter the spiritual world.

CHAPTER 3.9
THE BIRTH OF THE PARTZUFIM

Behina Dalet is scalled *Malchut* (Kingship) because it has the greatest will to receive. When it is filled with Light, it is called *Ein Sof* (No End), because it receives Light without limitation. *Malchut* is therefore the only creature. Its parts are called "worlds" (the Hebrew word for it is *Olam*, from the word *Ha'alama* (concealment) because they conceal the Light of the Creator from the creatures). The concealment of each world corresponds to the measurement of Light the creatures can receive with the screen.

When *Behina Dalet* received the Light of *Ein Sof* she felt that the Light came from the Giver. The sensation of the Giver awakened in her such shame and torment that she decided never to receive again. A decision in the Upper One becomes a binding law for all the following situations. Hence, even if some part of *Malchut* wants to receive for itself, it is unable to because *Malchut* controls all her parts. Any new decision is a result of the weakness of the degree; therefore it operates only on the lower degrees.

After the First Restriction, *Reshimot* remain in *Malchut* from the Light and the vessel. But the Light still wants to fill *Malchut* because the intention of the Creator to delight the Creature doesn't change. This

Thought of the Creator is the only active thing in the entire Creation, even when reality appears to not be working in our favor.

The *Malchut* that stands at the *Peh de Rosh* of the *Partzuf* feels the Desire of the Creator to please it, as with the example of the host and the guest. But *Malchut* feels that she is not giving the Creator anything. Therefore, she decides to receive so that the Creator will enjoy her reception.

Using the *Reshimot de Hitlabshut* and *Reshimot de Aviut* from the previous filling, *Malchut* can calculate how much she can receive in order to please the Creator and not to please herself.

A *Reshimo de Hitlabshut* is a *Reshimo* from the Light that filled *Malchut*. The screen with which she received that Light has now been refined, and the screen hasn't the strength to receive the same amount of Light again. All that's left of it is the *Reshimo de Hitlabshut*. The *Rosh de Hitlabshut* of the new *Partzuf* is born on top of the *Reshimo de Hitlabshut* from the previous *Partzuf*.

At that point, the screen performs a *Zivug* (spiritual mating) on the *Reshimo de Aviut*. That creates the second *Rosh*, named *Rosh de Aviut*, and from there the Light expands to the *Guf* (body), which is the *Hitlabshut* of the Light in *Malchut*.

The part where *Malchut* decides how much of the Upper Light she can receive in order to bestow is called *Rosh*. Once the decision in the *Rosh* has been made, *Malchut* receives the amount of Light she had decided on inside the *Partzuf*. That Light is called *Taamim*. When the Light of *Taamim* stops entering the *Guf*, the screen that drew the Light stops drawing it into the *Partzuf*.

The screen stops the Light from entering because the decision in *Malchut* is a decision about the maximum amount she can receive without taking for herself. If she receives any more, it would be in order to please herself.

Thus, in the place where the screen stops receiving, *Malchut* feels a further urge by the Upper Light to receive it. That place is called *Tabur*. If *Malchut* receives any more Light, it will be for her own pleasure. Hence, she has no choice but to stop receiving any Light.

The decisions are always taken at the *Rosh* of the *Partzuf* and only afterward are they executed in the *Guf*. And so it is here: once a decision has been made to stop receiving, the screen rises from the *Tabur* to the *Peh* and pushes the Lights out of the *Guf* of the *Partzuf*.

The screen arrives at the *Peh* along with the *Reshimo* of the Light that filled the *Partzuf* and a *Reshimo de Aviut* that remains in the screen. The encounter of the screen with the Upper Light reawakens the screen to want to receive Light in order to bestow, hence new *Reshimot* awaken in it. It performs a *Zivug de Hakaa* with the Light and creates the next *Partzuf*.

In each *Partzuf* there are two screens: one that rejects the Light and one that receives it. The screen that rejects the Light always remains at the *Peh* of the *Partzuf*. It rejects all the Light that wants to enter the *Partzuf*, and by that it adheres to the condition of the First Restriction.

Once the first screen has rejected all the Light and is certain that receiving will not be done for self, but only with the intention of pleasing the Creator, the second screen is activated. The second screen weighs how much of the Upper Light that arrives can be received in order to bestow.

Once the decision has been made, the receiving screen begins to receive Light. It drops from the *Peh*, followed by the Light that enters the *Partzuf*. When the amount of Light in the *Partzuf* has reached the decided-upon amount, the screen in the *Guf* stops because the *Guf* screen always executes the orders of the *Rosh* screen. Thus, a new *Partzuf* is born out of the first.

The calculation is performed at the screen in the *Rosh*. But because the *Aviut* in the new *Partzuf* is smaller than in the previous *Partzuf*, the screen drops from the *Peh* of the old *Partzuf* to its *Chazeh* (Chest). It happens because the *Aviut* in the new *Partzuf* is of the third degree, not of the fourth as it was in the first *Partzuf*.

Therefore, once the screen rises from *Tabur* to *Peh* and takes the desire for a new *Zivug*, it drops to the *Chazeh* and calculates how much it can receive. That calculation creates the *Rosh* of the second *Partzuf*. Once the decision has been made, the screen drops from the *Peh* to as low as it had decided to descend in order to receive Light. That place will become the *Tabur* of the new *Partzuf*.

From the *Tabur* and below, down to the *Sium Raglin* (End of Legs, the end of the *Partzuf*), the vessels remain empty. This is because the screen doesn't fill them due to a lack of sufficient resistance. The second *Partzuf*, like all the other *Partzufim* in the world of *Adam Kadmon*, cannot reach below the *Tabur* of the first *Partzuf* due to the weakness of their screen.

After the second *Partzuf*, called AB, is born and receives what it decides to receive in the *Rosh*, the same *Bitush* (the vigorous pressure of Inner Light and Surrounding Light on the Screen at the *Tabur*) that occurred in the first *Partzuf* occurs again. Here, too, the screen realizes that it cannot remain at the *Tabur* because it lacks sufficient strength to receive any more in order to bestow. If it remains that way, then the purpose of Creation will not be realized.

Because of that, the second *Partzuf* also decides to refine itself and rises to the *Peh*. Again, there is a *Reshimo* left in the screen, and when it is once more included in the *Peh*, it reawakens to receive Light. The last *Reshimo de Aviut*, that of *Behina Gimel*, disappears from the screen and the *Reshimo de Aviut* of *Behina Bet* appears. The screen drops once more to the *Chazeh* and performs *Zivug de Hakaa* to create the new *Partzuf*, called SAG.

The same process now repeats: once *Partzuf* SAG is born, its screen in the *Guf* refines as a result of the *Bitush* of the Inner and Surrounding Lights. The screen rises to the *Peh*, drops to the *Chazeh*, and creates the new *Partzuf* in *Aviut Aleph*, called MA, or Upper MA.

When *Partzuf* MA stops the expansion of the Light into it, it feels the *Bitush* of the Internal and Surrounding Lights and decides to refine itself. It returns to the *Peh* with *Aviut Shoresh* (root coarseness) because there is no more strength left in the screen to receive Light in order to bestow. It can no longer create new *Partzufim*, but only a *Rosh*. At this point, the process of creating the *Partzufim* stops.

CHAPTER 3.10
REALITY IN GENERAL

After the restriction, *Malchut* decides to receive in order to give to the Creator. This intention is called a "screen." A series of *Partzufim* then comes out on this screen:

- *Partzuf Galgalta* is emanated on the screen that can receive Light with fourth-degree coarseness.

- *Partzuf AB* is emanated on the screen that can receive Light with third-degree coarseness.

- *Partzuf SAG* is emanated on the screen that can receive Light with second-degree coarseness.

- *Partzuf MA* is emanated on the screen that can receive Light with first-degree coarseness.

- *Partzuf BON* is emanated on the screen that can receive Light with root-degree coarseness.

The names of the *Partzufim* are given according to the quality and the quantity of the Lights that fill them. *Malchut* emerges as *Behina Dalet*, meaning the fifth in the evolution of the Light of the Creator's essence. For that reason, she receives from her previous phases and consists of them. This is also the reason why *Malchut* has five phases of desire, from the smallest (*Behinat Shoresh*) to the greatest (*Behina Dalet*) and she can take Light indefinitely.

After the restriction, *Malchut* decides to receive Light only in order to give to the Creator. This kind of reception goes against her natural desire. Therefore, she cannot receive indefinitely and cannot receive the Light all at once as before. For that reason, she decides to receive this Light in small portions. In the end, though, she will be filled to the top and attain the purpose of Creation.

Each part inside *Malchut* consists of five parts of will to receive, just like the general *Malchut*, because there cannot be a desire if there aren't four degrees of expansion of Light that precede it.

For that reason, there is a fixed formation according to the five degrees of *Aviut*: *Shoresh, Aleph, Bet, Gimel, Dalet*. In terms of *Sefirot* they are called *K'eter, Hochma, Bina, ZA, Malchut*, which are also named (in Hebrew letters)—the tip of the *Yod* (·), *Yod* (י), *Hey* (ה), *Vav* (ו), *Hey* (ה).

There are five worlds, each consisting of five *Partzufim*. In each *Partzuf* there are five *Sefirot*, thus the sum total of degrees turns out to be $5^3 = 125$ degrees or *Sefirot* that each soul must go through on its way from our world to the world of *Ein Sof*, and the adhesion with the Creator.

Each degree, *Sefira, Partzuf*, or world, any part of *Malchut de Ein Sof*, and even the smallest particles of reality, consist of five parts of the will to receive, a screen over it, and Light received by the screen. The strength of the screen determines the kind and the degree of the use of the desire.

There is not a single object, spiritual or physical, that is not comprised of these five parts, the tip of the *Yod* (·), *Yod* (י), *Hey* (ה), *Vav* (ו), *Hey* (ה). These Hebrew letters comprise the name of the Creator; it is the mold in which He created the creature. The creature feels and names the Creator according to how it feels the Light.

Every vessel is named according to the extent that it feels the Creator. That is why each degree has its own name, starting with this world, the lowest degree, through the world of *Ein Sof*. When a soul ascends a degree, it means that it receives the Light in that degree, meaning it fills up its *Yod* (י), *Hey* (ה), *Vav* (ו), *Hey* (ה), also known as *HaVaYaH* with a certain filling. That specific Light, together with the *HaVaYaH*, makes up the name of the degree.

It is written that everyone must attain the degree called "Moses." All the names in the Torah are holy names, because they are appellations of manifestations of the Light; i.e. the Creator. That is why the whole Torah is comprised of names of the Creator, including such names as Pharaoh, Balak, and Balaam etc.

A name of a degree is determined by the Light that fills the *Partzuf*, the *HaVaYaH*. For example: if the vessel is filled with the Light of Wisdom, and the sign for that Light is the letter *Yod*, it turns out that the filling of the letters (how they're spelt in Hebrew) would be:

Yod (י)	Hey (ה)	Vav (ו)	Hey (ה)
Yod-Vav-Dalet	Hey-Yod	Vav-Yod-Vav	Hey-Yod

That is because each letter in the Hebrew alphabet has its own numerical value (when two Hebrew letters appear, the left marks the form of that letter at the end of a word. They are called "final letters"):

Aleph: א = 1	Zayin: ז = 7	Mem: מ/ם = 40	Kuf: ק = 100
Bet: ב = 2	Het: ח = 8	Nun: נ/ן = 50	Reish: ר = 200
Gimel: ג = 3	Tet: ט = 9	Samech: ס = 60	Shin: ש = 300
Dalet: ד = 4	Yod: י = 10	Ayin: ע = 70	Tav: ת = 400
Hey: ה = 5	Chaf: כ/ך = 20	Peh: פ/ף = 80	
Vav: ו = 6	Lamed: ל = 30	Tzadik: צ/ץ = 90	

Thus, summing up the value of the letters of the name *HaVaYaH* spelled this way—*Yod-Vav-Dalet* (10+6+4) + *Hey-Yod* (10+5) + *Vav-Yod-Vav* (6+10+6) + *Hey-Yod* (10+5) = 72, or pronounced in letters: *AB* (ע"ב). Hence *Partzuf Hochma* is called *AB* (ע"ב).

A *Partzuf* that receives the Light of Mercy (*Hassadim*) is called *SAG* (ס"ג)—*Yod-Vav-Dalet* (10+6+4) + *Hey-Yod* (10+5) + *Vav-Aleph-Vav* (6+1+6) + *Hey-Yod* (10+5) = 63, or pronounced in letters: *SAG* (ס"ג).

All the degrees in all the worlds are given these names. Thus, in order to know the name of each degree we need only know the name for each type of Light. Then, when we read the Torah, we will understand which spiritual degrees, actions and places it talks about.

Then we will no longer be led to think that the Torah speaks of anything lower than the spiritual world. We will know that it doesn't speak of our corporeal life, about history, or about how to get on in the physical world. We will know that all the books in the Torah are in fact instructions for man that explain how to attain the purpose of our lives, while living in this world, so that we do not have to return to it time after time and suffer again and again from this empty, purposeless life.

A *Partzuf* consists of ten *Sefirot*: *Keter, Hochma, Bina, Zeir Anpin,* and *Malchut*. Expressed in letters it would be: *Yod–Hochma, Hey–Bina, Vav–Zeir Anpin, Hey–Malchut*.

But the degree of a *Partzuf* (*Nefesh, Ruach, Neshama, Haya,* and *Yechida*) is not clarified by the name *HaVaYaH*. The letters of *HaVaYaH* make up ten *Sefirot*, the skeleton of the vessel. They explain the state of the empty vessel, without the Upper Light. The degree of the vessel is determined by the power of the screen. The screen fills up the ten *Sefirot* of *HaVaYaH* with Lights. The screen can fill up the vessel with the Lights of *Nefesh, Ruach, Neshama, Haya* or *Yechida*. The amount of Light in the vessel determines its degree.

There are actually only two Lights: the Light of *Hochma* (Wisdom) and the Light of *Hassadim* (Mercy). The sign for *Hochma* is the letter *Yod* (י), and the sign for *Hassadim* is *Hey* (ה).

A. The degree of *Yechida* (*Keter*) is written as *HaVaYaH* without any filling: *Yod* (י), *Hey* (ה), *Vav* (ו), *Hey* (ה) = 10+5+6+5=26.

B. The degree of *Haya* (*Hochma*) is *HaVaYaH* filled with *Yod*: *Yod-Vav-Dalet* (10+6+4) + *Hey-Yod* (10+5) + *Vav-Yod-Vav* (6+10+6) + *Hey-Yod* (10+5) = 72, or pronounced in letters: *AB* (ע"ב). Hence *Partzuf Hochma* is called *AB* (ע"ב).

C. The degree of *Neshama* (*Bina*) is *HaVaYaH* filled with *Hey*, except that in the letter *Vav* it is filled with *Aleph* and in the letter *Hey*, it is filled with *Yod*: *Yod-Vav-Dalet* (10+6+4) + *Hey-*

190

Yod (10+5) + Vav-Aleph-Vav (6+1+6) + Hey-Yod (10+5) = 63, or pronounced in letters: SAG (ס״ג).

D. The degree of Ruach (Zeir Anpin) is HaVaYaH filled with Hey, but only the letter Vav is filled with Aleph: Yod-Vav-Dalet (10+6+4) + Hey-Aleph (5+1) + Vav-Aleph-Vav (6+1+6) + Hey-Aleph (5+1) = 45, or pronounced in letters: MA (מ״ה).

E. The degree of Nefesh (Malchut) is HaVaYaH filled with Hey, except in the letter Vav which remains without any filling: Yod-Vav-Dalet (10+6+4) + Hey-Hey (5+5) + Vav-Vav (6+6) + Hey-Hey (5+5) = 52, or pronounced in letters: BON (ב״ן).

CHAPTER 3.11
NEKUDOT DE SAG

After the First Restriction Malchut decides to fill herself with Light in order to bestow using the Reshimot that remained from the world of Ein Sof. Reception in order to bestow goes against the nature of the creature, therefore Malchut cannot receive the Upper Light that filled her in the world of Ein Sof all at once, but only in small portions, called Partzufim. That way Malchut receives five portions of Light: Galgalta, AB, SAG, upper MA, and upper BON. That concludes the surfacing of her Reshimot and the expansion comes to a halt.

The third Partzuf is SAG. Its nature is that of Bina. Hence, it has no desire to receive anything for itself and "delights in mercy." Because of that, this Partzuf can descend below Tabur de Galgalta and fill the Sof de Galgalta (End of Galgalta) with its Lights.

Partzuf SAG comes out on Reshimot 3/2 (3rd degree of Hitlabshut and 2nd of Aviut). The result is that there is the Light of Wisdom in its Taamim. Having a Light of Wisdom makes it impossible for it to go below Tabur de Galgalta. Only when Partzuf SAG begins to refine itself does the Light of Wisdom retreat, and as the screen refines from Tabur to Peh, the Partzuf Nekudot de SAG emerges. In this Partzuf there is only Light of

Mercy, and it can therefore descend below *Tabur de Galgalta* and fill the *Sof de Galgalta* with Light of Mercy.

The entire reality stems from *Behinat Shoresh*, which is the desire of the Creator to delight His Creatures. In accordance with this desire, the Light expands by way of cause and consequence to execute the thought of Creation inside the vessels, so that they will receive the Light.

In *Behina Aleph*, consisting of the entire Light, there is the complete intent of the Creator to create a vessel and fill it with Light. Anything that comes out after *Behina Aleph* is a consequence of it. This is how the thought of the Creator is executed. The Creator imprinted the possibility to bring Creation to its goal, i.e. raise it to the degree of the Creator in the nature of the vessels and the Lights.

After the First Restriction, *Malchut de Ein Sof* decides to receive with the screen and produces five *Partzufim*: *Galgalta*, AB, SAG, upper MA, and upper BON. That concludes the surfacing of all the *Reshimot*. The screen then loses its strength, though only a part of *Malchut* has been filled.

If *Nekudot de SAG* had not descended in order to fill the *Sof de Galgalta*, *Malchut de Ein Sof* would never have been filled. That is because *Malchut* is only a will to receive, without any mixture of desires for bestowal. But when *Nekudot de SAG*, which consists of the nature of *Bina*, descends below *Tabur* to the *Sof de Galgalta*, it creates a mixture of *Malchut* and *Bina*. Thus, *Malchut* gets an opportunity to acquire a desire (vessel) for bestowal, correct herself, and be filled with Light.

After the First Restriction *Malchut de Ein Sof* decides to receive only through the screen to the extent of her ability to receive in order to bestow. She makes a *Zivug* on *Reshimot* 4/4 (4th degree of *Hitlabshut* and 4th of *Aviut*) that are left in her after the restriction, and receives a part of the Light of *Ein Sof*. That part of *Malchut de Ein Sof* that was filled by this *Zivug* is called *Galgalta*, or *Partzuf Keter*.

192

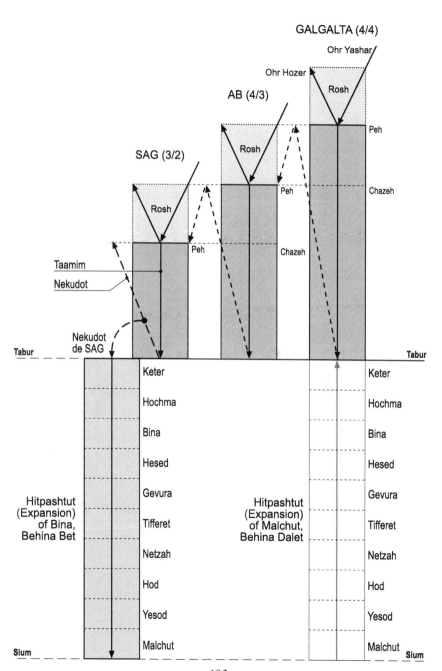

After that, *Malchut* receives yet another portion of the Light of *Ein Sof* in order to bestow. The part of *Malchut* that was filled by this *Zivug* over the *Reshimot* of 4/3 that remained after *Galgalta* is called AB, or *Partzuf Hochma*.

The part of *Malchut de Ein Sof* that was filled in the next phase by the *Zivug* on the *Reshimot* 3/2, that remain after *Partzuf AB*, is called SAG, or *Partzuf Bina*. *Partzuf SAG* is the same *Malchut*, the same will to receive, but now it cannot receive in order to bestow with the screen like the *Partzufim* of *Galgalta* and AB. It can only resemble itself to *Behina Bet*, to *Bina*.

Bina does not want to receive Light; by nature, she only wants to give. There is no limitation on the act of giving, therefore *Partzuf SAG* fills with its Light the part of *Malchut* that is still left empty.

Bina consists of three parts:

A. The expansion of the Light of Wisdom.

B. The decision of *Bina* that she doesn't want to receive any Light of Wisdom, only to give, hence in *Bina* there is only Light of Mercy.

C. The receiving by *Bina* of a small amount of Light of Wisdom, not for herself, but in order to give to *Partzuf Zeir Anpin*.

The upper part of *Bina* is still *Hochma*. The desire to bestow manifests only from the lower part. Hence, she can fill the part of *Malchut de Ein Sof* below *Tabur* that hasn't been filled yet.

Partzuf SAG begins to receive Light in its *Toch* (its internal part) by performing a *Zivug* on 3/2. The presence of *Reshimo Gimel* (3) *de Hitlabshut* makes for the expansion of the Light of Wisdom in his *Taamim*. Therefore, that part of SAG cannot go below *Tabur de Galgalta*.

But once the screen begins to refine itself and rises from *Tabur* to *Peh*, the part of the *Partzuf* that is only *Bina* can descend below *Tabur de Galgalta*, because it is pure Light of Mercy (pleasure from bestowal) without any Wisdom (pleasure from reception).

Hence, that part of *Partzuf SAG*, called *Nekudot de SAG*, descends below the *Tabur de Galgalta* and clothes its *Sof*.

CHAPTER 3.12

THE SECOND RESTRICTION

*N*ekudot *de SAG* went below *Tabur de Galgalta* and filled the empty vessels of the *Sof de Galgalta* with Light of Mercy. They felt that in the empty vessels of *Galgalta* there were *Reshimot* from the Light that filled the *Sof de Galgalta* before it had been refined.

The Light that filled the *Sof de Galgalta* was a Light of Mercy with a little bit of Wisdom. After the refining of the screen there were *Reshimot* that were left there: they were *Reshimot* of the Light of *Dalet* (4) *de Hitlabshut* and *Gimel* (3) *de Aviut*. The *Sof de Galgalta* rejected the Light from expanding in it, like *Bina*. In that, it is much like *Nekudot de SAG*. Because of that, *Nekudot de SAG* mix with the *Sof de Galgalta* and fill up the empty vessels.

From the mixture of *Nekudot de SAG* with *Sof de Galgalta*, they receive *Reshimot* that remained at the *Sof de Galgalta*. The *Reshimot* from *Galgalta* are stronger than the power in the screen of *Nekudot de SAG*, which makes *Nekudot de SAG* begin to want to receive the pleasure that was in *Galgalta* for themselves. A spiritual law says that if the pleasure that is felt in the will to receive is stronger than the strength of the screen, the vessel wants to receive it for itself, because the strong (screen or desire) rules.

All the worlds and the *Partzufim* are parts of *Malchut de Ein Sof*. *Malchut* restricted herself and decided never to receive again if it is for her own pleasure. Therefore, when a desire to receive for itself awakens in *Partzuf Nekudot de SAG*, the *Malchut* that performed the First Restriction and stood at the *Sof de Galgalta* rises to the place in *Nekudot de SAG*, from which *Nekudot de SAG* began to want to receive the Light for itself.

Each *Partzuf* consists of ten *Sefirot—Keter, Hochma, Bina, Hesed, Gevura, Tifferet, Netzah, Hod, Yesod, Malchut.*

Nekudot de SAG is *Partzuf Bina. Bina* consists of two parts:

A. An upper part, comprised of *Keter, Hochma, Bina, Hesed, Gevura,* and *Tifferet.* These *Sefirot* want only to give and receive nothing in return.

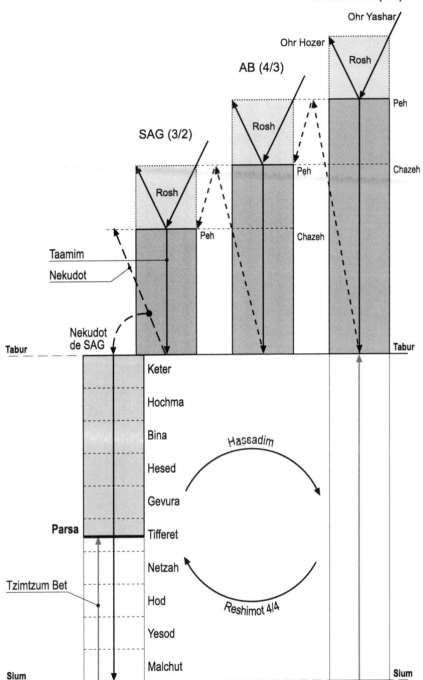

B. A lower part, comprised of *Netzah, Hod, Yesod*, and *Malchut*. These *Sefirot* do not belong to *Bina*. Their role is only to receive Light of Wisdom from *Hochma* and pass it on to the lower one. *Sefirot Netzah, Hod, Yesod* and *Malchut* do have a will to receive Light. They have a screen to receive the Light not for themselves, but only in order to pass it to the lower one. But if the screen is gone, the *Sefirot*, meaning those desires, will immediately want to receive the Light for themselves.

Example: A man was accustomed to receiving a regular sum of money in order to give to the poor. One day, he received a much larger sum than usual. He felt he couldn't give the money to the poor now because he wanted it for himself. He couldn't resist the temptation for such great potential pleasure.

The man could resist temptation only as long as the sum of money was smaller than his screen, because the pleasure from giving the money was greater than the pleasure of stealing. But when the pleasure from reception became greater than that of giving, he immediately wanted to receive it for himself.

This is how the will to receive works in every creature, because we are all made of a will to receive. And if we do bestow, it is only because it brings us more benefit than receiving.

This is what happens in *Partzuf Nekudot de SAG*. When the part of the *Partzuf* that should receive in order to bestow to the lower ones became exposed to a greater pleasure than its screen could resist, the screen was immediately canceled and the *Partzuf* wanted to receive for itself.

The will to receive for self was awakened in *Partzuf Nekudot de SAG* from *Tifferet* and below, because the *Sefirot Keter, Hochma* and *Bina* belong to the *Rosh* and therefore do not want to receive. *Hesed, Gevura*, and *Tifferet* have the same function as *Keter, Hochma* and *Bina* respectively, except they are at the *Guf* of the *Partzuf*. Thus, *Tifferet* is like *Bina* in the *Guf* of the *Partzuf*.

Each *Sefira* consists of ten inner *Sefirot*. Hence the *Sefira Tifferet* has its own ten inner *Sefirot*, that like *Bina*, are divided into two parts:

- Parts that do not receive in *Tifferet*: *Keter, Hochma, Bina, Hesed, Gevura,* and *Tifferet*.

- Parts that do receive include the lower part of *Bina* and the *Sefirot Netzah, Hod, Yesod* and *Malchut*.

Partzuf Nekudot de SAG is divided into vessels of bestowal and vessels of reception. The line that separates them is in the inner *Tifferet* of *Tifferet*. That place is called the *Chazeh* (chest) of *Partzuf Nekudot de SAG*.

Some of the vessels of *Nekudot de SAG* received a greater will to receive than their screen. Hence, *Malchut* of the First Restriction that was maintaining the First Restriction, rose precisely to the point of the *Chazeh*, and did not let the Light go under that point. The border for the expansion of the Light below that point is called *Parsa*.

The rising of *Malchut* to the *Chazeh* of *Nekudot de SAG* in order to limit the expansion of Light below is called "the Second Restriction." The First Restriction is the prohibition on receiving the Light of Wisdom in order to receive. The Second Restriction, however, is the prohibition on receiving any Light of Wisdom, because from *Partzuf Nekudot de SAG* onward there isn't enough strength to receive that Light in order to bestow.

A desire in the Upper World becomes a binding law in the lower one. Hence, in all the *Partzufim* that emanated after the Second Restriction is a *Parsa* (border, separating line) that will not let any Light of Wisdom into the vessels of reception.

As a result of that, the area below *Tabur de Galgalta* was divided into four parts:

1. The place of the world of *Atzilut*, where Light of Wisdom can shine.

2. The place of the world of *Beria* under the *Parsa*. No Light of Wisdom is allowed there, only Light of Mercy.

3. The place of the world of *Yetzira* below the world of *Beria*.

4. The place of the world of *Assiya* below the world of *Yetzira*.

Holiness ends at the end of the world of *Assiya*. Below it there are:

1. The barrier—the border between spirituality and corporeality, which separates the world of *Assiya* from the point of "This World."

2. The place of "This World."

3. Our world.

CHAPTER 3.13
THE WORLD OF NEKUDIM

The entire process of the descent of *Nekudot de SAG* below *Tabur de Galgalta*, their mixture with *Sof de Galgalta* and the Second Restriction, occurred while the screen of *SAG* was rising from the *Tabur* to the *Peh*. Thus, when the screen arrived at the *Peh*, the *Reshimot* of everything that happened in *Nekudot de SAG*, and in *Tabur de Galgalta*, where already there.

Once *Partzuf Galgalta* was refined, there were *Reshimot* of *Dalet de Hitlabshut* that remained in the screen from the Light that was in *Galgalta*, and *Reshimot* of *Gimel de Aviut* in the screen that remained. After the refining of *Partzuf AB*, the same process occurs, but now the *Reshimot* drop one level; i.e., *Gimel de Hitlabshut* and *Bet de Aviut*. So we see that after the refining of the *Partzuf* there are pairs of *Reshimot* left in the screen: one *Reshimo de Hitlabshut* and one of *Aviut*.

But after the refining of *Partzuf SAG* there are three pairs of *Reshimot* that remain in the screen that come from the *Tabur* to the *Peh*. The screen then performs three *Zivugim* (plural for *Zivug*) on them, in descending order of importance:

1. A *Zivug* on *Reshimot Bet de Hitlabshut* and *Aleph de Aviut* from *Taamim de SAG*. That produces a *Partzuf* in the degree of *Zeir Anpin* above the *Tabur* called Upper MA.

2. A *Zivug* on *Reshimot Bet de Hitlabshut* and *Aleph de Aviut* from *Nekudot de SAG* that went below *Tabur de Galgalta*. These *Reshimot* come after the Second Restriction that was done on *Nekudot de SAG* below *Tabur*. Everything that existed in the *Partzuf* becomes *Reshimot*. Hence there is a "memory" of the prohibition of the Second Restriction never to use the vessels of reception that is imprinted in the *Reshimot* from *Nekudot de SAG*.

3. In order to adhere to that condition, as the *Reshimot* dictate, the screen of *Rosh de SAG* rises from the *Peh* to *Nikvey Eynaim* and performs a *Zivug de Hakaa* with the Upper Light, on *Reshimot Bet de Hitlabshut* and *Aleph de Aviut*. The place in the *Rosh* where the screen performs the *Zivug de Hakaa* with the Upper Light determines the unique way that the Lights extend to the *Guf* of the *Partzuf*.

The screen had to rise to *Nikvey Eynaim* (NE) because of the prohibition on receiving Light in the vessels of reception. The Light can only reach as far as the *Chazeh* in each *Partzuf* because the vessels of bestowal only reach as low as the *Chazeh*. From the *Chazeh* and below begin the vessels of reception of the *Partzuf*.

The screen that performs the *Zivug* on the restricted *Reshimot* produces a *Partzuf*. The Light expands in the *Partzuf*, but fills only the vessels of bestowal. It doesn't fill the vessels for the reception of Light and they remain empty. The *Partzuf* can use only a part of its vessels, hence the name *Katan* (Small).

Question: Why does the screen rise, as the *Reshimot* dictate, from the *Peh* to *Nikvey Eynaim* and performs the *Zivug* there?

Answer: Because the *Reshimot* dictate that a *Zivug* be done only on the vessels of bestowal. That is why the screen must rise to the middle of *Bina* of *Rosh de SAG*, where the vessels of bestowal end in the *Rosh*, and make a *Zivug* on *Reshimot* of *Bet de Hitlabshut* and *Aleph de Aviut*.

The *Reshimot* below *Tabur* want to draw Light only in vessels of bestowal. But how can a *Partzuf* be produced with only the vessels of bestowal? Any *Partzuf* must have its ten *Sefirot*. However, there can be a *Partzuf* that uses only a part of its *Sefirot*. For that purpose, *Rosh de SAG* must produce a *Partzuf* whose vessels of reception are inactive. Those vessels are the lower half of *Bina*, *Zeir Anpin* and *Malchut*.

The screen of SAG must produce the *Partzuf* in this manner so as to prevent it from using its vessels of reception in the *Toch* to begin with, so that these vessels will not be filled. For that, the screen must perform a *Zivug* for the production of a *Partzuf* with only the vessels of bestowal in the *Rosh*.

The vessels of the *Rosh* are called:

Keter – Galgalta
Hochma – Eynaim
Bina – Awzen
Zeir Anpin – Hotem
Malchut – Peh

CHAPTER 3.14
THE DIVISION OF ROSH DE SAG TO FIVE PHASES

The vessels *Keter*, *Hochma*, and the upper half of *Bina* are referred to as *Galgalta ve Eynaim* (GE), or vessels of bestowal. The upper half of *Bina* belongs to the vessels of bestowal because it is filled with Light of Wisdom, and hence wants to receive nothing for itself, wishing only to have the Light of Mercy. But the lower half of *Bina* wants to receive Light for *Zeir Anpin*. *Partzuf Nekudot de SAG* is *Partzuf Bina*. From the lower half of *Partzuf Bina*, meaning from *Tifferet de Nekudot de SAG* and below, there are vessels of reception:

- The lower half of *Bina* wants to receive Light for *Zeir Anpin*.

- *Zeir Anpin* wants to receive the Light of Mercy with illumination of wisdom.

- *Malchut* wants to receive the entire Light of Wisdom.

That is why that part of *Partzuf Nekudot de SAG* consists of a will to receive in order to receive.

THE DIVISION OF PARTZUF NEKUDOT DE SAG
TO GALGALTA EYNAIM AND AHP

The place where the screen of the *Rosh* stands determines the form of the new *Partzuf*:

- If the screen wants to produce a *Partzuf* that will receive Light in all its ten *Sefirot*, it must perform a *Zivug* in the *Peh*. When the screen is situated in the *Peh*, the *Kashtut* (Hardness) of the screen determines its degree, meaning to what extent the screen will be using its vessels.

- If the screen wants to produce a *Partzuf* that will receive only in its vessels of bestowal, meaning using only half the *Partzuf*, it should stand at the *Nikvey Eynaim* and not in the *Peh de Rosh*, because that is the upper half of the *Rosh*. Then the vessels of bestowal will be above the screen, meaning they will be taken into account by the screen.

Once the screen stands at the *Nikvey Eynaim*, the *Kashiut* of the screen determines what percentage of its vessels of bestowal the screen will use. When a *Partzuf* is produced under these restrictions, it is called *Partzuf Katnut* (smallness) of *Olam HaNekudim* (the world of *Nekudim*).

Once a *Zivug* has been made on the restricted *Reshimot* of *Bet de Hitlabshut* and *Aleph de Aviut* in *Rosh de SAG*, the *Partzuf* descends to the place where the *Reshimot* came from. It goes under *Tabur de Galgalta* and expands there complete with *Rosh* and *Guf*. *Rosh de Hitlabshut* is called *Keter*; *Rosh de Aviut* is called *Abba ve Ima* (AVI, lit. Father and Mother) and the *Guf* is called ZON (*Zeir Anpin* and *Nukva*).

Its overall structure, *Rosh* and *Guf*, as well as any other part of it, is divided into two parts, GE and AHP.

- GE are vessels of bestowal. They are always active because only the Light of Wisdom was restricted, not the Light of Mercy.

- AHP are vessels of reception. After the Second Restriction in *Partzuf Nekudot de SAG*, no *Partzuf* has the sufficient strength to receive Light of Wisdom in its AHP in order to bestow.

A third pair of *Reshimot* that rose to *Rosh de SAG* along with the screen are *Reshimot* that moved to *Nekudot de SAG* from *Sof* of *Galgalta—Dalet de Hitlabshut* and *Gimel de Aviut*. *Partzuf Nekudot de SAG* received those *Reshimot* when it filled the end of *Galgalta*. Those *Reshimot* are the ones that need the Light of Wisdom.

Once the *Partzuf* of *Katnut* of the world of *Nekudim* descended to its place from *Tabur de Galgalta* through the *Parsa*, *Rosh de SAG* gave it the remaining *Reshimo* of *Dalet de Hitlabshut* and *Gimel de Aviut*. In response to the demand of these *Reshimot*, the screen that stood at *Nikvey Eynaim* of AVI drops and performs a *Zivug* on *Reshimot* 4/3 (*Dalet de Hitlabshut* and *Gimel de Aviut*). Because of that *Zivug*, the Light of Wisdom drops to the *Guf*, reaches the *Parsa* and crosses it on its way down.

The *Rosh* of AVI assumes, judging by the demand of *Reshimot* 4/3, that the vessels of reception below *Parsa* can receive in order to bestow. Because of that, *Partzuf* AVI makes a *Zivug* on *Gadlut*, meaning on *Reshimot* 4/3. For that purpose, it joins the vessels of GE with the AHP in its *Rosh* and the *Guf*, which is ZON, and the Light of Wisdom expands from it down to ZON.

CHAPTER 3.15
THE BIRTH OF A PARTZUF—KATNUT AND GADLUT OF NEKUDIM

*K*eter and AVI don't know that the Light of *AB SAG* that comes from Above and gives the vessel the power to go from *Katnut* to *Gadlut*, cannot go under the *Parsa*. That is why, until now, the *Parsa* was not canceled. But now, when Light of Wisdom begins to fill the vessels below the *Parsa*, the vessels begin to break, as they are still working in order to receive.

When *Rosh de AVI* makes a *Zivug* on *Reshimot* 4/3 there is Light of Wisdom that stems from them and enters the *Guf* of *Nekudim*. The Light that extends through GE wants to go through the *Parsa* and enter the AHP of the *Guf*. At that point, the vessels of AHP begin to receive the

Light of Wisdom in order to receive. The vessels of GE that stand above the *Parsa* join with the vessels of the *AHP* below the *Parsa* to form one *Guf*. Hence, the GE break as well, the vessels of bestowal, along with the *AHP*, the vessels of reception.

When Light of Wisdom comes from the *Peh* of *AVI* and expands to the *Guf* of *Nekudim*, comprised of both GE and *AHP*, this creates the first *Partzuf* of *Gadlut* of *Nekudim* and it breaks into two phases:

A. The *Guf* vessels lose their screen.

B. They fall from their previous degrees because they want to receive in order to receive.

The breaking makes the screen of the *Partzuf* in *Gadlut* (*AVI*) refine and rise along with *Reshimot* 3/2 that remain in it to the *Rosh de AVI*, perform a *Zivug de Hakaa* on these *Reshimot*, and produce the next *Partzuf*, whose *Rosh* is called YESHSUT (*Israel Saba ve Tvuna*). Once the *Rosh* comes out, it calculates and produces a *Guf*. *Partzuf* YESHSUT breaks and dies as well. Because of that, the screen once more refines and rises to the *Peh* of YESHSUT with *Reshimot* 2/1. These *Reshimot* can no longer produce a *Guf* because there isn't sufficient *Aviut* to receive Light.

Thus we see that the two *Partzufim* that came out, AVI and ZON, were broken. Four *Partzufim* of *Nekudot* were produced in the process of the refining of each *Partzuf*. These went on to produce a total of eight *Partzufim*, named "the Eight Kings," because they are controlled by *Malchut* (kingship); i.e., the will to receive in order to receive.

Each *Partzuf* consists of *HaVaYaH*, or four parts, which is the structure of every creature. Each part consists of its own ten *Sefirot* hence the total number of parts adds up to 8x4x10=320 (8 kings, 4 *HaVaYaH*, 10 *Sefirot*, and 320 parts). In *Gimatria* (numerical value of the letters) this number is called *Shach*, comprised of two Hebrew letters: *Shin* (**ש**) = 300 and *Chaf* (**כ**) = 20.

The breaking occurred in all the *Sefirot*. They were all mixed with one another so that in each broken piece were 320 parts. Therefore, the entire work of the correction is in sorting out each of the broken pieces.

The sorting happens by taking the least broken of the 320 broken pieces and sorting out its inner parts of *Malchut*, which caused the breaking. The 320 parts consist of nine *Sefirot* of ZON *de Nekudim*, and *Malchut* as the tenth part in those ten *Sefirot*. Thus, in the 320 parts there are 32 parts of *Malchut*.

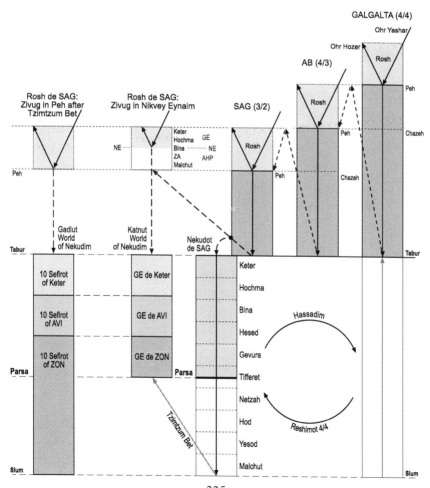

The Light of Wisdom performs the sorting of the parts of *Malchut*. When it shines on each of the broken parts, it can only shine to nine of the *Sefirot*, meaning to 320 − 32 = 288 parts, excluding the tenth *Sefira*, meaning the 32 parts of *Malchut*.

Malchut is the only bad part, denying man the entrance to spirituality. We naturally stay away from evil and learn to hate it, because in spirituality, hate separates, and therefore we separate ourselves from this evil (the will to receive for self).

Man is then left with 288 parts worthy of correction, called *Rapach*, comprised of *Resh* (ר) = 200, *Peh* (פ) = 80, and *Het* (ח) = 8, which together make up 288, and 32 parts that are unworthy of correction (i.e. parts that the creature cannot correct) made of the Hebrew letters *Lamed* (ל) = 30 and *Bet* (ב) = 2, which together make up 32 parts, also known as the Stony Heart.

After the sorting of the above 32 parts of *Malchut* that cannot be used, 288 parts of the broken pieces of the upper nine *Sefirot* remain. The first to be sorted of those vessels are the vessels of bestowal, the GE (*Galgalta* and *Eynaim*). They comprise the ZON of the world of *Atzilut*.

Just as there are ten *Sefirot* in the expansion of the Light in the vessel from Above downward, so there are ten *Sefirot* inside the vessel. These were created as a consequence of the mixture of the *Sefirot* with the Returning Light. The ten inner *Sefirot* are called:

Keter — *Mocha* (Marrow)
Hochma — *Atzamot* (Bones)
Bina — *Gidin* (Tendons)
Zeir Anpin — *Bassar* (Flesh)
Malchut — *Or* (Skin)

The rule of the Second Restriction acts in them just as it does in the longitudinal *Sefirot*.

CHAPTER 3.16
THE WORLD OF CORRECTION

Several thing unfold after the breaking in the world of *Nekudim*:

- The Lights that filled *Partzuf Gadlut* of the world of *Nekudim* rise to the *Rosh* of *Partzuf Nekudim*.

- The *Reshimot* that remained in the screen rose to the *Rosh* of *Partzuf Nekudim* and to *Rosh de SAG*.

- The *Nitzotzin* (Sparks, parts of Returning Light, the broken screen) fell into the broken vessels that lost their screens and returned to the will to receive in order to receive. It is considered that they fell to the place of BYA, below *Parsa*.

The difference between the refining of the *Partzuf* by the beating (*Bitush*) of the Inner and Surrounding Lights and the refining of the Lights invoked by the breaking of the vessels, is that after the breaking, the vessels must be corrected. Only then can new *Zivugim* (couplings for production of new *Partzufim* or reception of Light) be carried out for the purpose of producing new *Partzufim* and filling them with Light.

The *Rosh* of the world of *Nekudim* intended to receive the entire Light of the purpose of Creation in order to bestow. By filling the *Sof* of *Galgalta*, it would attain the complete filling of *Malchut de Ein Sof*. Therefore, when the broken vessels are corrected, all the vessels of reception will be corrected for bestowal, and the end of correction will be accomplished.

But that would still not correct the entire *Malchut de Ein Sof*, but only a part of it—*Behinot Shoresh, Aleph, Bet* and *Gimel*. *Behina Dalet*, which is in fact, the only creature, would not be affected. *Behinot Shoresh, Aleph, Bet* and *Gimel*, come from its mixture with the Upper Nine, or the Creator's influence on *Malchut*, whereas a "creature" is a will to receive that is entirely separated from the Creator and stands on its own.

Only *Behina Dalet* in *Behina Dalet* is a will to receive in order to receive that feels independent. Hence, she is the only one who needs to restrict her will to receive. After the restriction, the *Partzufim* and the worlds intend to fill the desires of the root, 1st, 2nd, and 3rd degree desires in *Behina Dalet*, but not *Behina Dalet* of *Dalet*.

But if what needs to be corrected is *Behina Dalet* in *Dalet* and not *Behinot Shoresh*, *Aleph*, *Bet* and *Gimel*, then why do these desires take Lights? These desires are not the creature's, but are properties and forces of the Creator.

The Creator uses those Lights to guide and lead the creature, the *Behina Dalet* of *Dalet*. These forces fill all the spiritual worlds, except for man's soul.

Behina Dalet itself, which is man's soul, can't actually correct itself to receive in order to bestow. The entire correction of the creature occurs by examining one's own attributes vs. those of the Creator, and preferring those of the Creator. One doesn't use one's own attribute, such as the stony heart, but only the Upper Nine, the *Rapach Behinot*. One sorts and raises them after the breaking for the purpose of unification with the Creator.

All the *Zivugim* performed after the First Restrictions are performed on those desires. These *Zivugim* produce the *Partzufim*, the worlds and everything in them, and expand downward. The five worlds with the five *Partzufim* in each world become the ladder from the Creator (the Giver) to the creature (the receiver). The degrees are measurements of equivalence of desires between the creature and the Creator.

The emanation of the *Partzufim* and the worlds from Above downward builds the degrees, which are like covers over the Light of *Ein Sof*. Each *Partzuf* covers the Light and hides it from its lower *Partzufim* to the extent that it receives in order to bestow.

We can compare the *Partzufim* and the worlds to the layers of an onion: round, contained in one another, and the deeper the layer, the more the Light is covered. Thus, at the bottom of the ladder, in the middle point in the onion, there is the point of darkness.

For the creature to have free will and want to equalize with the Creator, clinging to Him of free choice, and to rise from its original state to that of the Creator, the creature must be born in the point of darkness.

The possibility of correcting one's desire must also be created, but because of the creature's weakness, the correction is a gradual process. That is what the ladder was prepared for—the five worlds with five *Partzufim* in each world and five *Sefirot* in each *Partzuf* make up a ladder of 125 degrees from the preliminary state of the creature, to its final completion. Thus the worlds have two functions:

A. To gradually hide the Light of *Ein Sof*. This is done by the descent of the worlds from Above downward. That is why the degrees of concealment are called "worlds" (Heb: *Olamot*, from the word, *Ha'alama*—concealment).

B. To provide the souls (creatures) with corrections with which they can climb the degrees of the worlds from below upward. Each degree they acquire is a *Partzuf* that was created during the descent from Above downward. In order to rise in the spiritual degrees, the creature must be helped by the degree it wants to attain. When the creature receives that help, it uses that force to attain a screen and rise to that degree. When the creature rises to that degree it is given the name of that degree.

This teaches us that all the worlds, with everything in them, are but a ladder that the Creator had prepared for man's ascent. When man climbs these degrees the worlds rise with him, because all the worlds and everything in them are inside man. Thus, aside from the attaining creature, the only thing that exists is the Creator.

Around us, there is only the simple Light in a state of complete rest. That means that the intent of the Creator is unchanging, but that in all His Acts, He intends just one thing—to benefit man. But man can feel the Creator only to the extent that he equalizes his attributes with the Creator's attribute of bestowal.

If man's attributes (desires, intentions) are completely opposite to those of the Creator, then he has no sensation of the Creator whatsoever. This state is called "This World." If one can change even one attribute to having some measure of equivalence with the Creator's attribute of bestowal, it will be considered that one has risen from "This World" to the "Spiritual World." This is considered stepping on the first rung in the ladder that leads to closeness with the Creator.

All changes occur inside us, in our vessels of reception, and depend on the measure of the correction of the screen. Besides us, there is only the unchanging Upper Light. By obtaining some of the Upper Light, one attains and feels a part of the Creator, naming the Creator according to that feeling—Merciful, Gracious, Glorious, etc.

The Torah is a documentation of what one who attains spirituality feels, meaning what a person who comes nearer the Creator feels. The entire Torah is comprised of appellations of the Creator. One who attains the Torah attains a portion of the collective Light.

The degrees of the attainment are called by the names of the *Sefirot* (the *Partzufim* or the worlds) or by the names of the Lights that one receives (*NRNHY*).

Besides man, there is only the Creator. Hence, what we all feel, want, and think, comes from the Creator. Everything we always feel is only the Creator.

When the creature climbs from the lowest point (this world) toward the Creator, until it attains complete equivalence of form with Him (the end of correction), it will go through 620 degrees, also called the 613 *Mitzvot* of the Torah, and the seven *Mitzvot* of our sages. A *Zivug* (mating) with the Upper Light in the screen is called a *Mitzva*.

The Light that the creature obtains inside his vessel is called "Inner Light," or the Light of *Taamim*, or Torah. That is why Kabbalists always say, "Taste and see that the Lord is good."

The creature, *Behina Dalet* of *Dalet*, corrects its will to receive in order to be able to bestow. The correction is not of the desire itself, but in the way it is used—it must be done with the intention to give. That correction, the setting up of the intention to bestow, is done with small bits of the desire of the creature, from the smallest to the greatest, but not on all of the desires at once.

Thus, the creature rises from one degree to the next in the ladder of degrees. The worlds are in fact the degrees by which man climbs from below upward.

The correction of the will to receive in order to bestow is a very hard one to make because it goes against the very nature of the creature. Hence, the Creator has divided the way into 613 smaller degrees. He also split the creature into 600,000 small parts called "souls." When the souls come together they are referred to as "The Collective Soul" or the "First Man."

However, the correction of the desire begins even before that, in an even lower state called "Our World." In this state, there is no sensation of a Creator whatsoever, or of spirituality. In this state, there is not even the sensation of a need to recognize the Creator. We are all born in that degree. It is comprised solely of desires for pleasures that we can feel in our five physical senses.

The world is led by the orders of the Creator. We call this leadership, "Nature." In it, the will to receive pleasure in every degree (still, vegetative, animate, and speaking), necessarily determines our every reaction. The law is that every creature always chooses the greater pleasure and escapes pain.

In every generation there are people in whom the Creator plants a "Point in the Heart," a desire to feel the Creator. Such a person begins to seek satisfaction for this new need, not knowing that it is a need for the Creator, which can only be satisfied by the Upper Light.

The *Partzufim* that emerge after the breaking are called the "World of Correction." Everything that happens must be and is necessary for the evolution of the creature, so that he will be able to attain the perfection of the acts of the Creator, and delight in what the Creator had prepared for him.

Hence, the breaking of the World of *Nekudim*, also called the "breaking of the Worlds," and the breaking of the First Man, also called "the breaking of the Souls" were both premeditated. In the breaking of the World of *Nekudim*, the vessels of reception were mixed with the vessels of bestowal in such a way that each of them contained all 320 parts of the desire inside it. In consequence, the vessels of reception will be corrected by being contained in vessels of bestowal, and each desire will now consist of NRNHY of Lights instead of just the Light of *Nefesh* that was there previously.

Without the mixture caused by the breaking, the vessels of reception would have no way of receiving Light, but would always be separated from the Light by the *Parsa*. Now, however, after the breaking, they can be brought up to *Atzilut* (by a process called *AHP de Aliah*, raising the *AHP*) and filled there.

The breaking of the world of *Nekudim* is also called "the breaking of the worlds," because *Malchut de Ein Sof* consists of five parts, four of which produce the worlds and everything in them as they evolve from above downward. They comprise the entire Creation, except for man, who was born from *Behina Dalet* of *Dalet*, from the last part of *Malchut*, the actual will to receive. This independent part was completely detached from the Creator's desire to bestow.

Hence, it is only man that is the goal and the purpose of Creation. Besides man, the rest of Creation is not independent. It belongs to the Creator because it is He Who determines its behavior and actions, just as the inanimate, vegetative, animate, and speaking behave in our world.

Man's desire isn't fundamentally different from that of animals. Only a person who shows a desire for the Creator, a part of the desire of the first man, is called "man." A person who does not show that desire has nothing to correct, and doesn't feel the need to come closer to the Creator.

The entire reality is divided in this world into the four parts of Creation, which are still, vegetative, animate, and speaking, ranked by the intensity of the will to receive, and hence by the ability to harm or benefit.

A person in this world must go through four phases of development: still, vegetative, animate, and speaking. Each phase increases and develops man's will to receive, until the Creator finally creates a "Point in the Heart," a desire to attain the goal.

Therefore, humanity has been under Nature's press for thousands of years, developing the will to receive from the still degree to that of speaking, in the evolution of the generations as we know it.

From generation to generation, each and every soul in humanity goes through four phases of development of the will to receive:

1. Populace–the "still" in the human species. Through desire they develop the degree of "Rich."

2. The Rich–the "vegetative" in the human species. Through the inclination for honors (government) they develop to the degree of "heroes."

3. Heroes–the "animate" in the human species. Through the inclination for knowledge they develop to the degree of "educated."

4. The Educated–the "speaking" degree in man. In the "speaking" degree in man, the desire is unlimited by space and time. One becomes jealous of past events, of previous generations, of things one does not need simply because others have them. Because these people want what they see in others, they can increase their will to receive indefinitely, and thus become worthy of attaining the purpose of Creation.

If the Creator "plants" the "Point in the Heart," man begins the search for the Creator and the root of his soul. The order of correction from below upward is as follows: To receive in order to receive in our world, to bestow in order to receive in our world, to bestow in order to bestow in the worlds of BYA, and to receive in order to bestow in the world of Atzilut. The entire system of Creation is corrected by the world of Atzilut. Hence, the world of Atzilut is also called the World of Correction.

CHAPTER 3.17
THE WORLD OF ATZILUT

Once broken, the screen refined and rose to AVI together with the Reshimot. The Reshimot in the screen demanded to be corrected and to have a Zivug over them for the reception of the Light. But the Rosh of AVI de Nekudim returned to a state of Katnut and could not do it; hence, the screen rose to the Partzuf of the adjacent Partzuf, that of Rosh de SAG.

There is no difference between the refining screen from the Bitush (beating) of the Inner Light and the Surrounding Light, and the screen that refined after the breaking. After the breaking there were also Reshimot left in the screen that demanded to be realized:

- Restricted Reshimot Aleph de Hitlabshut and Shoresh de Aviut that remained from Partzuf Nekudim.
- Reshimot Dalet de Hitlabshut and Gimel de Aviut from the end of Partzuf Galgalta.

The restricted Reshimot Aleph de Hitlabshut and Shoresh de Aviut came from Partzuf Nekudim itself; hence, the screen performs its first Zivug on them. Once a Partzuf is realized from them, the screen would satisfy the 4/3 Reshimot that produced the exit of the Gadlut of the Partzuf.

Therefore, once the screen rose to Rosh de SAG, it continues to rise by the Reshimo de Aviut Shoresh that was restricted to Bina of Keter de SAG. The five Behinot of the Rosh are called:

Keter – Galgalta – Aviut Shoresh
Hochma – Eynaim – Aviut Aleph
Bina – Awzen – Aviut Bet
Zeir Anpin – Hotem – Aviut Gimel
Malchut – Peh – Aviut Dalet

In each of the Sefirot of the Rosh are five inner Sefirot: Keter, Hoch-ma, Bina, Zeir Anpin, and Malchut. The restricted Reshimo of Aviut Shoresh demands a Zivug only on the vessels of bestowal. The Reshimo wants to create a Partzuf that would work only with vessels of bestowal, GE of Aviut Shoresh. Hence the screen that creates that Partzuf must perform a Zivug only on the vessels of bestowal of Aviut Shoresh in the Rosh.

Because of that, the screen rises from the Peh to Keter of Rosh de SAG and farther up from there to Bina de Keter and stands above the Sefirot KHB de Keter. It turns out that above the screen are only the vessels of bestowal of Keter, meaning those of Aviut Shoresh. The place where the screen now stands is called Metzach (forehead).

The Partzuf that was created, as a result of the Zivug on the restricted Reshimo de Aviut Shoresh, is called a "fetus." There cannot be any lesser degree than that in spirituality; this is the minimal degree. Once born, the Partzuf descends to the place where the Reshimot come from, meaning below Tabur de Galgalta, and expands there from Tabur and below.

Once the Partzuf of the fetus has taken its place, Reshimot Dalet de Hitlabshut and Gimel de Aviut (from the Sof of Galgalta) awaken in it. It is over these Reshimot that the Gadlut of the Partzuf comes out: the screen performs a Zivug on Reshimot 4/3 and the degree of Gadlut expands from Tabur de Galgalta to the Parsa. That Partzuf is called Atik (meaning Detached, but also Ancient), because it is detached from the attainment of the lower ones, or the souls.

Atik is the first of a series of new Partzufim called the "world of Atzilut." Partzuf Atik serves as the Keter of the new world.

Once Partzuf Atik comes out in Gadlut, Rosh de SAG passes it all the Reshimot that rose to it after the breaking. Of all these Reshimot, Atik chooses the finest *Reshimo*, makes a *Zivug* on it, and creates the next *Partzuf*. It first creates it in the fetus degree, and then performs a *Zivug* on *Gadlut* for it (4/3). The new *Partzuf* expands from the *Peh* of *Atik* to the *Parsa*. It is called *Partzuf Hochma*, or *Arich Anpin* (AA).

Once the *Gadlut* of *Arich Anpin* expands, *Partzuf Atik* gives all the remaining *Reshimot* from among those that rose to *Rosh de SAG*. *Arich Anpin* chooses the finest of the *Reshimot* among them, performs a *Zivug*, which creates *Partzuf Bina* in the world of *Atzilut*, first in *Katnut* and then in *Gadlut*. That *Partzuf* expands from the *Peh* of *Arich Anpin* to *Tabur* of *Arich Anpin*. It is named *Abba ve Ima* (AVI), literally meaning, "Father" and "Mother."

After *Partzuf AVI* is created in *Gadlut*, *Arich Anpin* gives it the remaining *Reshimot*. Of all the *Reshimot* that *Arich Anpin* gives it, AVI chooses the finest and performs a *Zivug*, which creates *Partzuf Zeir Anpin* of the world of *Atzilut*. Here, for the first time, there are three situations: Fetus, *Katnut*, and *Gadlut*. *Partzuf Zeir Anpin* takes its place from *Tabur* of *Arich Anpin* to the *Parsa*.

Once *Partzuf Zeir Anpin* is out, it is given all the remaining *Reshimot*. *Zeir Anpin* performs a *Zivug* on them and creates *Partzuf Malchut* of the world of *Atzilut*. That concludes all the *Zivugim* (couplings) that can be performed on the *Reshimot* that rose to *Rosh de SAG* after the breaking of the vessels.

The permanent state of the world of *Atzilut* is *Katnut*, or GE, vessels of bestowal. There cannot be any less than that in *Atzilut*. In that state, it is exactly the same as the world of *Nekudim* was in *Katnut* before it broke. But the world of *Atzilut* came about in order to bring Creation to the end of correction, so that *Malchut de Ein Sof* would be filled with the Light of *Ein Sof* with the intent to bestow, and that hasn't been accomplished yet.

The breaking of the vessels caused the vessels of reception to mix with the vessels of bestowal and create four distinctions in each vessel:

A. Vessels of bestowal.

B. Vessels of bestowal inside vessels of reception.

C. Vessels of reception inside vessels of bestowal.

D. Vessels of reception.

The **first sorting** is done by selecting the vessels of bestowal from the mixture. They are used to construct the *Katnut* of the world of *Atzilut*.

The **second sorting** sorts the vessels of bestowal inside the vessels of reception. They construct the world of *BYA*. These worlds are vessels of bestowal, *GE* just like the world of *Atzilut*, but they remained contained in the *AHP*, the vessels of reception. But in and of themselves, these vessels are vessels of bestowal, hence the Light can expand in them.

Therefore, once the world of *Atzilut* comes out, *Malchut* of *Atzilut* rises to *AVI* and performs a *Zivug* on the vessels of bestowal inside the vessels of reception. She creates the world of *Beria*, then the world of *Yetzira*, and then the world of *Assiya*. The *Zivug* on *GE* in the vessels of reception of *Bet de Aviut* creates the world, *Beria*; the *Zivug* on *GE* in the vessels of reception of *Gimel de Aviut* creates the world, *Yetzira*; and the *Zivug* on *GE* in the vessels of receptions of *Dalet de Aviut* creates the world, *Assiya*.

The **third sorting** takes out the vessels of reception that were mixed with the vessels of bestowal. That sorting and correction is done by souls of people. They sort these vessels and raise them above the *Parsa* to the world of *Atzilut*. This work is called an "awakening from below," because it is done by the souls. The broken vessels that rise to *Atzilut* are called "*AHP de Aliah*" (The Raised *AHP*).

The **fourth sorting** is the sorting of the vessels of reception that were not mixed with the vessels of bestowal. Those are sorted out as ones that remain in their attribute of reception and hence are disqualified for use. Those vessels are called *Klipot* (shells), or *Lev HaEven* (the stony heart) because they cannot be corrected before the end of correction.

CHAPTER 3.18
THE WORLDS OF BYA

The *Zivug* for the creation of the world of *Beria* was performed in *Bina* of *Atzilut*, and hence took the place of *Zeir Anpin* of *Atzilut*.

The world of *Yetzira*, which was created after the world *Beria*, expands below it in the place of *Malchut* of *Atzilut*. *Partzuf Malchut of Atzilut* clothes only the four lowest *Sefirot* of *Partzuf Zeir Anpin* (NHYM) so that only the first four *Sefirot* of *Malchut*, KHB and *Tifferet* are in *Atzilut* facing the four *Sefirot* NHYM of *Zeir Anpin*. The *Sefirot Gevura*, *Tifferet*, and NHYM of *Partzuf Malchut* are below *Parsa*.

Hence, when the world of *Yetzira* was created, its first four *Sefirot* dressed the four first *Sefirot* of *Malchut*, while its six lower *Sefirot* came in the place of the bottom six *Sefirot* of *Beria*. The place of BYA consists of 30 *Sefirot*.

In the future, after the sin of the First Man, the worlds of BYA descend to this place. The place where the lower six *Sefirot* of *Yetzira* end is called the *Chazeh* of the place of the world of *Beria*. After the breaking of the soul of the First Man, that would become the *Chazeh of Beria*.

After the world of *Yetzira* was created and took its place, *Malchut* of *Atzilut* created the world of *Assiya*. It expanded below the world of *Yetzira*, meaning from the *Chazeh* of the place of the world of *Beria* to the *Chazeh* of the world of *Yetzira*.

The *Chazeh* of the place of the world of *Yetzira* is called "the *Chazeh* of the place of the worlds of BYA." In that place the expansion of the worlds of BYA stops. Below that place there is no Light. In that place, from the *Chazeh* of the place of the world of *Yetzira* and under, it is called *Mador HaKlipot* (the "shell section"). Under it there is the point of "This World."

A place (in spirituality) means desire. The point of "This World" is a will to receive in order to receive for oneself, a desire to enjoy pleasures in worldly clothes, such as sex, respect, control, and envy. The shells are higher up than that, because they wish to take pleasure in the Creator.

In the wisdom of Kabbalah, the reference point is always that which is to be attained. Hence, those who learn that their desires are aimed only at reception in order to receive, and never to bestow, can be referred to as "attainees." They are in the state of "This World." But those who do not learn that all desires are directed at reception in order to receive are not in this place (desire). They are even lower down than that, i.c. even before that discovery. They exist in a place (desire) called "Our World," unconscious of their own desires, and do not feel their unconsciousness.

Humanity as a whole is in the degree of "Our World," or unconsciousness. From this degree begins the evolution of the desire to receive. The evolution is a natural process, pushing everyone through the harsh force of *Din* (judgment) toward correction.

Man's entire history is a generation-by-generation evolution of the will to receive, promoted by three factors: envy, desire, and the pursuit of glory.

The reason for all the suffering in the world is the will to receive; therefore, suffering will bring man and the whole of mankind to the decision to leave it. Those whose will to receive has evolved enough will receive a push from Above to want something beyond this world. That push makes man begin to search for the source of satisfaction for this new desire, until the right teacher is found. It often takes years, and sometimes an entire lifetime is not enough.

But if the Creator brings one to a place where Kabbalah is taught, as He did with me, it is a sign that one is given a chance fron Above to correct one's soul and attain the goal.

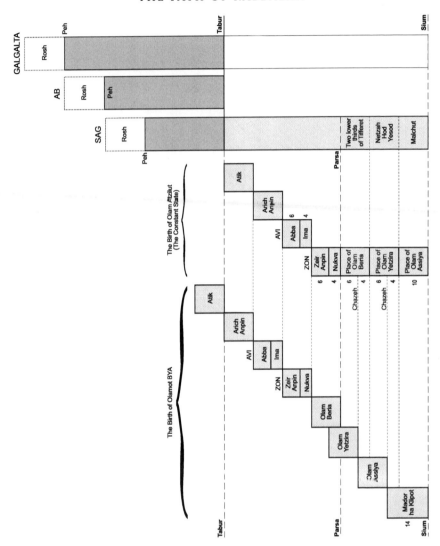

CHAPTER 3.19
THE FIRST MAN

The First Man is a different creation from anything that preceded it. He is the only one that was created from the actual *Malchut de Ein Sof*, and is therefore the only one that can be called a "real" creature. He, too, was created by *Malchut de Atzilut*, which rose to AVI. She (*Malchut*) created *Partzuf Adam ha Rishon* just as she had created the worlds of BYA. Consequently, *Adam ha Rishon* is always inside the worlds of BYA.

The worlds of *BYA* were created standing at *AVI*, and continued down to the "*Chazeh* of the place of the world of *Yetzira*," with *Adam ha Rishon* contained in them. When born, he was at the height of all three worlds of *BYA* and received from *BYA* the Lights of *Nefesh, Ruach, Neshama* (*NRN*). *Adam ha Rishon* received additional Lights—*NRN de Atzilut*, because *BYA* were in *Atzilut*.

The state of the worlds at the time of the birth of *Adam ha Rishon* is called the *Erev Shabbat* (Friday morning). Then, by an awakening from Above, the worlds rose one degree (meaning ten *Sefirot*) along with *Adam ha Rishon*, so that the end of *BYA* rose along with *Adam ha Rishon* to the "*Chazeh* of the place of the world of *Beria*."

In that situation, *Adam ha Rishon* wanted to receive all the Lights in order to bestow, as it was before the breaking of the vessels in the world of *Nekudim*. But back in *Nekudim*, *Rosh* of *AVI* didn't understand that *ZON* were not corrected, and hence gave them Lights of *Gadlut*. Consequently, *ZON* broke.

That understanding was lacking here with *Adam ha Rishon* as well, but this differed from the first breaking, as after the first reception, an innocent mistake on the part of *Adam ha Rishon*, he wanted to receive a second time. This time he was aware that it was a sin (an act of reception in order to receive), but he could no longer stop himself from receiving for self-pleasure.

Hence, this breaking produced the shells—the desires to receive in order to receive. The worlds of *BYA* fell below *Parsa* to their permanent state, from *Parsa* to the end of *Galgalta*. The "permanent state" is called by that name because there cannot be any lower state than that for the worlds of *BYA*. But they are not fixed in this place; they do have a possibility to go up and back down.

Besides the descent of *BYA* to their permanent place, as a result of the breaking of *Adam ha Rishon*, the impure worlds of *BYA* were created as well. They consist of weaknesses and stand opposite *BYA*. Because of that, *BYA* are clear of any will to receive and are therefore named the "Holy *BYA*." Their opposite worlds are therefore named the "impure *BYA*."

The impure worlds (shells) are called:

- *Esh Mitlakachat* (Erupting Fire)—opposite the world of *Beria*.
- *Anan Gadol* (Great Cloud)—opposite the world of *Yetzira*.
- *Ruach Se'ara* (Stormy Wind)—opposite the world of *Assiya*.

After the sin, *Partzuf Adam ha Rishon* broke into 600,000 pieces. The pieces continued to break (the Torah describes them as the killing of Abel, the flood, Babylon, and more). Consequently, all that was left of *Partzuf Adam ha Rishon* were fragments with a will to receive in order to receive, with just a spark of Light. These parts with sparks in them clothe people in this world and awaken them to spirituality, to the Light, to the Creator. This is how people are pushed to join groups of Kabbalah students.

There is yet another shell, called *Klipat Noga* (the Noga Shell). It consists of a mixture of good and evil. The term, "mixed," indicates that when this shell receives Light, it receives it in the good part, but immediately passes it to the evil part. The correction of the entire reality concentrates solely on the correction of the Noga Shell: to detach it from the three impure *Klipot—Ruach Se'ara, Anan Gadol,* and *Esh Mitlakachat*—that it is connected with in the evil part, and join it with the good part to holiness, to *Atzilut*.

CHAPTER 3.20
THE RISING OF THE WORLDS

The real place of all the worlds is the phases before the sin: *Zeir Anpin* occupies the place of *Arich Anpin*; *Malchut*, the place of *AVI*; *Beria*, the place of *YESHSUT*; and *Yetzira* stands in the place of *Zeir Anpin*.

The first four *Sefirot* of the world of *Assiya* occupy the place of *Nukva* of *Atzilut*, dressed over *TNHYM* of the world *Yetzira*. The last six *Sefirot* of the world of *Assiya* stand in the place of the world of *Beria*,

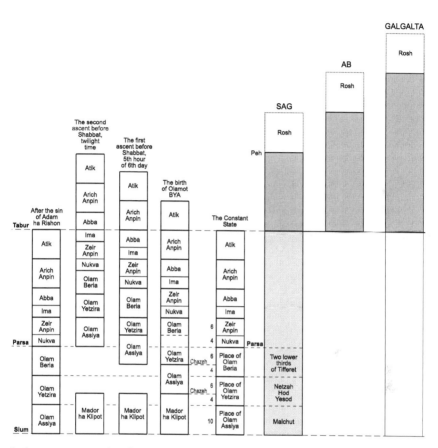

below *Parsa*. Lastly, the first six *Sefirot* of the place of the world of *Beria*, meaning the place from *Parsa* to the "*Chazeh* of the place of the world of *Beria*," is called the "outskirts of the city," because they belong to the world of *Atzilut*, called *Ir* (city).

The *Parsa* is called the "wall of the city." From the *Chazeh* of the place of the world of *Beria* to the general *Sium* (end) there are twenty-four *Sefirot*, a space vacant of Light.

The sixteen *Sefirot* from the *Parsa* to the *Chazeh* of *Yetzira* are called the "Shabbat Zone." It consists of the outskirts of the city plus ten more *Sefirot* from *Chazeh* of *Beria* to *Chazeh* of *Yetzira*.

Every ten *Sefirot* are called 2000 *Amah* (measurement unit). Hence the entire place of the worlds of *BYA* is called 6,000 *Amah*, or 6,000 years of the life of the world.

The 14 *Sefirot* from the *Chazeh* of *Yetzira* to the *Sof* of *Galgalta* are called the "shell section." That is where the shells reside prior to the sin of the First Man, but after the sin they become the four worlds of the impure *ABYA*.

CAUSE & CONSEQUENCE

The Four Phases of Direct Light:

1. *Behinat Shoresh*: Light stems from His Essence, or His desire to delight His creatures. Because He has a desire to benefit, He creates *Behina Aleph*, which is the will to receive, the desire to take pleasure in the Light.

2. *Behina Aleph*: once it feels that it is receiving, *Behina Aleph* decides to stop receiving. That new desire is called *Behina Bet*.

3. *Behina Bet*: once completely empty of the Light of Wisdom, *Behina Bet* feels the lack of it and decides to receive a little bit of Light of Wisdom clothed in the Light of Mercy, thus creating *Behina Gimel*.

4. *Behina Gimel*: upon receiving Light of Wisdom and the Light of Mercy, *Behina Gimel* decides that it wants to receive all the Light, and this is *Behina Dalet*, also called *Malchut* (Kingship) because the will to receive dominates it.

5. *Behina Dalet*: *Behina Dalet* wants to receive Light like *Behina Aleph* did, but with a supplement. The additional desire is a new vessel, called "yearning," which is the sensation of *Malchut* that its desire is an independent one, coming directly from within. Thus, *Behina Dalet* receives all the Light without limitation, and is consequently called *Olam Ein Sof* (the world of no end).

The First Restriction: *Behina Dalet* makes the First Restriction. The restricted *Behina Dalet* is called the world of *Tzimtzum* (the restricted world).

The work of the screen: *Behina Dalet, Malchut,* decides to receive Lights in her desires for bestowal, meaning in her inner *Behinot Shoresh, Aleph, Bet, Gimel,* but not in her *Behina Dalet,* which is pure will to receive.

Partzuf Galgalta: *Malchut,* using the screen with the *Reshimot* of *Dalet de Hitlabshut* and *Dalet de Aviut,* makes a *Zivug* with the Upper Light that was removed because of the restriction. Mating with the Upper Light, the screen decides how much Light it can receive inside *Malchut.*

Once the decision has been made, it descends to the *Guf* with the amount of Light it decided to receive. The Lights that enter the *Partzuf* are called *Taamim.* The place where the screen stops descending and limits the reception of the Light is called *Tabur.*

The Light that enters the *Partzuf* is called Inner Light. The part of the Light that remains outside the vessel is called Surrounding Light. The screen that stands at the *Tabur* goes under the *Bitush* (beating) of the Surrounding Light and Inner Light, as they both want to remove the limitation on the reception.

The screen decides not to use the *Reshimo* of *Aviut Dalet* and become refined. It rises from *Tabur* to *Peh* and the Inner Light leaves the *Partzuf.* The departing Lights are called *Nekudot.* The entire *Partzuf,* from the first *Zivug* in the *Rosh* to the end of its refining is called *Partzuf Galgalta.*

Partzuf AB: The screen of *Partzuf Galgalta* that rose to the *Rosh* of *Galgalta* is contained in the perpetual *Zivug* in the screen at the *Peh.* The encounter of the screen with the Upper Light in the *Rosh* makes the screen want to receive a part of the Light in the *Rosh* according to its own *Reshimot,* meaning those of *Dalet de Hitlabshut* and *Gimel de Aviut.* The last *Reshimo de Aviut* (for the reception of the Light) disappears as a consequence of the decision to stop receiving.

Following the *Reshimo* of *Gimel de Aviut*, the screen descends to *Chazeh* of *Galgalta* and makes a *Zivug* on *Reshimo Dalet de Hitlabshut* and *Gimel de Aviut*. This is the place of the *Peh* of the next *Partzuf*. After the *Zivug*, the screen descends from the *Peh* down to the *Tabur* of the new *Partzuf*, and the Lights of *Taamim* enter the *Toch* of the *Partzuf*.

The screen that stands at the *Tabur* is being "*Bitushed*" in order to cancel the limitation. The screen then decides to refine, the *Reshimo* of *Gimel de Aviut* disappears and the screen rises from *Tabur* to *Peh*. The exiting Lights are called *Nekudot* of AB.

Partzuf SAG: When the screen reached the *Peh*, it was included in the constant *Zivug* with the Upper Light that exists there, and wanted to receive a part of the Light in the *Rosh*. Hence, the screen descends to the "*Chazeh* of *Partzuf AB*" and makes a *Zivug* on the *Reshimot* of *Gimel de Hitlabshut* and *Bet de Aviut*.

It receives Light and stops in the place it had decided on in the *Rosh*–the *Tabur*. The *Bitush* of the Inner Light and Surrounding Light happens immediately because the Lights want to cancel the limitation that the screen sets in the *Toch*, the screen decides to refine.

Nekudot de SAG: The Lights created during the refining of the screen are called *Nekudot*. *Nekudot de SAG* are of *Bet de Hitlabshut* and *Bet de Aviut*. This is the nature of *Bina*. These Lights can appear anywhere (in any desire), and hence the Lights of *Nekudot* descend below *Tabur de Galgalta*, and fill the *Sof* of *Galgalta*.

The *Sof* of *Galgalta* and *Nekudot de SAG* mix. *Partzuf Nekudot de SAG*, which is *Partzuf Bina*, divides to GAR *de Bina* and ZAT *de Bina* (the upper three of *Bina* and the lower seven of *Bina*). ZAT *de Bina*, which are vessels of reception, are influenced by the *Reshimot* at the *Sof* of *Galgalta* and want to receive those Lights in order to receive. This is because the power of the screen of *Nekudot de SAG* is of *Bet de Aviut*, and the *Reshimot* at the *Sof* of *Galgalta* are 4/3, meaning stronger than the resistance power at the screen.

That situation creates a will to receive in order to receive from "Chazeh of Nekudot de SAG" and below. That necessitates Malchut, which performed the First Restriction to rise from the Sof of Galgalta to Chazeh of Nekudot de SAG, and limits the expansion of the Light below the Chazeh.

All these processes at Nekudot de SAG took place during the rising of the screen of Guf de SAG, from Tabur de SAG to its Rosh. But now the Reshimot from the First Restriction and from the Sof of Galgalta were added to it.

The Second Restriction: The rising of Malchut of the First Restriction to the Chazeh of Nekudot de SAG is called the Second Restriction.

MA and BON above Tabur de Galgalta: When the screen at the Guf de SAG reaches the Peh, it mates on Reshimot Bet de Hitlabshut and Aleph de Aviut that remain from the Lights of Taamim de SAG, above the Tabur, and creates Partzuf MA Elyon (upper MA) from Peh de SAG to Tabur de Galgalta. After the refining of Partzuf MA Elyon, Partzuf BON Elyon (upper BON) comes out from Peh of MA to Tabur de Galgalta.

The world of Nekudim (Katnut): When the screen of Guf de SAG rises in its refining to Peh de SAG, and wants to make a Zivug on its Reshimot (Bet de Hitlabshut and Aleph de Aviut), it rises from the Peh to Nikvey Eynaim of Rosh de SAG because the Reshimot 2/1 are restricted. This means that they want to receive Light only in their vessels of bestowal.

Hence, the screen stands below the vessels of bestowal at the Rosh, below Keter and Hochma at Rosh de SAG. The screen always mates on the Behinot at the Rosh, which are above it. Therefore, it stands at the Rosh, where it wants to receive the Light into the Guf.

After the Zivug, the screen passes what it received to the Guf. The Light expands to the place where the restricted Reshimot 2/1 originate, meaning below Tabur de Galgalta. That Partzuf is called Partzuf Nekudim because it is created on Reshimot from Nekudot de SAG. The Partzuf consists of Rosh de Hitlabshut called Keter, Rosh de Aviut called Abba ve Ima

227

(AVI), and *Guf*, called ZON (*Zeir Anpin* and *Nukva*). Each contains only vessels of bestowal. Their vessels of reception are concealed.

Gadlut of the world of Nekudim: When the *Katnut* of the world of *Nekudim* is complete, the screen at the *Rosh de SAG* descends (because the *Reshimot* 4/3 demand it) to *Peh de SAG* and mates. This *Zivug* brings Light of Wisdom to *Rosh* of *Keter* of *Nekudim* and to *Abba* of the *Rosh* of AVI. *Ima* is *Bina*, who doesn't want any Light of Wisdom, except if ZON asks for it. The Light of Wisdom shines from the *Rosh* of *Nekudim*, even as far as the *Sof* of *Galgalta*. This is where the request comes from, through ZON of *Nekudim*, for AVI to give them *Gadlut*, the Light of Wisdom. When ZON asks of AVI, they mate and bring Light of Wisdom to ZON.

The breaking of the vessels: Light of Wisdom expands from *Rosh* of AVI to ZON and crosses the GE down to the *Parsa*. When the Light wants to reach under the *Parsa* and fill the vessels of AHP *de* ZON, it encounters the will to receive and rises. The vessels of GE and AHP break together and 320 broken pieces fall below the *Parsa*.

The vessels of reception and the vessels of bestowal were mixed in the breaking and created four types of vessels:

1. GE created GE *de* ZON of *Atzilut*.

2. The mixture of GE with AHP created the worlds of BYA.

3. The mixture of AHP with GE created the AHP *de Aliyah* (the raised AHP).

4. AHP created the shells, desires to receive in order to receive, unworthy of receiving Light. They consist of 32 *Malchuts*, of the 320 parts, which couldn't be corrected before the end of correction (using them to receive in order to bestow). Those thirty-two *Malchuts* are called the "stony heart." Their correction is to separate them from the other 320 parts and refrain from using them.

288 (320 - 32) of the 320 parts in every broken piece can be corrected because they are not parts of *Malchut*, but of the upper nine *Sefirot*. Those that belong to the GE need only be sorted and taken out of the pile, as they are vessels of bestowal in and of themselves. They are the ones that construct *Katnut* of *ZON de Atzilut*.

CHAPTER 3.21

THE FORMATION OF THE WORLDS OF ABYA

THE FORMATION OF THE WORLD OF ATZILUT

A*tik*: The screen rose along with the *Reshimot* to *Rosh* of *Nekudim* and from there to *Rosh de SAG*. The screen sorted the finest *Reshimot—Aleph de Hitlabshut* and *Shoresh de Aviut*, and rose from *Peh* to *Keter* of *Rosh de SAG*, and from there, even higher up to *Bina de Keter*. There it stopped above the *Sefirot KHB HGT* of *Keter*, so that above the screen there are only vessels of bestowal of *Keter*, meaning those of *Aviut Shoresh*. That place is called *Metzach* (forehead). The screen mates there, creating *Partzuf Keter* of *Atzilut*, called *Partzuf Atik*.

The *Partzuf* that is created by this *Zivug* is called a "fetus" because it has only vessels of bestowal in *Aviut Shoresh*. There cannot be less than that in spirituality. Once created, the *Partzuf* descends to the place where the *Reshimot* came from, meaning below *Tabur de Galgalta*.

When *Partzuf Atik* is born and descends to its place, the *Reshimot* 4/3 awaken in it and demand *Gadlut* from the *Partzuf*. The screen mates with the Light on these *Reshimot* and builds the degree of *Atik* in *Gadlut*. That *Partzuf* expands from *Tabur de Galgalta* to the *Sium* of *Galgalta*. It reaches lower than the *Parsa*, because *Partzuf Keter* still belongs to the First Restriction. Thus the name, *Atik* (Ancient, but also Detached) means detachment from the lower ones the lower *Partzufim*.

Arich Anpin: When *Partzuf Atik* was created in *Gadlut*, *Rosh de SAG* passed it all the *Reshimot* that it took after the breaking. From among those *Reshimot*, *Atik* selected the finest ones and made a *Zivug* on them,

229

creating the next *Partzuf* in line—*Partzuf Hochma*, first in the "fetus" degree and then in *Gadlut*. That *Partzuf* expanded from *Peh* of *Atik* to the *Parsa* and was named *Arich Anpin* (AA).

Abba VeIma: When *Partzuf Arich Anpin* was created in *Gadlut*, *Atik* passed it all the remaining *Reshimot* from among those that rose after the breaking to *Rosh de SAG*. *Arich Anpin* selected the finest ones and made a *Zivug* on them, creating the next *Partzuf* in line, *Partzuf Bina* of *Atzilut*, first in the "fetus" degree and then in *Gadlut*. That *Partzuf* expanded from *Peh* of *Arich Anpin* to its *Tabur*.

Zeir Anpin: When *Partzuf Abba ve Ima* was created in *Gadlut*, *Arich Anpin* passed it all the remaining *Reshimot*. *Arich Anpin* selected the finest ones and made a *Zivug* on them, creating *Partzuf Zeir Anpin* of *Atzilut*, first in the "fetus" degree, then in *Katnut*, and then in *Gadlut*. *Partzuf Zeir Anpin* expanded from *Tabur* of *Arich Anpin* to the *Parsa*.

Malchut: When *Partzuf Zeir Anpin* was created in *Katnut*, *Abba ve Ima* passed it all the remaining *Reshimot* that had not been corrected by the previous *Partzufim*. *Zeir Anpin* selected the finest ones and made a *Zivug* on them, creating *Partzuf Malchut* of *Atzilut* as a dot, as it was in the world of *Nekudim*. That concludes the corrections of all the *Reshimot* of *Katnut* of the world *Nekudim* that rose to *Rosh de SAG*.

THE FORMATION OF THE WORLDS OF BYA

The *Partzufim* of GAR, of the world of *Atzilut*, came out on *Reshimot* of *Rosh* of *Nekudim* that refined, but did not break. From ZON of *Nekudim* and under, the birth of any *Partzuf* is done by sorting and correcting the broken pieces. This is because the breaking of the vessels in the world of *Nekudim* mixed the vessels of bestowal above the *Parsa* with the vessels of reception. Therefore, in each of the 320 broken pieces there are four types of vessels:

1. Vessels of bestowal.

2. Vessels of bestowal inside vessels of reception.

3. Vessels of reception inside vessels of bestowal.

4. Vessels of reception.

The vessels of bestowal were sorted out first off the 320 parts, by order of coarseness, from fine to coarse, and corrected, i.e. a *Zivug* was performed over them. The screen that descends from *Rosh de SAG* created all the *Partzufim* in the world of *Atzilut* in *Katnut*, and then in *Gadlut*. *Katnut* of the world of *Atzilut* is parallel to *Katnut* of the world of *Nekudim*.

ZON de Atzilut then rose to *Abba ve Ima* of *Atzilut*: *Zeir Anpin* becomes like *Abba* and *Malchut* becomes like *Ima*. A lower degree that rises to the upper degree becomes like the upper one. Consequently, *Malchut* attained the degree of *Bina* so that she could mate on the Light of Wisdom and create new *Partzufim*.

When *Malchut de Atzilut* rose to *Ima*, she took the vessels of bestowal that were inside the vessels of reception from each of the 320 parts, in order of coarseness from fine to coarse. In that order, she then created new *Partzufim*:

- From the sorting and mating on the vessels of bestowal that fell in the part of *Bina*, under the *Parsa* (GE included in *Bet de Aviut* of the AHP), emerged five *Partzufim*: *Keter–Atik, Hochma–Arich Anpin, Bina–Abba ve Ima, Zeir Anpin–Zeir Anpin, Malchut–Nukva* of the world of *Beria*.

- From the sorting and mating on the vessels of bestowal that fell in the vessels of *Zeir Anpin*, under the *Parsa* (GE included in *Gimel de Aviut* of the AHP), emerged five *Partzufim*: *Keter–Atik, Hochma–Arich Anpin, Bina–Abba ve Ima, Zeir Anpin–Zeir Anpin, Malchut–Nukva* of the world of *Yetzira*.

- From the sorting and mating on the vessels of bestowal that fell in *Malchut*, under the *Parsa* (GE included in *Dalet de Aviut* of the AHP), emerged five *Partzufim*: *Keter–Atik, Hochma–Arich Anpin, Bina–Abba ve Ima, Zeir Anpin–Zeir Anpin, Malchut–Nukva* of the world of *Assiya*.

Malchut of *Atzilut* performs those couplings standing at the place of *Ima de Atzilut*. Hence, the world of *Beria* stands below her, in the place of *Zeir Anpin* of *Atzilut*.

The world of *Yetzira*, created from *Malchut* of *Atzilut*, after the world of *Beria*, comes from her and takes its place below the world of *Beria*, taking the place of the four *Sefirot* of *Malchut* of *Atzilut* and six *Sefirot* of the place of the world of *Beria*.

The world of *Assiya*, created by *Malchut* of *Atzilut* after the world *Yetzira*, takes its place below the world of *Yetzira*, from the *Chazeh* of the world of *Beria*, to the "*Chazeh* of the world of *Yetzira*."

The worlds end at "*Chazeh* of the world *Yetzira*," because all the vessels of bestowal, and the vessels of bestowal inside the vessels of reception, have been sorted out from the broken pieces. Below *Chazeh* of *Yetzira* begins the *AHP* of the place of *BYA*, the place of the vessels of reception that were included in the vessels of bestowal and the vessels of reception ("the stony heart").

The raised AHP: The sorting and correction of the vessels of reception that were included in the vessels of bestowal, adds vessels of *AHP* to the world of *Atzilut*. Those vessels take the Light of Wisdom and the world of *Atzilut* attains Gadlut.

The Light of Wisdom expands only in genuine vessels of reception, whereas here there are vessels of reception that were included in the vessels of bestowal during the breaking. Hence, the Light that expands on the couplings of these vessels is not a real Light of Wisdom, but an illumination of wisdom.

There is a special correction in the *Rosh* of the world of *Atzilut* that guarantees there will never be another breaking, as in the case of the world of *Nekudim*. There is a limitation in the *Rosh* of *Partzuf Arich Anpin*, so that from *Arich Anpin* and below, there will not be a *Zivug* on the actual *Malchut*, but only on the *Malchut* that is included in the *Sefirot* above it, in the desires for bestowal.

Consequently, the world of *Atzilut* is born in *Katnut*, and every *Partzuf* has only the vessels of bestowal, the vessels of GE. The vessels of reception (*AHP*) remain below the *Parsa*. It is impossible to join the *AHP* with the GE and make a *Zivug* on the entire ten *Sefirot* in their actual place, as it was in the world of *Nekudim*, because it causes the vessels to break.

Hence, any addition of vessels of reception to *Atzilut* is done by raising some of the vessels of reception included in the vessels of bestowal. The ascent is from under the *Parsa* to over it, thus adding parts of *AHP* to *Atzilut*, which brings illumination of wisdom to *Atzilut*.

This is how the vessels of reception rise from under the *Parsa* and join *Atzilut*. All the vessels of reception that can join the vessels of *Atzilut*, meaning vessels of reception that are included in the vessels of bestowal, rise in order of coarseness, from fine to coarse.

THE CORRECTION OF THE STONY HEART

After all the above corrections, only vessels of reception remain in *BYA*, called the "stony heart." They are not included in the vessels of bestowal, and hence cannot be corrected. Their correction is in being separated and excluded every time there is a sorting of the 320 broken parts. In each sorting there are thirty-two parts of that nature.

When using the 288 remaining parts and building *Partzufim*, a decision must be made to refrain from using the stony heart that belongs to that part. Once the correction of the 288 parts is completed, a Light of Wisdom will come from Above, named Messiah, to correct these vessels by giving them a screen. Then the entire *Malchut de Ein Sof* will be corrected with a screen. That state of *Malchut* is defined as the "end of correction."

All the vessels in the worlds of *BYA*, except the stony heart, are corrected from the finest to the coarsest. In each of the worlds of *BYA* there are 2,000 phases of correction, named "years" or "degrees." All together, there are 6,000 degrees in the three worlds of *BYA*, called the "six days of the week." The worlds of *BYA* are considered the weekdays and the world of *Atzilut* is the holy *Shabbat*.

Once all the worlds of *BYA* and the stony heart are corrected, the world of *Atzilut* will expand below the *Parsa* to "this world." That state will be called "the seventh millennium." Afterwards, the worlds of *ABYA* will rise to *SAG* and that will be called "the eighth millennium." Then the worlds of *ABYA* will rise to *AB* and that will be called "the ninth millennium." Finally, the worlds of *ABYA* will rise to *Galgalta* and that will be called "the tenth millennium."

Thus, after the correction of *Malchut de Ein Sof* is completed, she will be filled as prior to the First Restriction. In addition, she will benefit from the endless ascents in the degrees of bestowal to the Creator.

But because the wisdom of Kabbalah teaches only those acts concerning man's correction, these situations are not taught. They do not even appear in books of Kabbalah because they belong to a part that is forbidden to be told, called "The Secrets of Torah." Only a chosen few practice them, and under strict conditions.

CHAPTER 3.22
THE BIRTH AND THE BREAKING OF ADAM HA RISHON

Throughout the corrections of *Malchut* that we have been discussing, *Malchut* of *Malchut* still has not been filled, the central *Malchut* of all the worlds. Everything that happened up until now, the First and Second Restrictions, the breaking of the vessels, and corrections were all done on the Upper Nine *Sefirot* of *Malchut*, not on *Malchut* itself, *Behina Dalet* of *Dalet*. That is because she was restricted not to receive anything inside it, meaning within the will to receive.

Any Light that is received after the First Restriction is received only in the vessels of bestowal, or the vessels of *Malchut de Ein Sof*. These were impressed with the upper nine from the will to bestow of the Upper Light.

Malchut of Malchut will be corrected and filled with the Light of Wisdom, as before the First Restriction, only if Malchut will obtain desires for bestowal, and mix with Malchut's desires for reception. Malchut was mixed with its Upper Nine Sefirot in the breaking of the vessels, consequently creating the worlds. But that still corrected nothing of Malchut itself, because she did not mix with the desires for bestowal.

After the descent of the worlds of BYA, Malchut of Atzilut (which stands at the place of Ima) makes a Zivug on Katnut, on the joining of the vessels of bestowal with Behina Dalet of Dalet. That is why this Partzuf is strictly forbidden to use its vessels of reception, its AHP.

This Partzuf is called Adam ha Rishon (the First Man), who was forbidden to eat from the tree of knowledge, meaning to make a Zivug on the vessels of reception, the AHP.

At the birth of Adam ha Rishon, the worlds of BYA expanded to the place of Chazeh of Yetzira. Then came the Light from Ein Sof, named "awakening from Above," which elevated all the worlds by one degree. Therefore, the end of the world of Assiya rose from the place of Chazeh of Yetzira to the place of Chazeh of Beria. Then came another awakening from Above, elevating the worlds one more degree, so that the end of the world of Assiya rose above Parsa.

Being inside the worlds of BYA, Adam ha Rishon rose along with them to Atzilut. He thought that now he could receive all the Light in his vessels of reception in order to bestow, meaning in the AHP, the Behina Dalet of Behina Dalet.

But just as in the case of the breaking of the vessels in the world of Nekudim, when he drew the Light of Wisdom into the vessels of reception, he lost the screen, the aim to bestow. His body was broken into 600,000 pieces, called "organs" or "souls," that fell into the shells and received an aim to receive in order to receive.

All the parts together, and each separate part, fell deeper down (those are the sins that the Torah tells us about in the first generations after the sin of Adam ha Rishon). These parts are dressed in people of our world. A person who has such a part feels the desire to rise and unite with his origin at Adam ha Rishon. That origin is called "the root of man's soul."

In order for the creature to earn that name (creature), it must become independent, meaning not influenced by the Creator. Therefore, the Creator hides Himself, thus helping the creatures equalize with Him through their own labor. It turns out that a person in our world, whose soul clothes a part of the First Man, is the creature.

A creature is a part of *Adam ha Rishon* that is inside a person of our world. All creatures, meaning souls, are parts of the body of *Adam ha Rishon*. They all need to correct their breaking, thus returning to the state that was before the sin, and add adhesion with the Creator. They sort the parts from within the shells.

All of us must come to the roots of our souls while in this physical world. Otherwise, we will return here until we realize the purpose of our creation.

CHAPTER 3.23
BASIC TERMS

Sefirot: properties, clothes that the Creator "wears" in order to appear before His Creatures. They are *not* His real properties and there is nothing we can say about them, because we cannot grasp their meaning. We can only grasp what He wants to reveal to us. We regard these external properties as "attributes" or "*Sefirot*."

We feel the properties of the Creator as a certain Light that awakens a unique feeling in us. We name each *Sefira* according to that feeling. Every Light that comes from the Creator is a certain form or providence, a sign that awakens a certain response. Generally speaking, all the forms of Light that emanate from the Creator toward us are called "the Light of divinity."

One feels the Light of the Creator to the extent that one attains corrections. Without a single mended property, we cannot feel the Light that comes from the Creator, although unknowingly we are still controlled by Him. When that is the case, we cannot believe that the Creator exists.

One feels that Light comes from the Creator only to the extent that one's own attributes resemble His. Then one begins to understand that the Creator's influences are forms of bestowal of love and mercy. Even formerly "negative" emotions, such as fear and cruelty, will now be interpreted this way.

All the Light-forms of the *Sefirot* are monitored signs of how the Creator relates to His Creation. That means that the *Sefirot* convey the Creator's rule to mankind. These Light-forms, these *Sefirot* are different forms by which the Creator watches over us and relates to us. Those forms are divided by ten primary types, ten *Sefirot*.

The wisdom of Kabbalah teaches what the Creator extends to His creatures, meaning the ten *Sefirot*. That is why the fundamental textbook of Kabbalah is titled, "*The Study of the Ten Sefirot*."

There are ten forms (*Sefirot*) through which the Light emanates from the Creator. These forms beget Creation. The vast variety of creatures in Creation stems from various combinations of the properties of these ten *Sefirot*, because these combinations create ten inner *Sefirot* in each *Sefira*. Inside of these are another ten *Sefirot* and another inner ten *Sefirot* and so on indefinitely.

Every property in Creation stems from the properties contained in those ten *Sefirot*. That is the reason for the differences between people. The various branches of Creation are interconnected and thus create new branches. It is therefore possible to compare Creation to a tree that has a root. This is the source, while a trunk and branches and leaves are replicas of the root.

In fact, everything that happens in the root will happen later in the branches. There cannot be an event in the branches that does not happen first in the root.

Restriction: This is the Law of Creation. It states that the creatures were not created perfect, but with a certain flaw. Perfection is a complete match (identicalness) between every creature and the Creator.

The world of *Ein Sof*, the collective form of Creation, which is the beginning of everything, was created perfect by the Creator. But the perfection is concealed from the creatures. They must discover it gradually, according to their individual desires.

Therefore, although Creation is complete, eternal, and in utter bliss, one cannot feel it at first, but only when one changes one's attributes to match those of the *Sefirot*, the Light. Then one begins to feel the actual reality denominated "the next world."

The entire Creation is made in such a way that it is compelled to discover its real state. This is how the Creator uses the *Sefirot* to control Creation.

Place: A place is an absence. The concealment of the Creator creates a "place"—a feeling of emptiness. The Creator created that sensation of emptiness deliberately, so that one would strive to feel the Creator independently and discover Him by himself, through the properties that he corrects to match the *Sefirot*.

The World of Restriction: First the Creator created everything in its complete and final state. Afterwards, He concealed Himself from the creatures, thus creating a vacant space, an absence called "The World of Restriction."

Reshimot (1): These are reflections, recollections that remain from the past, after everything is no longer felt. It is a memory of what life could be like if it hadn't all disappeared.

It is through these *Reshimot* that His creatures can survive inside the empty space, without being filled with the Light of the Creator. Without any pleasure, the creatures would simply cease to exist. The *Reshimot* keep changing, and it is those changes that urge us to move, to want, and to obtain whatever it is the *Reshimot* awaken in us. The changes of the *Reshimot* give us the sensation of movement, time and life.

The *Reshimot* make both good and bad things appear in our senses equally, and it is for us to understand that they are equal and determine which way the *Reshimot* will evolve through thoughts and acts in a positive direction. The *Reshimot* give us the freedom of choice, the ability to decide between the two, because if there is too much good feeling, or too much bad, then everything is predetermined.

For instance, if the Creator were not concealed and His Perfection was exposed, we would not be able to make a single independent act through our own choice. We would have to act like the Creator does; His Perfection would compel us to.

Line: This is a form of the Creator's leadership by which His Creatures are corrected and regain their completeness. The line is a part of the perfection that all the creatures will feel in the future. This will occur once they are corrected through the providence of the Creator that descends on them through the line, depending on their momentary state.

There are *Reshimot* in the creatures, and the Light pours on them from above through the world of *Ein Sof* that is filled with Light. The line fills the creature according to the *Reshimot* and gives it a certain portion of its own perfect state in the world of *Ein Sof*. The purpose of Creation is to perfect man's imperfection, the sensation of the absence of the Creator and the absence of the Light in the creatures.

In order to bring us to that perfect state, the Creator uses a providence of good and bad. Although man can feel only good and bad, since the providence of the Creator is always of benevolence, it is our corrupted properties that make the absolute good feel like bad.

It is according to our degree of correction that we can begin to discern the "bad" providence as good. That is why it is said that within the providence of "good" and "bad" there is the providence of the "Absolute Good."

Reshimot (2): *Reshimot* are a part of the collective and complete Light of *Ein Sof*. The line transmits the Light to the creatures that are in the empty space, concealed from the Creator and feeling incompletion in accordance with the nature of the *Reshimot* in this or that creature.

That is why it is said that the *Reshimot* awaken and move the body (desire). But the line does more than just fulfill the body. While fulfilling the desire, it corrects it in accordance with the *Reshimot*.

A "tube" is a Light that comes from the world of *Ein Sof* and descends to the creatures in the empty space that are feeling incompleteness. The Light fills them according to the line, and the creatures then unite with the Creator.

The Creator gives to all creatures, regardless of the Light that passes through the tube. However, His Leadership is felt only by those who are already in the Upper Worlds, according to their labors.

At the end of correction, the Creator will once again reveal Himself to all creatures as the Absolute Benevolent Leader of the world. He will not appear through the tube, according to our personal attributes, but as the Absolute Good Who is equally good to everyone at all times.

This is the state of the end of correction, a time when everyone feels the absolute good, love, eternity, absolute knowledge, and perfection. That state has been prepared for us ahead of time by the Creator in the world of *Ein Sof*, and all creatures will see it according to their individual degrees of perfection.

Inner Light and Surrounding Light: When the Light comes from *Ein Sof* to the creatures, it divides into Inner Light and Surrounding Light, or a filling Light and a casing Light. Inner Light is what the Creator reveals to the creature by filling it with this Light. The Surrounding Light is what the creature has yet to attain from the perfection.

Hence, the entire Light of *Ein Sof*, meaning that perfect state that the creature will reach in the future, is divided into a partial state that the creature has already attained by acquiring a certain degree in the spiritual world. A part of the perfection that is not yet attained, and since the creature does not receive the entire Light, but limits the amount it receives, the partial Light received is measured against the Light of *Ein Sof*. The measurement unit that is used is the five Lights NRNHY (*Nefesh, Ruach, Neshama, Haya,* and *Yechida*).

Adam Kadmon: This is the first and the highest of the spiritual worlds. Since all the other worlds are "lower" than *Adam Kadmon*, they descend from it. Thus, it is obvious that the properties received from the Light, transmitted through it from the world of *Ein Sof*, also contain the properties of the world of *Adam Kadmon*.

Otiot (letters): *Otiot* are vessels. The Light from *Partzuf AB* does not carry with it any *Otiot* because the *Otiot* are already so filled with Light, they are completely satiated. The Light from *Partzuf SAG* is expressed in the letter *Hey* (ה), which represents the root of the future vessel. The

Light that comes from *Zeir Anpin* contains the letter *Vav* (ו), which is the actual beginning of the future vessel.

The Light that comes down from *Partzuf BON* contains *Otiot*, especially on their departure from the *Partzuf*, when they collide and vanish, thus begetting the twenty-two Hebrew *Otiot*, or vessels.

After the breaking of the vessels in the world of *Nekudim*, each vessel is left with *Reshimot* from the breaking. These stay with it until the end of correction. Each Light leaves its vessel during the breaking, which creates the flaws in the vessels. This is where the domination of the body over the soul originates, as the extent of the body's control over the soul is related to the amount of corruption of the body, meaning the amount of desire.

But that domination of the body over the soul happened deliberately to create the egoism in us, our independent desire to take pleasure in the Light of the Creator. However, that domination also creates the conditions to correct the body-desire. In the end, that will result in the beginning of the process of correction, which will end when we attain the level of the Soul-Light. At that time, there will be no difference between the body and the soul, or between man's desire and the Creator's.

The end of this process is when the body-desire declines even further, until finally it declines to the level of a beast (animate degree). This is all preordained in the breaking of the vessels in the world of *Nekudim*. However, since the corrected state is also preordained even before the breaking of the vessels, every desire will be reconstructed to resemble the Light, and the more identical it is to the Light, the more Light will enter it.

During the 6,000 years, meaning before the souls complete their correction and a few individuals become Kabbalists, spirituality (the revelation of the Creator) will not be felt in this world. But when all the souls are corrected, we will come to a state called "the end of correction." Then, the Creator will be evident to everyone in this world and this world will become a perfect place. The Light from the world of *Ein Sof* will come down to it and the *Parsa* in the world of *Atzilut* will no longer be an obstacle to its expansion. That state is called "the seventh millennium."

Since the desires of the body (the *AHP*) consist of egoistic desires that contain three degrees of *Aviut*—*Bet*, *Gimel* and *Dalet*—their correction is not like that of the raised *AHP*, but occurs gradually.

The correction of *Aviut Bet* and its filling in its place below the *Parsa* is called "the eighth millennium." The correction of *Aviut Gimel* and its filling in its own place under the *Parsa* is called "the ninth millennium." The correction of *Aviut Dalet* and its filling in its place under the *Parsa* is called "the tenth millennium."

No one can know what will happen at the end of the correction of all the souls, when the Light of the Creator becomes evident in our world. Even Kabbalists who rose through all the degrees of the spiritual worlds can only attain the degree of the seventh millennium. But they cannot know how the Creator will appear in our world after that.

However, Baal HaSulam writes that there are souls that do attain these situations. These souls come to our world once every ten generations and his soul is one of them. However, he cannot explain how it happens, because that is a situation that we must learn by ourselves.

The state of the end of correction is characterized by the original desire (the egoism) obtaining an identical nature to that of the Light, something that presently is unimaginable.

Providence operates through the worlds of *ABYA*, but these will exist only while there is concealment.

The world of *Nekudim* is the root and origin of the evil in our world. The Creator uses it to show how "Light excelleth darkness" by inverting the darkness to become like the Light. All the worlds exist for the sole purpose of revealing the perfection of the Creator, both in man and in Creation. Therefore, there are two kinds of worlds: in the beginning there is concealment, and afterwards there is completeness.

The worlds of *BYA* were created from the broken vessels of the world of *Nekudim*. The vessels of the *Rosh*, meaning the three upper *Sefirot* continue to the world of *Atzilut*. After that, the world of *Atzilut* completes itself at the expense of the vessels of the worlds of *BYA*.

Shabbat and Holiday: These are states of *Katnut* and *Gadlut* of *Zeir Anpin* of the world of *Atzilut*. The state of *Katnut* means "suckling" (breast feeding). The state of *Gadlut* means "redemption." However, these states are only temporary and last only as long as correction is still needed.

Image of the Creator: The Creator demonstrates His leadership in the form of "circles" and "straight lines." During His descent from Above, He demonstrates His Power and the marks of His Leadership. "Superior" means stronger and greater; it is defined as "the inner circles," when at the very center there is our world.

Malchut: *Malchut* is called the "similitude of God" because that is the only place where we can feel the Creator, with attributes that were given to us from Above. We attain in our innermost feeling, in our *Malchut*. However, we do it with the attributes we receive from Above.

CHAPTER 3.24
QUESTIONS & ANSWERS

WHAT IS KABBALAH?

Q: What is Kabbalah?

A: Kabbalah is an ancient teaching that covers a number of languages and many forms of expression. There is the language of tales that the Bible uses and the language of rules that the Talmud uses. There is also the language of Kabbalah itself, which uses drawings, formulas, and matrices. Kabbalah utilizes pure mathematical rules in order to express spiritual phenomena. There are many ways to depict our sensations and feelings, but the language of Kabbalah is the most accurate and scientific of all.

It is also possible to convey spiritual sensations through music. Though we do not know the music that former Kabbalists composed, we know that music and songs did exist and that Kabbalists used it to convey feelings that relate to the spiritual world. The latest Kabbalistic music, the only original music that has reached us, is that of Rabbi Ye-

243

huda Ashlag and his eldest son, Rabbi Baruch Ashlag. The advantage of music over text is that it reaches everyone's ears, even if the listener is completely unfamiliar with regard to the language of Kabbalah. It also allows a person who does not feel the spiritual realm to feel and participate in the emotions and experiences that the Kabbalist felt while being in the spiritual world.

Q: What are the principles of the wisdom of Kabbalah?

A: The only law that exists in reality is the maximum pleasure that Creation derives from the Creator. All other laws are based on that law and are actual examples of it. Everything that happens in reality is an implementation of that law. Anything in the universe at any given moment is motivated by the power that drives mankind to reach the state of ultimate delight, the filling of the creature with the Light of the Creator.

The Creator acts like gravity: He is at the center of the universe. First, He pushes the souls to a distance of five worlds from Him: *Adam Kadmon, Atzilut, Beria, Yetzira* and *Assiya*, and the farthest point is called "this world." Later, He begins to pull us towards Him.

We feel this process as compulsory, accompanied by all kinds of torments and pain. That anguish is intended to motivate us to replace our egoistic nature with an altruistic one. The Creator is altruistic by nature. Nearing or distancing from the Creator means changing our spiritual attributes to altruism or egoism respectively. The more altruistic we become, the more intensely we are drawn to Creator, and the more egoistic we are, the farther we draw from Him.

If we strain ourselves to obtain spiritual nearness with the Creator and not wait until His pulling Force affects us painfully, we will be able to reduce our pain and feel His pulling Force as good and pleasurable. If, however, we insist on remaining corrupted and refuse to adopt the altruistic nature of the Creator, we will be pushed to it by means of financial problems, sickness, and death.

The wisdom of Kabbalah allows us to realize ourselves in every way, so that we can consciously advance toward the Creator and not need the influence of His harsh, compelling Force. Those who study Kabbalah increase their spiritual strength and knowledge until they are able to approach the Creator quickly and easily. By doing that, they spare themselves pain, distressing events, and wars. All the negative events in our world are a consequence of that compelling power of the Creator pushing us toward correction.

You, the readers, are already taking part in the conduct of the Upper World by the very fact that you have begun to think, analyze, and argue, agree or disagree with what you are reading. As you awaken the point of connection with the Creator in your soul, you draw the correcting Light to our world. That process softens Providence and turns it from rougher to softer. That is why the wisdom of Kabbalah is the most practical science of all; it explains how we can all "live well."

Q: What is the mathematical structure of the wisdom of Kabbalah?

A: The mathematical structure of the wisdom of Kabbalah is very complex. It consists mostly of *Gimatria*, but there are tables and complex interdependencies and formulas as well. There are mathematic-type sequences in it, and there are also Hebrew letters involved. In fact, it is impossible to understand the entire system before one begins to feel emotions that relate to the situations being taught.

Kabbalah is not a theoretical study of the spiritual world, the heavens, as many like to think. It is *the most* practical science of all because it is taught and understood only by the influences it bears on each student. This means that one not only learns about some spiritual operations, but actually experiences them.

Only the student can know precisely what he or she is doing, and only the student can feel the consequences of any actions taken. These feelings are conveyable to others only through a unique language, but only one who can repeat the operation can experience it. That is why the wisdom of Kabbalah is a guide to spiritual operations.

THE CREATOR

Q: What is the difference between the perspective of the Creator and the perspective of the creature?

A: The perspective of the Creator means that the entire Creation emanates from His Thought. It is created through four phases (*Behinot*) of Direct Light that finally reach a state entitled "the world of *Ein Sof*." Creation is already completed in the world of *Ein Sof*, but the creatures will be able to feel it only when they rise from below, from this world to the world of *Ein Sof* in their emotions. Then the creatures will also see what has always been there and can judge it from the perspective of the Creator.

Q: What is the work of God and why is it called by that name?

A: God's work is the work that God does. If that is the case, why do we normally think that it means our work? All work from Above downward was done by the Creator. However, if we want the Creator to do the same work on the way up, we must demand this work to be done by a higher spiritual degree than our own.

All of Creation begins with the Creator. There is a Superior Force that wants to create a creature that equalizes with His Completeness. If that Complete Force had created an incomplete Creation, that would mean that He was incomplete.

Thus, the purpose of the Creator is to create a creature that is as complete as He is, since He cannot create anything else. That desire is imprinted in the Light; it is entitled, "the purpose of Creation." This purpose determines the entire evolution of Creation, from beginning to end. Everything that happens in every single step in the spiritual worlds, all the agony the creatures feel in this world, serves a single objective—to bring the creature to its complete, best possible state.

There is no other creature but man. We will not only read about it in books but also feel it and see it in every level of Creation, not just in our world, but in every single world. If the Creator is complete, His operations are also complete and final. However, as long as we are in our intermediary phases, when we are suffering, when there is injustice in the world, can we honestly say that He is complete?

The intermediary situations are also complete, even those we are in right now. Our only problem is that we cannot experience them as such. This stems from the system of the impure forces, which makes it impossible for us to feel the state we are in as perfect.

The wisdom of Kabbalah allows each person to neutralize the influence of the impure forces and, according to the degree of that neutralization, feel eternity in every situation, not just in our tiny limited world.

Q: What is the meaning of the name *HaVaYaH*?

A: The meaning of the name *HaVaYaH* is that the Creator creates and revives in the past, present and the future, meaning above time, just as we must attain the Creator in the spirit, above time.

Q: What is the difference between the names of the Creator and His appellations?

A: The names of the Creator are what we call "the ten names that cannot be erased." These correspond to the ten *Sefirot*: *El, Elokim HaVaYaH* etc. The appellations are the attributes of the Creator: "Gracious," "Merciful," "Keeping mercy unto the thousandth," and so on. These attributes were given to Him according to what Kabbalists attained of Him.

Q: Does the Creator have a concept of "benevolence"?

A: The concept of benevolence is a little different with regards to the Creator than the concept we normally think of. That is because we regard as "good and doest good" everything that satisfies our egoistic desires. I regard as "good" anything that is *good for me*, and as "bad," anything that is *bad for me*. These are measured according to my level of development.

Q: What does *Heichal HaShem* (the Palace of the Lord) mean?

A: The word *Heichal* (Palace, Hall) consists of two words: *Hey* (the letter that represents the Creator), and *Kol* (everything). When put together, they form the word. *Heichal*. This means that anyone who enters the King's palace receives everything the Creator had prepared. If one attains an inner state called *Heichal*, one attains eternal and complete connection with the Creator. Until this state is attained, one's soul continues to experience gradual corrections of attributes.

The Creator is also called *Makom* (Place). A place is the distance between man and the Creator. Therefore, we must come to a state where we will be completely cleaved to the Creator, blending with Him. The border that we feel between us and the Creator is also called *Makom*.

When we complete our corrections and cleave to the Creator, we enter a state called "the revival of the dead," meaning the revival of our own attributes. The revival of the dead is also called *Kima* (rising), hence the word *Makom*, and our sensation of the Creator and the sensation of our own attributes we feel as *Heichal*.

WORLDS

Q: What is "our world"?

A: Our world is what we feel in our egoistic sensations, the corrupted ones that haven't been corrected. We begin to feel a more external world as we progress in the correction of our egos.

Q: What is the meaning of the term, "this world"?

A: The state called "this world" designates the farthest point from the Creator (in terms of properties). That is what we should feel when we begin to work on ourselves and study Kabbalah, when the Surrounding Light begins to shine on us. We awaken the illumination of that Light on ourselves during our studies, and gradually begin to feel ourselves as more and more corrupted (a process known as "the recognition of evil"). This is the consequence of the comparison that we begin to make between ourselves and the Light.

When that Light shines in full power in this world, we will feel ourselves completely opposite to the Creator, and then we'll shout for help. In response, the Creator will save us from this world and take us across the barrier to the first degree of the spiritual world.

We can see that our problem is actually to acknowledge our own egoism as bad, as our own nature. The only way to come to that is through the effect of the Light of the Torah, or the Surrounding Light that shines on us when we study Kabbalah. The Light is given the name "Surrounding" because as long as there is evil in us, it cannot enter and therefore stays around us on the outside.

Q: Why are we and our world built the way we are?

A: The Light that comes from the Creator passes through four phases, during which it increases its density before finally creating a "vessel," or the desire to receive the Light and enjoy it.

That desire is the fifth phase. But the minute this fifth phase, meaning *Malchut*, begins to feel the Light inside it, it decides to try and resemble it. That is why it tries to resemble the four previous phases, which is also why the fifth phase has five inner phases. The fifth phase resembles the previous four as much as it can. The parts it cannot resemble remain unchanged.

The third phase is divided into six subdivisions, which is why we count ten parts in each creature, or ten *Sefirot*. They are also called *Shoresh, Neshama, Guf, Levush,* and *Heichal* (root, soul, body, clothing, and palace—respectively). The first three unite in man's body, while the remaining two exist separately, like clothes and the world around us. This is a result of the Second Restriction, since the remaining two (*Levush, Heichal*) designate the vessels of reception that were forbidden to be used after the Second Restriction.

Q: Why are there so many worlds?

A: There are many worlds because an egoistic desire is built in a gradual process of increasing remoteness from the Creator. The first world is *Ein Sof*. It is a desire, the root of the creature to be. The will to receive for self is created after the Second Restriction, but the desire also restricts itself from doing it. Afterwards, when the breaking of the vessels occurs, the impure desires, or "shells" appear, which already want to use the egoistic desire.

After the sin of *Adam ha Rishon* there are entire worlds of impure forces created. The impure system consists of the same structure, but is opposite to the system of the pure worlds. The creature is in between them to be given the conditions for free choice.

Q: What are "parallel worlds"?

A: There are no other worlds. All five worlds—*Adam Kadmon, Atzilut, Beria, Yetzira* and *Assiya*—are parallel. Try and imagine five rings with a joint center. Imagine the same picture in parallel, one under the other, five times. What we get is five parallel areas, each consisting of five inner circles. All the areas are worlds entitled, *Adam Kadmon, Atzilut, Beria, Yetzira* and *Assiya*.

Now, imagine taking these areas and putting next to them another area with five circles. That new area will be called *Ein Sof*. There are five worlds between us and the world of *Ein Sof*, and we cannot gradually connect with these worlds and attain equivalence of form (properties) with the world of *Ein Sof*. We feel the transitions from world to world according to the changes in our inner properties (inner feelings). We begin with feeling ourselves in this world, and gradually come to feel ourselves as completely identical to the world of *Ein Sof*, to the Creator.

Q: Do we feel our souls rather than our physical bodies?

A: The physical body is an illusion. We must obtain a state where we will feel our souls. That is what Kabbalah initiates—the sensation of our own souls. Afterwards, we can continue developing it to become an immense vessel that the Creator can fill.

Q: How can a spiritual object divide into ten *Sefirot* indefinitely?

A: Each part in the spiritual world, even the smallest particle, can be isolated and divided once more to ten inner parts. It is an indefinite process. The desire that the Creator created does not change. What does change is the measurement of its use with the aim to give to the Creator. It depends on the screen. A spiritual object is a part of the uniform and unique desire that the Creator created and that must be given a screen.

LIGHTS & VESSELS

Q: What is the Upper Force?

A: It is the Absolute Good, the Benevolent Force that leads us. However, because we are not corrected, we feel this power as bad and harmful.

Q: Does the wisdom of Kabbalah teach sorcery? Is it permitted and if so, how do we practice "practical Kabbalah"?

A: The wisdom of Kabbalah strictly prohibits any of this kind of activity. The purpose of the study of Kabbalah is to give one a desire and spiritual power, to be able to evolve to the spiritual degree of the Creator.

Q: What is a vessel?

A: A vessel is a desire that has been corrected by the screen. Using the screen (aim), the vessel is able to receive in order to benefit the Creator, and thus fulfill the desire for pleasure. A desire without a screen is still not considered a vessel, but is called a *Reshimo* or a shell.

MALE & FEMALE

Q: Why is the Light of Wisdom assigned a male gender and the Light of Mercy a female, motherly gender?

A: The Light of Wisdom is the root of the male properties and the Light of *Bina* is the root of the female properties. Men and women differ in properties, skin texture, physiology, etc. You can even see the differences in their handwriting. What separates the two genders are the

(Hebrew) letters *Yod* (י) for male and *Hey* (ה) for female. The letter *Yod* represents the *Sefira* of *Hochma*, while the letter *Hey* designates the *Sefira* of *Bina*, in *Malchut*.

Since all parts of reality are interconnected and complement one another, and each part contains something of the other, we can always explain each part or property that we examine in different ways. However, it will always be about the Four Phases of Direct Light

Q: **Why is the Light of Wisdom the principal Light, and not the Light of Mercy?**

A: The Light that extends from the Creator is called "the Light of Wisdom." It has been written: "Form the Light, and create darkness," referring to the lack of the Light of Wisdom. That is why the eyes are the highest vessels of the *Partzuf*. It is also why it is said that a "bride whose eyes are beautiful needs no further examination," because the eyes are the highest degree of the *Guf* (body) of the *Partzuf*.

The lowest and darkest part is *Malchut*. It transfers Light from itself to the eyes of the lower *Partzuf*, which demonstrates the difference between the *Partzufim*.

Q: **Why are we born as a man or a woman?**

A: These questions relate to the mechanism of the superior providence, called ZON of the world of *Atzilut*. That system consists of two parts: *Zeir Anpin* and *Nukva*, meaning males and females that have their own relationship. That relationship creates "time" (days, weeks, months and years) and their mating creates the souls. The properties of the souls define the characteristics of the physical body that the soul clothes. The soul is created and descends to this world even before a child is born into it.

I am using earthly terms of time, space and motion, although they do not exist in the spiritual world. We must understand that relationship between the male and female parts of ZON of the world of *Atzilut* determines everything that happens in our world. There is no other way to easily explain the variety of possibilities for the relationship between these two parts, how they connect and how they clothe one another, how they mate and how they create new souls. It is a very complex system. Nearly 1600 of the 2000 pages of *The Study of the Ten Sefirot* are dedicated to the description of ZON of the world of *Atzilut*.

Part Four: Proper Study

CHAPTER 4.1
ABOUT THE STUDY

WHO IS PERMITTED TO STUDY?

Every person, regardless of sex, is permitted to study the wisdom of Kabbalah. For that reason, Kabbalists have always tried to circulate this wisdom in both Israel and the world over, to bring this option to everyone's awareness. This is especially true of those whose souls are ripe for the study of the wisdom of Kabbalah. Through study, they can correct themselves and attain the purpose of Creation. Others who still don't feel it necessary to study Kabbalah should be aware of this system, should they want to study it later. This allows them to accelerate their progress toward the correction phase.

If we read *The Study of the Ten Sefirot*, one of Kabbalah's most prominent works, written by Baal HaSulam in the previous century, we will see that from the very first page, Rabbi Yehuda Ashlag (Baal HaSulam) explains that every individual can and should study Kabbalah. It is absolutely necessary for those who have a single question burning in their hearts: "What is the meaning of my life?"

Although the wisdom of Kabbalah is a vast and complex science, Rabbi Ashlag opens his book with a simple, humane question, one we can all recognize. Those who feel dissatisfied with the answer can find the answer in the wisdom of Kabbalah, and only there. There is no other way! A person who does not ask, "What is the meaning of my life?" will not benefit from the wisdom of Kabbalah.

PAST PROHIBITIONS

In the past, men under forty years of age who were not married, and women, were forbidden to study Kabbalah. But it was the Ari who determined that from his generation onward, the Kabbalah should be permitted to all men, women, and children, provided they are imbued with a desire for spirituality, testifying to the maturity of their souls.

Our desire and passion for spirituality, and our search for the meaning of life are the only testimonials to our readiness to study the wisdom of Kabbalah. Moreover, Rabbi Kook answered the question of, "Who can study Kabbalah?" with the simple words: "Anyone who wishes it."

PRIOR KNOWLEDGE

There is no need for any prior knowledge in order to study Kabbalah. It is a science that deals with one's spiritual contact with the Creator. If one feels a need to study the Upper World, the knowledge acquired in this world will be of little help. The students wish to understand the laws of the Upper World, not the laws of this world. Therefore, such people should not be met with demands or prior conditions of certain courses needed before they can begin their studies.

The only requirement is to read the right books and to have a genuine desire for spirituality. That is, the Light is attained only by the desire for the correction of the desire. The human mind acts as an aid to carry out our egoistic desires. If we try to understand the Torah only through the intellect, we will be able to perceive the science of it, but not the Light.

Therefore, people who learn only about the practical laws of the Torah and perform them mechanically, without correcting their hearts, are called Gentiles. They have the knowledge, but not the Light. The Torah is the Light of the Creator that enters one's corrected vessels, while knowledge is a proficiency in what is written where and how. One can be proficient in the entire Torah, know the entire Talmud by heart, but still not have any real spiritual attainment.

This phenomenon exists in the study of Kabbalah, too: one can be proficient in all the texts of Kabbalah and master the text like a university professor, but that does not mean that all one's desires have been corrected, or that one has replaced egoism with altruism.

That is the true purpose of our Creation and the purpose of the giving of the Torah. If we learn and apply the text we study, we correct our nature. Only then is it considered to be studying Torah. But if we learn only to acquire knowledge, this is all we are considered doing.

Therefore, a real teacher does not demand proficiency from his students. On the contrary, he wants to see their doubts, their weakness, their sensation of lack of understanding, and their dependency on the Creator. These signs testify to the beginning of our process of equalizing with the Upper Forces.

If beginning students become proud of their knowledge and demonstrate confidence and self-esteem, it is because the more they learn the more proficient they become, just as in any other knowledge. However, the wisdom of Kabbalah, unlike any other study, and against common sense, should not increase one's knowledge, but the sensation of the lack of it.

DURING THE STUDY

Baal HaSulam, *Introduction to the Study of the Ten Sefirot*, item 155:

> "Therefore we must ask, why then did the Kabbalists obligate each person to delve in the wisdom of Kabbalah? Indeed there is a weighty thing here, worthy of being publicized, that there is a magnificent, invaluable remedy for those who delve in the wisdom of Kabbalah. Although they do not understand what they are learning, through yearning and the great desire to understand what they are learning, they awaken upon themselves the Lights that surround their souls.
>
> This means that every man from Israel is guaranteed the ultimate attainment of all these wonderful attainments that God resolved, in the Thought of Creation, to grant each creature. But he who has not attained it in this life will attain it in the next and so on, until he has completed that which He preliminary thought of.
>
> And while man has not attained perfection, these Lights, that are destined to come to him, are deemed Surrounding Lights. That means

*that they stand ready for him, awaiting his attainment of the vessels
of reception. Then these Lights will clothe within the able vessels.*

*Thus, even when the vessels are absent, when we delve in this wis-
dom, mentioning the names of the Lights and the vessels related
to our souls, we are immediately illuminated to a certain degree.
However, they illuminate us without dressing in the internality of
our souls, since we do not have the vessels needed to receive them.
Indeed, the illumination we receive time and again when studying,
draws to us grace from Above, imparting us with a bounty of sanctity
and purity, greatly furthering us toward our perfection."*

A SPIRITUAL GUIDE

It is hard to tell a genuine spiritual teacher from one who pretends to
be such. These days, everyone wants cheap and easy fun, quick answers,
and quick solutions. People can easily be misled by eloquent speakers
and overlook the properties of spiritual guidance, which by nature are
not theatrical.

If that is the case, how can we identify a spiritual teacher in this
generation? A spiritual teacher may be proficient in many fields—science,
religious laws and customs, education, etc.

However, it is not enough to know what is written in the Kabbalah
books to become a spiritual guide. Such a person can only understand
the wisdom, and our sages warn us: "Wisdom in the Gentiles, believe'
Torah (Light) in the Gentiles, do not believe."

The word "gentile" refers not to a non-Jew, but to an egoist yet to
be corrected. Such a person may display impressive knowledge in Kabbalah and boast about it before one's students, displaying knowledge
with accurate citations from the texts, etc.

This display of knowledge may at first lead beginners to consider
this rabbi a spiritual person. This is because beginning students cannot
see what spirituality is, and without it there is no way to examine its ab-

sence or presence in anyone. A beginner goes through such fundamental changes in the beginning of the journey that it is difficult to understand what is going on within, much less assess another person correctly.

A beginning student is illiterate even with regard to the written Torah, and might take any person for a great teacher. However, there is a fundamental difference between a Kabbalist and a person proficient in the Torah: in Kabbalah, a rabbi is more than just a rabbi, he is a spiritual guide. The meaning of the Hebrew word *Rabbi* is "Great." The teacher and the student experience the spiritual path simultaneously.

The purpose of the teacher is not that his students will fear and respect him; on the contrary, he wants them to study in such a way that they will develop fear, respect, and love for the Creator, he wants to place them face to face with His Power. He wants to teach them how to turn directly to the Creator. Those who go through spiritual development will feel at some point the sensation of ignobility, weakness, egoism, and the vileness of their own desires.

After we experience these feelings, we can no longer be proud of ourselves, since we begin to see that everything we receive comes from the Creator. That is why a Kabbalah teacher is a modest person who lives a daily life just like every one of us, not a sage who is disconnected from this world.

That is why neither a Kabbalistic teacher nor his students are arrogant; they do not force their ideas on others, nor do they preach. The purpose of the rabbi is to turn the student toward the Creator in every single matter, not toward himself. In all other methods, even when they pretend to be Kabbalists, students begin to feel awe toward the teacher, not toward the Creator.

The wisdom of Kabbalah is the most practical science of all. Everything is subject for experimentation by the student. That is why a Kabbalistic spiritual guide is not just any rabbi, but a guide, a coach who works alongside his student. Even when the student does not feel it, the rabbi always helps him and directs him.

WHERE IS A TEACHER FOUND?

Finding a spiritual guide is a pretty tough task. I've already pointed out the fact that finding my rabbi was a great miracle. Our world is headed toward correction, whether we like it or not. The general design of the Creator is carried out even against our will. He has developed us to the point where we can listen to what He wants to tell us.

For that to happen, we had to develop our minds and technology to believe the possibility of an infinite speed, of energy and thoughts traveling great distances, and of one substance being transformed into another. We had to be brought to the point where we could believe in the possibility of space warps and time warps, and other once unimaginable scenarios.

Mankind achieved this, and now is on the border of understanding his egoistic desire. We think that there are advantages to this development, but we are approaching the exact opposite: the understanding that evolution should be internal, spiritual, and not external.

The Creator has us develop our technology while sustaining our internal evolution, both as individuals and in the whole of mankind. The Creator uses messengers for that purpose, secret Kabbalists who live among us.

While we are unaware of their existence, they are around us, next to us, working and living just like we do. They absorb our desires, thoughts, pleasures and pains, mingle our egoistic egos with their altruistic desires and thus pass the correction on, so as to bring each and every one of us to listen to and accept spiritual ideas.

The spiritual altruistic desires of these secret Kabbalists and their vessels are huge compared to our egoistic desires, because their desire is to give everything to the Creator, whereas ours is only to delight in what we find before our eyes in this world. Thus, a secret Kabbalist can easily absorb the desires of millions of people, correct them on a general level and promote them to a state where each person will begin his or her individual correction.

Furthermore, and this is difficult to understand, our world exists because of these people. These individuals need kindergartens for their children, books, clothes, etc. Those needs justify the existence of these items in our world.

In fact, this is the justification for the existence of anything. That is why all these things exist and are corrected later on. These words may sound untrue, exaggerated, or disconnected from reality, but time will prove that this is precisely how the world is managed.

It is impossible to find these Kabbalists because it is their task to stay in hiding and work secretly with all mankind. So how does one find a teacher? Everyone must search for himself. Where one ends up is where that person belongs.

The most important thing about this search is not to lie to yourself that you are in the right place at this time. Do not make compromises with yourself and do not follow others' examples. The only way for a person to find the right place for himself is to listen to himself and not to others. One must examine one's soul to see if that is where one feels at ease, if that is where the soul finds its nourishment.

There are people among us who look at others and try to follow them; they silence the voice of their souls' demands for spiritual evolution. They shut their eyes and settle for academic wisdom instead of spiritual development.

Naturally, as soon as one mingles with the collective, one feels confidence, but that is self-deceit, as this feeling should only come from a direct and personal contact with the Creator!

Therefore, those who take the path of individual growth feel less secure and more dependent. These sensations are sent by the Creator precisely so that one will need Him! Then one's own egoism will seek the connection with the Creator, attempting to find confidence and peace, and connection with the Creator is indeed the purpose of Creation.

A WISE DISCIPLE

A wise disciple is a person who wishes to learn from the Creator Himself. But what can we learn from the Creator? The Creator's sole property is His Desire to delight His creatures. To the extent that one wishes to acquire this precise property, meaning to delight the Creator, one merits the title "a wise disciple," meaning the disciple of the Wise (the Creator).

Students must labor intensely in their spiritual work in order for their prayers to equalize their attributes with those of the Creator to be heard. Those whose hearts are empty and who seemingly want to attain spirituality, but only display their work before others, will receive nothing! One cannot deceive the Creator or one's own heart.

When we want nothing but the Creator and make every effort possible to attain this goal, then our desires will be granted by the Creator.

Those who take the spiritual path are forbidden to speak about the degree they have achieved, because where feeling begins, words end. They must first and foremost know what they need for their correction, because we still don't understand the nature of the vessel that is worthy of receiving the Upper Light, or even the nature of the Light itself.

Those who attend lessons gradually begin to feel that they do not understand anything. That is already the attainment of a basic truth. The Creator gives them that feeling because He wants to bring them near to Him. When the Creator does not want someone near Him, He gives that person satisfaction in life, in family, and in work. In fact, it is only possible to evolve through a perpetual sensation of dissatisfaction.

There is another way to evolve, or better phrased, "to be educated": by developing a sense of completeness within. In that way, the educator prevents any ascents or descents from the disciple. This is the basis for traditional upbringing. When one has a sense of completeness, one is tempted to halt one's progress, as the ego is satisfied.

It is the intensity of dissatisfaction that creates the desire to break one's indolent routine. This is important in spirituality, for dissatisfaction is the power that pushes us toward the spiritual growth. Only sufficient effort and labor in both quality and quantity, unique to each person, can bring us to our desired goal. Therefore, any form of teaching Kabbalah and circulating wisdom will benefit those who practice it, because practitioners act as tubes through which the knowledge of the Creator can pour into our world.

Kabbalistic knowledge is not valid before it goes through one's heart, one's emotions. We may study any science in the world without changing our attributes; there is not a single science that demands scientists to change their views and correct themselves. This is because all sciences revolve around accumulating knowledge about the outer part of our world, though even science is beginning to find out about the dependency between the results of an experiment and the attributes of the scientist who held it. In the future, scientists will discover that any real knowledge can be attained only if researchers equalize their own properties with those of the subject of study.

Therefore, if we wish to understand the structure of the world in the degree where these events are formed, where our souls dwell before they come down to this world, and to where they ultimately return, if we want to see the picture of reality as it is, without depending on time, which controls our lives (the dream of many physicists), then we must come to be like that Upper Reality by ourselves.

Kabbalah teaches us how we can learn to sense the upper layers of reality. A Light of Wisdom can be felt only by a vessel that has been made ready for it, by progress in a state called "faith above reason." The interesting and beautiful thing about this entire process is that a spiritual vessel originates only when one actually performs actions aimed at bestowal. But those who study and remain at the level of their own reason, and with the knowledge they had acquired at the animate level, will find

THE PATH OF KABBALAH

that their knowledge only feeds their egoism, and does not support the creation of a vessel with a screen.

We should monitor the desires that surface within us. Our every desire is sent to us from Above, including the desire for the Light, for honor, for money, for knowledge, and so on. Each of us must scrutinize the desires that surface in us every single moment and choose the one we must realize according to the principles of Kabbalah, and not according to our own "gut feelings."

It appears to be extremely difficult for us to give up the pleasures of this world when we are offered them so abundantly that all we have to do is to reach out and grab them. It doesn't seem possible that we can give them up in favor of some future spiritual pleasure we don't understand.

However, once our properties are a little closer to those of the Creator, we will see the illusion of our worldly pleasures, the futility and meaninglessness of them compared to even the tiniest drop we receive through our adhesion with the Creator. At that point, we will naturally prefer the egoistic spiritual delight to the egoistic corporeal delight.

We are all given many chances to begin to progress in the right direction. It is important to identify these opportunities and not to miss out any that we are given by the Creator. We must strive for Him alone and try to see His Guidance in everything that happens to us, in every thought that comes to our mind.

The greatest Kabbalists wrote of how one must advance toward the spiritual world. The Creator gives us so much more than we need to advance we must be thankful to Him and to the Kabbalists for having given all this to us.

The teachers that have conveyed to us the desire of the Creator and the purpose of His Guidance, were at such a high spiritual degree, it is beyond our imagination, all the more so before we attain even the first and lowest spiritual degrees.

The concept of receiving for myself doesn't even exist in the degrees our spiritual leaders have achieved. They find pleasure from the contact with Him back to Him! The great Kabbalists found special words to describe the operations of the Creator for us; they clothed His Light and His actions in words and phrases. The Kabbalists wrote on a level we could understand at the beginning of our journeys, so that afterwards, through our hard work and by delving into the text, we will be able to feel His Light directly and completely.

THE LEARNING ENVIRONMENT

According to the design of Creation, we must come to a state where we can live by spiritual laws. The troubles we all experience, the global disasters and catastrophes, all come in order to bring each of us as individuals, and mankind as a whole, to keep the spiritual commandments while still living in this world.

Baal HaSulam writes about Kabbalah that it is a method for "the revelation of His Godliness to His creatures in this world" (*The Revelation of Godliness*). He doesn't write about what happens after death, but specifically of what must happen to us while we are here in this world. Kabbalah is only about the things we need in this world, the things we must attain if we don't want our lives to be wasted and have to reincarnate and finish what we did not finish before. That is why the wisdom of Kabbalah is the most practical and necessary science there is.

It is inescapable; life itself compels us to operate this way, and at the end of all the suffering, we still have to complete our individual corrections. It is not as if anything will really change at the end of correction; it will be the same universe, with the same stars, the same birds, and the same trees. But our consciousness will change! Our perception of the world around us will change because we will be different inside. Nothing else needs to change, but need only continue naturally, guided by the Creator. The only difference will be that man will become a real Man, instead of the beast he is today.

This can be attained by studying in a special group, with the right books and guided by a real spiritual guide. It is written that the more a teacher's students understand what their teacher is required to do, the closer both students and teacher are to achieving perfection. That is what Baal HaSulam writes about; he describes how we should be in our corrected state.

First, we learn about the concatenation of the worlds, *Partzufim* and *Sefirot* from Above downward. Second, one must begin to climb the spiritual degrees that have been prepared in advance from below, in order to achieve correction while living in our world. Altogether, there are 125 degrees that separate us from the Creator and that we must ascend in the spiritual worlds. Those degrees are the phases of the attainment of the Creator.

In my current state I operate according to the understanding of my egoistic nature. I regard this or that thing as good or bad; I learn from my environment and act accordingly.

The more I connect with my surroundings, the freer I feel in this world, and I see that the world around us changes according to how we want to see it.

Every generation is characterized by its unique souls. We see how different each generation is by seeing how different our parents are from us. That is because souls accumulate more and more experience in every life cycle, and their demands increase, compared to the former generation. Because of that, each generation wants new discoveries, which induce even greater progress in every generation.

When we begin to question our spiritual world, we begin to want to move our environment and the entire world toward equivalence with the Creator. The last phase of this change will be that the world will attain absolute equivalence with the Creator. That generation is called "the last generation," not because there won't be anything afterwards, but because this generation will be the most perfect, one that needs no further correction.

Kabbalah does not speak about the evolution that will come after that; this part belongs to the secrets of Torah. The Torah (Kabbalah) speaks only about how to climb the 125 degrees of the attainment of the Creator.

On the one hand, our environment is the place where we keep the spiritual laws and change our surroundings. On the other hand, we can always change ourselves along with the environmental changes. Changes to our environment affect us in proportion to the number of people in that environment. For example, a group of students is both a place for correction and a source of power for each of its members. Even if someone is not strong and cannot contribute to the group at a given time, that member will still receive strength from the group towards self-correction.

That is why each person must build the right personal environment. In this way, one can receive forces for spiritual correction and can ascend after each descent. In a group that is not yet able to provide sufficient forces for correction, there will be many low-spirited people who haven't the strength for progress. In an able environment, though these situations do appear, they will not last.

Each degree consists of the following: "on the right" is the altruistic power of the Creator; "on the left" is the egoistic force of desire created by Him. In between there is the creature. Now the creature must take the right amount of forces from the right and left sides and use them to rise to the next degree.

The terms "right" and "left" are symbolic, as are all other Kabbalistic symbols, but we use them to help define characteristics of the Upper Worlds.

This process of right, left, and middle continues until the 125th degree. These degrees are divided into five worlds, with twenty-five inner degrees in each. The first spiritual world from the bottom, the one that is above us, is called the world of *Assiya*. Above it are the worlds of *Yetzira*,

Beria, Atzilut and finally *Adam Kadmon*. Our world is below the lowest degree of the world of *Assiya* and is separated from it by a barrier.

The powers of both "right" and "left" help us overcome difficulties in our passage from one degree to the next. When we begin to work against our egoism, we feel the power and desire to ascend. This is the first phase, the right side, that of the powers of the Creator.

The second phase is simply when we turn to the "left" and add more egoism to work with. Now, we are in a completely opposite state than in the "right": we are low-spirited, depressed, and weak. However, being on the "right" side depends on the Creator, not on us.

It is necessary to be on the "left" side so we will feel egoism, but the time we remain there depends solely on us. We can shorten it to the minimum.

The length of time that we'll feel bad depends on how long we remain in the "left line." If we understand that our present "bad" state comes only to correct our future, we will regard the situation as good, and we will experience any pain as a necessity and therefore good.

This is how our perception of good and bad will change: The group and the environment can help correct these feelings, because we can take spiritual forces from them until we, too, have entered the spiritual world. All creations are actually parts of the body of *Adam ha Rishon*, and only our uncorrected desires, or bodies, separate us from Him.

When egoism is removed, we can receive knowledge from other souls. We can feel them because everyone is willing to do whatever is needed for each other. A group must be built with only one goal in mind: to become a whole unit with a uniform spirit. An even level should be strictly kept among all members of the group. Everyone should be willing to help each other and mingle with one another at all times.

We actually receive a spiritual "charge" from our group to the extent that we are willing to nullify our own egos before each member and before the group as a whole. A lower may receive from the upper, but for that to happen, each member must regard the others as higher than himself.

The focus of the group should always be "the greatness of the Creator." That goal must dictate every move. When that happens, everyone will be able to receive the spiritual charge from the group and the descents will pass by smoothly.

Each degree of souls builds for itself the right environment for its degree. It all depends on the degree, meaning on the inner level of the souls.

A good group is a flexible one, enabling the principle of change to dominate it, even if that means constant changes that indicate its progress. Life, work, family, the physical life in the corporeal body, all must change according to the spirituality of the members of the group. That is what the Creator wants from us.

Our bodies will be in this world, while our souls will be in the spiritual world. The more frequently the soul performs spiritual activities, the better the physical body will accustom itself to spiritual laws. At the end of our spiritual development, family and group member relationships must be built according to the laws of the world of *Atzilut*.

Adam ha Rishon was deliberately made with its body-desire consisting of nine *Sefirot*, and the *Malchut* divided to a part that can absorb and adopt the properties of the upper nine *Sefirot*. These include the properties of the Creator, and a part that cannot adopt these properties, called "the stony heart."

Adam ha Rishon sinned hoping to receive the Light into *Malchut* from the upper nine *Sefirot* in order to bestow to the Creator. However, because *Malchut* was unable to acquire that property, that altruistic aim, he received the Light in order to receive. As a result, his soul disintegrated into 600,000 separate souls that cannot feel the complete soul that they comprised, or one another.

Each part of that soul is a will to receive pleasure. It is called "ego" and needs to be corrected. It is corrected by raising it by 125 degrees, meaning each correction is a correction of 1/125 in each of the 600,000 souls-desires. Each time a part goes from the right side to the left and returns to the middle, it takes the power of the Creator from the right, meaning the will to bestow, and acquires a will to receive from the left. The middle line is the summation: a will to receive in order to bestow.

One always gets sufficient power from Above with which to over-power the egoism of the left side, correcting the relevant egoistic part from working in order to receive to working in order to bestow. One gets only what one can take. If an individual does not get the strength from Above, a bad situation will not be sent to that person.

If a member of the group wishes to become more spiritual, that member must always be able to take from the group both spiritual power and egoism. For that reason, these two properties must always go hand in hand in the group.

A person who comes to Kabbalah is normally very egoistic and very independent. That person needs time to begin to want the Creator and understand the importance of the purpose of Creation. Only then can the ego begin to lessen before the group in order for one to both give to it and receive from it.

At first, there might be an unwillingness to contribute to the group, but the collective cause must obligate each member to do so. If everyone understands that there is nothing more important than the purpose of Creation, it will be easier for all to become beneficial to the group.

If one still cares more about worldly pleasures and cannot break free from them, it means that the time has not yet come for membership in the group. This person's soul isn't ready yet to take upon itself the spiritual laws. When one finishes all the pleasures of this world, then one is pushed to spirituality. There is no need to have every possible experience in this world before deciding one doesn't need them. This knowledge is attained by receiving proof from Above of the baseness of the beastly pleasure hunt.

What attracts us about spirituality is the relatively greater pleasure that we find in it, compared to the corporeal world. That is the reason we want it, and it is genuine. Our entire world exists and is nourished by only a tiny spark of spiritual Light that broke through the barrier and penetrated our world. Now, picture a spiritual world that is completely filled with Light, billions and billions of times greater than the spark of this world. Imagine what pleasures exist there!

But how do we get over there? We know that to do so, we need to alter our egoistic natures from a will to receive to a will to bestow. But what we don't understand is this will to bestow. I personally haven't the words to explain it. Our minds simply do not have the "curves" to help us perceive something like that, because our minds operate in an egoistic system.

Furthermore, we are told that it is enough to change the aim of the desire, not the desire itself, in order to obtain the pleasure. This means that we are discussing a completely psychological concept, yet we will receive pleasure anyway. So what is the difference, and for whom do I receive it?

This brings up the question of "Where is that valve I need to turn, in order to receive it?" The "valve" is in the border between the egoism of our world and the altruism of the spiritual world. It is called "the barrier."

When we cross the barrier, we have completed our preparations. Our emotions are now ripe for the spiritual world. In order to come to such a state, we need a group and perseverance in our studies.

We need our group to help us develop the necessary intensity of desire for spirituality. Then, there is an inner breakthrough and we begin to receive the spiritual power and knowledge from Above.

BOOKS

In every generation, the Creator sends special souls to this world whose goal is to rectify it and convey His Knowledge to humanity. It is said that, "The Creator saw that there were not enough sages, so He planted them in every generation." That is why there are leaders and spiritual guides in every generation who adapt the wisdom of Kabbalah to the unique properties of their time.

There have been hundreds of books written over the years on the subject of the wisdom of Kabbalah. These began with the very first book on the wisdom of Kabbalah, *Raziel HaMalaach* (*The Angel Raziel*), written by *Adam ha Rishon*, and the second book, *Sefer Yetzira* (*Book of Creation*), written by Abraham the Patriarch. However, the most popular book in the wisdom of Kabbalah is the *Book of Zohar*. It was written in the second century AD by Rabbi Shimon Bar-Yochay.

The contemporary Kabbalist, Rabbi Yehuda Ashlag (1884-1954) wrote a commentary on the *Zohar* and on all the writings of the Ari in a contemporary language so that we could understand it. Today, the souls that descend to our world are such that only the *Zohar* and the books of the Ari, with the commentaries of Baal HaSulam (Rabbi Yehuda Ashlag) and his own books, can help us enter the spiritual world.

The commentary of Rabbi Ashlag is called the *Sulam* (*Ladder*) commentary because when one studies the *Book of Zohar*, one ascends spiritually from below as if on a ladder. The commentary that Rabbi Ashlag wrote on the Ari's *Tree Of Life* is called *The Study of the Ten Sefirot*. In addition, Rabbi Ashlag wrote a great number of complementary books, including *Matan Torah* (*The Giving of the Torah*), *The Book of Introductions*, *Beit Shaar Hakavanot* (*Gatehouse of Intentions*), and others.

I recommend studying Kabbalah only according to the books of this great Kabbalist, because they are written in a simple and clear language, and offer insight to all the hidden knowledge of the *Zohar* and the sources that preceded it. I also recommend reading the books of Rabbi

Baruch Ashlag and the books that I published. I don't recommend reading other sources for fear the text will be misunderstood.

However, once a student acquires the basics of the wisdom of Kabbalah through studies in the books of Rabbi Ashlag, any available literature can be read on Kabbalah, because the reader will know if the book is spiritual or not. The content of the book will be clear, and true sources will easily be distinguished from the false.

The correct order of reading the books of Baal HaSulam is: *Matan Torah, Preface to the Book of Zohar, Inner Reflection* of the first part of *The Study of the Ten Sefirot, Preface to the wisdom of Kabbalah, Introduction to the Study of the Ten Sefirot.*

LANGUAGE OF KABBALISTIC TEXTS

Kabbalists normally wrote in Hebrew or in Aramaic, so it is very difficult to study Kabbalah without knowing Hebrew. The Hebrew language has a special meaning. Each word, a combination of letters or a form of writing, conceals spiritual knowledge that cannot be translated to another language. One can only understand the Hebrew words and sentences according to the degree of one's spiritual development. That is because understanding relates to one's equivalence of properties with the hidden meaning of the words.

It is impossible to convey that information with a simple translation to another language, but it is certainly possible to begin the study of the wisdom of Kabbalah in a foreign language. Only afterwards will Hebrew be needed, according to one's spiritual progress. Having said that, students will be able to feel the spiritual degrees they are undergoing and understand them even without a language. For, as it is said, "One's soul shall teach him."

Most major Kabbalah texts were written in Hebrew. A profound study of these texts does require a minimal knowledge of Hebrew. However, Kabbalah can be written in any language. The *Zohar*, for example, was written in Aramaic, which was the spoken language in ancient Persia two thousand years ago. Kabbalah speaks of emotions and experiences we undergo, and these can be explained in any language, or even without it, such as through music or other means.

Everyone learns languages: musicians must know a little Italian, doctors need some basic Latin, and computer personnel must know English. Each science has its own language. The language of Kabbalah is Hebrew, though it could have been explained in other languages, as well.

WHEN TO STUDY?

The Kabbalah is studied at night when others are normally asleep and there are no obstructions from their egoistic thoughts. The efforts to awaken the physical body and subdue it for the spiritual purpose are rewarded from Above, and students obtain altruistic properties.

Kabbalists behave according to their objectives: they either isolate themselves and remain in hiding, or expose themselves to everyone with wide publicity in order to attract students and raise the next generation of Kabbalists. In the latter case, they establish a group of students. Group study is much more beneficial than is individual study.

It is said in the Introduction to *The Study of the Ten Sefirot*, item 155, that there is Surrounding Light that shines around every person who studies Kabbalah, which purifies and prepares the soul to receive the Inner Light. The intensity of that Light depends on the intensity of one's desire to attain the text being read.

You may have noticed that when we are in a group, we begin to take interest in the things that interest the people around us, just as our appetites increase when we watch someone else eating. A person who sees friends studying Kabbalah becomes envious of them. This promotes the development of spiritual desires and increases the power of one's Surrounding Light.

In addition, if a number of people study together, it does not mean that they are simply sitting in the same room reading from the same book. They share the same desires and the same intentions, and an aspiration to break free from their egoism and relate to their friends as they do to themselves. In that case, their desires for spiritual development unite and extend an immense amount of Surrounding Light, which affects every one of them. That is why it is so much easier to obtain good results in a group than when alone.

THE STUDY METHOD

The study method should be based on group work, and at the same time emphasize individual work. Baal HaSulam and Rabash wrote a great deal about how we must be attentive to the thoughts and desires of our friends. If a friend asks a question during class, each of the participants must try and understand that thought. It is called *Hitkalelut* (mingling, mixing) of one with the other. This way, the entire group lives inside each of its members.

In order to come to that, we must lessen our own value in our eyes compared to that of our friends, so that we can collect others' thoughts, desires, and internal and spiritual properties. Thus, each of us will gain and enrich ourselves. It is inadvisable to speak of spiritual issues when not in class. If you do speak, you can explain spiritual processes in the language of Kabbalah: *Partzufim, Sefirot,* worlds, which Lights go where, etc. It is all a science, and all knowledge.

That knowledge can be explained because it doesn't impose anything on anyone. You can convey your understanding of Kabbalah to others, but not your inner feelings and desires. At first, one wants things like health and wealth from the study, promotion at work and so on. One thinks, "Perhaps Kabbalah will help me tell the future so I could win the lottery."

In short, we want to better our lives. We seek self-gratification in everything we do in this world; that is our nature. Even when someone commits suicide, they do it because they don't want to feel pain, meaning they seek to better their situation.

These considerations keep changing, but the most important thing is to understand why we do what we do.

THE COURSE OF DEVELOPMENT

When we are at a certain degree, we determine how we are relating to what fills our vessels (what we want), meaning which desires are pure (altruistic) and which are not (egoistic). It is this examination that determines our spiritual degrees. By doing so, we improve our inner properties.

We do not climb up or down any ladder of spiritual degrees; all that changes is the ratio between our corrected and uncorrected parts. That is what determines our degrees and levels of our spiritual development. In the physical sense, everyone remains the same, but inside, everything changes. It is inside that we rise from this world to the world of *Assiya, Yetzira* and up to the world of *Ein Sof.*

There are five holy (pure) worlds, meaning five degrees in the evolution of the vessel, the screen: *Shoresh, Aleph, Bet, Gimel,* and *Dalet.* It is written in the *Introduction to the Study of the Ten Sefirot* that if one learns by the right method and makes every effort with the right intent, the spiritual world can be attained in three to five years.

This means we can correct ourselves and begin our actual spiritual ascent according to our actual abilities. It doesn't mean we must stop all other activities. On the contrary, we must work, study, raise families, and experience the problems and difficulties that life poses. That is how we evolve.

We must only labor as much as we can. It is not as if we are demanded to do something that is beyond our abilities. Let us say that we need 6-7 hours of sleep a day. We work about 8 hours, waste about two hours getting back and forth from work, eat, bathe, and give time to our families.

This is not what the Kabbalah requires from us. Kabbalah requires the time that remains after all the necessary occupations have been carried out. If we invest all our free time in Kabbalah, that will certainly be enough.

The most important thing about studying is to dedicate two or three hours in the morning before we go to work to these endeavors. We take that time only from ourselves. These 2-3 hours are enough. It is important to learn with the right intention; ask ourselves why we do it. Aim is the single most important thing!

As we mentioned earlier, spirituality can be attained within three to five years. However, that process may also take six years or longer. In any case, attaining spirituality is a must, because if we don't do it in this life, then we will do it in the lifetimes to come.

We must think what we are living for—every effort we make in this work, every thought is added to the general accounting of our spiritual labors. When the amount of labor is sufficient, we receive a "push" from Above and enter the spiritual world.

DEMANDING REWARDS

Why do you need to study, work, live, and where will all this ultimately take me?

We should regard the Creator in our every act and always want Him and cleave to Him. We must constantly think and examine what He wants from us. That purpose should be right in front of us every single moment. If the goal is always clear, that will turn us into Kabbalists and we can begin to feel the knowledge from the spiritual worlds.

Learning more or less of the text is of little importance. We use the knowledge to connect with the material; the more we study, the greater our demand for the Creator becomes and the more intense the question: "Why have I still got nothing? Where is the result of my efforts? I have put in so many hours of work, lost a lot of money because I don't work when I learn, I don't give enough time to my family, I could have had more fun in other places..."All those arguments only increase our egoistic demand of the Creator: "Why have I still got nothing?"

For that reason, we must claim a reward for every minute, every second that we put into Kabbalah. We should not say: "I am here because I am an altruist." We can be altruistic elsewhere, but in Kabbalah we should be completely stingy. We must question every minute given to Kabbalah: "Why? What for?"

Only then will we focus directly on the goal. If we do not demand a reward for every minute, it means that we do not need the next minute, that we make no demands from our studies. If that is the case, we will be left empty-handed.

Examining the reasons for our actions every minute is our greatest asset. Our minds and bodies vehemently revolt against it. We would do anything: draw pictures, learn meticulously about the *Sefirot*, the worlds, write articles about Kabbalah, anything to escape examining the aim, the primary question of our connection with the Creator.

The entire egoism is in the exact point between man and the Creator. You will have to extinguish your egoism to the exact measure that you want to cleave to Him. The Creator can be felt only where egoism is extinguished. That sums up our entire work, and that is precisely what we are forbidden to speak of to one another. We are forbidden to speak of the intent, the reasons for what exactly it is that we demand of the study. However, we can talk as much as we want about the study—the *Partzufim*, the *Sefirot*.

It is not important if our friends know the material or not. Do not be afraid of being told something incorrect; it is meaningless. The important thing is that you learned a little, and mainly that you did it with a friend. Therefore, if someone asks you something, do give the answer. Don't be afraid of being wrong, because it's not important.

However, do not slight your knowledge. This knowledge is very important because the result of the study will be a unification of the experiences, the inner feelings, and the feeling of the text being studied. You will begin to understand what a screen is, a desire, a Light, pleasure; you will begin to see how Light enters and how it leaves and pushes, and you will begin to feel these actions inside you. That is why we have to learn, because in the end, the study, the inner work, and the feelings will unite to create one big experience.

But in the beginning, when your studies are disconnected from your feelings, it is meaningless if someone knows more or less than you, or is correct or not. However, when the study becomes something you feel, then it is forbidden to pass it onto others! You might convey knowledge, but never feelings and emotions.

On the whole, only general topics should be discussed. Problems that relate to one's aim are personal problems, not topics for discussion. My students come to me only if they are completely bewildered. But if they turn their questions to others, they harm themselves and they harm their friends.

Man is born a tiny egoist. After labor, there is a little creature made of sheer egoism lying in bed howling. At this stage, man is no different from any other young animal. He develops using his five senses, lives, attains things in this world, perhaps becomes a scientist, is happy, and needs nothing more than that.

There are, however, a few differences between humans and animals: man wants to become rich and gain power and control, honor and knowledge. One doesn't need the Creator to attain these things, but if permeated with a little root of the future spiritual vessel from Above, one begins to seek something with which to fill this vessel.

The Creator seemingly implants the idea of a little source of Light, or a little need for Light, which is in fact the same. Blood cannot fill the need for Light and neither can wealth or power or honor. That need and its fulfillment do not belong to this world, but to the spiritual world. In every degree there is a special desire and its fulfilling. If one is permeated with corporeal desires, these desires can be satisfied in this world. It is not important if the filling is great or small, the important thing is that the filling exists in this world.

If one is permeated with desires that are not from this world, then one begins to search. One can search anywhere with these desires and

THE PATH OF KABBALAH

still not satisfy them. There is no worldly satisfaction for this need. It is given from Above, and therefore it is from here that its satiation must come.

One occasionally succeeds in shutting this desire off and going into a coma, which is how most people live. But something still nags: what can one do?

If one cannot contain this desire inside, the search begins and the seeker will ultimately find Kabbalah. From the moment one begins to study Kabbalah, problems begin. It takes work to fill a desire with pleasure. Let us say that in order to gain a certain amount of money, one must work hard for a certain number of years.

But to achieve fame, one must add another 20-30 years. It all depends on the level one is seeking. Any achievement requires effort. The efforts that we make in our world, along with the pleasures and desires that await us in the future, all appear to be on the same line—the more I do, the closer I become to what I want to get.

Another month, another year, another ten years, it is not important. I am headed toward it, I can see the picture clearly, and I can even say when I will accomplish my goal.

In Kabbalah is also a desire, but for what? That is something we don't know. The pleasure is in a higher level than our own. It is like giving a certain animal a desire for knowledge. In fact, this is even closer than the desire we are given.

When we are permeated with spiritual desire, we don't realize the kinds of efforts we will need to make to realize it. We do not see the final outcome of that desire, and we cannot even see what we need it for. We may feel our souls' desire, but if asked what we want, we cannot quite say. We only know we feel bad because we cannot satisfy ourselves.

It gets even worse when we try to realize this desire and we immediately get the opposite result of what we'd hoped for. We don't see any connection between the efforts we make and the goal we want to attain.

Normally, the closer we come to the goal, the clearer we see it, but that is not the case in Kabbalah. Things that were once clear suddenly become confusing, a good nature suddenly turns into a bad temper and nothing seems certain anymore.

We think we are taking the right path and expect to receive greater things in return for the pleasures of this world that we relinquish. After all, if our desires are that great, so should be our pleasure. We agree to work more than we do for this world, but in the end we must still see what it is we will receive.

But Kabbalah works in the exact opposite manner. One constantly gets bad responses and becomes depressed. Although we may be originally optimistic that things will work out, they don't. Instead of finding one's destination in Kabbalah, one either completely vanishes, or the studies become insipid, confusing and strange.

This turmoil is necessary in order to go from the level of the desires of this world to the level of the desires of the spiritual world. Man must become completely detached from any self-interest in the outcome of his work; this is true altruism. That is why one must experience a phase of complete discrepancy between effort and results.

Man's corporeal egoism has now been instilled with spiritual egoism, a spark of Light inside his egoism. The egoism abides by different rules in the spiritual world. For spiritual egoism to be fulfilled, we must reject our current level of egoism and ascend, so to speak, to the level of that spiritual desire.

When we are given a spiritual desire, no other feeling exists besides the absence of pleasure; it is the vessel in its purest form. For that reason, all the operations, all the efforts are only possible with the help of the body. It is the body that awakens us early in the morning, takes us to bed only late at night, and encourages reading and the occupying of our minds.

We work with bodies that belong to this level and it is in this level that the body wants to be rewarded. It immediately begins to present a just and natural claim—"What have I got for all my trouble?" Perhaps one has advanced in the spiritual level, but that is not an answer for the corporeal body; it cannot feel it. For the time being, it cannot even feel anything of the spiritual desire that was given from Above.

The bottom line is that one works, progresses, learns, but feels no concrete results in the mind or in the soul. This naturally brings the body to a state of depression, perplexity, and a lack of justification or reasoning that will enable the seeker to continue.

SENSATIONS & EMOTIONS

When one comes to that point, pain and torment result. The pain is given deliberately; if one overcomes this, a greater closeness to the truth will come. Overcoming means that even under the most unbearable corporeal pain, one must try and find the contact with the Creator, the Source of everything, and the One who can fulfill us all. These painful situations are crucial. They can become turning points along the way. After all these immense efforts, we receive a real reward!

There is only one reward: the sensation of the truth. If one wants only that, and cares nothing of physical pains, or the fact that no spiritual rewards have yet manifested, and instead focuses on attaining a greater sensation of truth than before, that person can progress and finally become a Kabbalist.

The road will be a hard one, you can be sure of that. Work, family, something will always go wrong, a feeling that everything is bad and a future that holds no promise. That feeling is given from Above deliberately so we will try to overcome these situations through the group and the books. There are times when we do not need to read books, but simply be with our thoughts.

In those moments, it is most important to simply keep oneself on track. What the mind can't heal, time will. One must be very strict: "I cannot see a thing, I cannot hear a thing, I feel bad, but all that doesn't matter. I study like an automatic machine, but I do."

This effort will bear the greatest spiritual fruits. There are situations when we are revived, when the Light begins to shine a little and we understand that we have found a real answer, though from a distance. Then, as efforts are increased, rewards arrive. However, this is followed by depression, as there is nothing in the world that pleases us, while we possess nothing of the spiritual world, either. This seesaw continues back and forth.

We must understand that the reward that we get for our efforts in this world is the sensation of truth; it is not the pleasure we are used to receiving. That is how the Creator accustoms us to love the truth more than anything, to go forward until we want to reject the entire corporeal egoism in favor of the truth.

Then we can ascend to the degree from which we were given spiritual desire. From this moment on, we will begin to receive spiritual knowledge, pleasure, and satisfaction from that degree. We will become Kabbalists and be born into the spiritual world. Therefore, if we choose to sense the truth over corporeal reward, we will become Kabbalists.

We cannot control our thoughts; they are sent to us deliberately from Above. We can only try to react to them correctly. But what does reacting correctly really mean? A student came to me recently saying he did not know anything anymore, he could not see anything, he felt bad, hesitant, nothing was working out for him. He wanted me to calm him down, pat him on the head, and tell him that there was a shining Light in his future.

But I could not tell him anything about his future. Any answer in these situations is like stealing what one is being given from Above. I have no right to extinguish the desire in him; in fact, I am forbidden to even soothe his disappointment a little. Yet all this is good; it is necessary and desirable. The only recommendation I could give him was to keep doing what he was doing mechanically, as he was doing it when he was in the good situation.

One gets all kinds of thoughts when at home, at work, or with family. Sometimes these thoughts obstruct the work. When that happens, one must disconnect from the thoughts about the purpose of Creation.

When I asked my rabbi the same question, he replied: "You see, that is why I was a construction worker, then a cobbler, and always tried to be a simple worker. I would rise at 1:00 a.m. and begin to study Kabbalah before work. When I was a clerk for the government, the truth is that sometimes I would fall asleep at work and spoil a report that I was working on, but what could I do? I was offered executive offices, but I knew that in a higher office they would take away my mind and my soul. For that reason, I kept choosing jobs that kept me to myself, though I could have earned more money. I have been poor my whole life. I kept trying to find a job that would keep my mind clean on the one hand, and would secure my future on the other, a job that would give me the minimal wages."

We live in a world where it is sometimes very difficult to choose the kind of work we want to do. Besides, man is a creative creature who tries to find sparks of creativity in what he does.

Sometimes the understanding that we are occupied with unnecessary things is taken away from us and then returned, and we suddenly ask: "What was I thinking of?" But these situations are given on purpose, so that we will see our actual situation, our real nature and degree. We must see what we must detach from and where we should go. We should acknowledge the lack of our own strength and our need for a connection with the Creator in order to save ourselves.

You will probably forget everything I am saying now in just a little while because it can only be absorbed though personal experience. I only want to stress one point: if you learn by the right books, you will always be a step ahead, whatever happens. We are forbidden to know everything in advance, but we must remember this: I was told to read these books, that's it!

Our desires come from Above. If there is some spiritual effect of these desires, then we begin to feel the Upper Force of the Creator controlling us. We begin to feel the entire reality and the One Who controls it.

Sensations do not have a language. We just call them by names such as sour, bitter, pleasant, or unpleasant. We cannot clearly define each of these sensations. Similarly, we cannot compare the feelings of different individuals. That is the problem with psychology and psychiatry. We are unable to accurately measure what we feel, duplicate it, repeat it, and compare it between different people.

As we've already said, only routine and persistent work without caring for our inner feelings will produce spiritual results. Baal HaSulam writes a story about it in item 133 of the *Introduction to the Study of the Ten Sefirot*:

There was a king who wanted to choose his most loyal and loving subjects in order to surround himself with them. He sent messengers throughout his kingdom to declare that anyone who wanted to work inside his palace doing special work was to come to the palace.

Explanation: it is like a person who gets a certain desire to draw nearer to the Creator, though without understanding the essence of that desire. Thus begins the search. It can be said that everyone in the world asked himself at least once about the purpose of his life. The answer to that question is the attainment of the spiritual world, meaning the attainment of the Creator.

Going back to our story: **In order to find who really loved him, the king placed guards on the roads leading to the palace to deliberately confuse and mislead the people who came there. Their job was to scare them and explain to them that it was not worthwhile to work for the king. When the people heard about the possibility of working for the king, they immediately began to move toward the palace.** (This is like people who want to attain apparent greater pleasures, instead of the little or no pleasure they have today).

If there is nothing that can satisfy your new desire, it means you need greater pleasure. When that happens, you will be willing to make all kinds of efforts that you would not make to satisfy other desires, such as leaving a good office, or giving up future progress or wealth, in order to attain spirituality.

The guards rejected the people who came to the king's palace, but many still managed to come close to the palace and would not listen to the scary stories of the guards that it was not worthwhile to work for the king. Our egos convince us that it is not worthwhile to serve the Creator. The Creator does this on purpose, because this is how the new vessel is built, precisely through these inner problems and observations. This is very important, and that is why these things must not be discussed outwardly with others. Even the rabbi is forbidden to explain anything to students about these situations. The student must experience this on his own, inside, however difficult it may be.

The guards at the gate were even crueler. They would not let anyone approach the gate. They rudely rejected anyone who tried to come near. The truth is that in the last phases before the entrance to spirituality, one feels rougher and rougher rejections despite accumulated experience. But this experience does not disappear, it is not taken away. One falls once, twice, and a third time; it accumulates. After some time, one gets used to these falls and no longer regards them as unbearable, because the need for them has become clear. These situations even bring some joy because they also bring the feeling that there is truth in the experience.

Only the most persistent of all continued to try and approach the king. They retreated under the pressure of the cruel guards and then struck again, trying to approach the king. These attempts to reach the king, followed by retreats under the influence of the cruel guards that told them that it was not worthwhile to work in the king's palace, lasted many years. Finally, the people weakened and left.

Only the strongest among them whose patience endured (patience, not any knowledge or philosophies), kept trying and defeated the cruel guards, opened the gates, and were immediately honored with seeing the King Himself, who gave each of them his rightful office. That is precisely what Baal HaSulam writes: "**them, whose patience endured defeated,**" meaning those who kept studying patiently. Nothing else helps because this is the only way to accumulate experience in the physical body.

Everything that happens in our world is done especially for us; we have no control over what happens. However, we must always think that we can choose our future actions. Here is where we should say to ourselves that we do have the freedom to choose. After we rise to a higher degree, we see that, in fact, we had no freedom of choice whatsoever.

In other words, as long as we are in a state where we must choose between alternatives, we must resolve whatever problems we are facing alone, and not say that it is the Creator's job to do this, that it is His Problem, not mine. The problem was given to me by the Creator, true. Do we really have a choice in any of it or is it done because of properties that the Creator permeated in us, or by social influence? All that should not interest us now. We must see what is ahead of us and resolve the problems with the means at our disposal.

We should always try and work out our problems by ourselves, and only afterwards, regardless of the result, should we think that all this came to us from the Creator and that the resolution was preordained. The contrast between the beginning and the end creates great confusion in our feelings.

We cannot understand how to relate to all that because we are conditioned by concepts such as past, present, and future. As long as we are confined by the boundaries of this world, and as long as our consciousness works by the principle of cause and effect, we will not be able to understand what eternity is in our animate degree, where nothing ever changes. Thus, while we are in that state, we must behave as though we know nothing, as though we own the situations and must do everything by ourselves.

IF I AM NOT FOR ME, WHO IS FOR ME?

It is written: "If I am not for me, who is for me?" On the other hand, it says, "I do nothing and everything is done not by me but by the Creator." These sentences seem to contradict each other, but when we examine them closely we will see that they can and must exist under one roof.

The Baal Shem Tov, a great Kabbalist from the 18th century, wrote that one should get up in the morning and go to work as though there were no Creator and he were on his own, as though there were no One Above to help him. And although he believes in the Creator, he should say that the Creator doesn't affect his behavior. Meaning, he should say, "I am the master of my own future."

There can only be one master of the world—is it man, or the Creator? In a place where I can choose, I am also the master; the Creator is not in it. This is how we should operate during the day. But in the evening, when we come home with earnings in hand, we should never say that it was we who earned it and it was we who were fortunate. The Creator planned it all in advance, and even if we'd been lying all day long in bed, we'd still have everything we earned.

But our minds cannot understand this and unite these two apparently contradictory ideas. Only after attaining spiritual properties can we unite these two primary, yet contradicting concepts.

The next day we should do the same. The next day, meaning the next moment, when faced with a choice, we must relate to it the same way: "It all depends on me." After our choice is realized without expectations and faith in God, however it turned out, we must say: "It was all done by the Creator."

There must be a clear separation, as though these are two different people, one who believes and another who does not, before the decision and after it.

CHAPTER 4.2
THE BEGINNING OF A KABBALIST'S WAY

When I first came to Rabbi Baruch Ashlag, he sent me to study with Hillel, his senior disciple. Before that, I tried studying with many other teachers but never received explanations that satisfied me. However, I was very pleased with studying with Hillel, because his explanations made sense and were clear and rational. At first it all seemed very clear to me: I thought that all I had to do was memorize the six volumes of The Study of the Ten Sefirot and that would be enough to take part in the upper leadership of myself and the entire world.

Then came the time when Rabbi Ashlag summoned me to participate in his classes. From that moment, everything I thought I understood became completely incomprehensible. New questions came up and remained unanswered. Not only did studying with Rabbi Ashlag not help me understand the text, it led me to recognize the fact that I understood nothing to begin with.

It took me a long time to realize that Rabbi Ashlag first provided theoretical knowledge to his students and only afterwards instructed them on how to take part in leadership. Since the passage to active participation in the upper leadership is not a rational process, and each person must attain it alone, that situation created an atmosphere of complete misunderstanding.

The rabbi did not teach his students for the purpose of accumulating theoretical knowledge of the names of spiritual concepts, or for the purpose of philosophizing without understanding the nature of things. Instead, he wanted to bring his students to a state where they would *feel* these concepts. This is an entirely different method than a theoretical study. In that method, the purpose is not the quantity of knowledge that the student acquires, but its quality, meaning, the extent to which the things the student hears help him approach the things he reads about by himself.

The rabbi did not teach beginners. Instead, he would send them to other students and monitor their progress. Students who were willing and diligent were summoned to study with him.

The human desire to understand, manage, and control is a very positive desire, because it adds desires to one's original desires. However, the only key that we should really acquire to enter spirituality is the screen and the Returning Light.

Baal HaSulam wrote *The Study of the Ten Sefirot* deliberately so that the more one reads, the more questions arise. It is necessary for one to be able to labor in something while maintaining a certain aim. The labor comes from below, from man, but the aim is given from Above, from the Creator.

However, the aim does not come before one feels that every effort has been exhausted and there is nowhere else to turn, that one is completely cornered. Only then does one sincerely ask the Creator to help, and then this prayer is answered.

The most important thing in spiritual work is to maintain determination and patience. Our prayers are defined by the state we are in and depend on the presence or absence of the sparks. Before we attain spirituality, we think that the less we strain ourselves, the better. But after we attain spirituality, we regret having done so little to attain it.

The way to attain spirituality involves our making an act of restriction. But what does it mean to restrict? Weight-watchers, for example, are people interested in losing weight. They understand that the pleasure that they will derive from losing weight is greater than the pleasure they derive from the food. There are cases where the food actually becomes an enemy for them, to the point of real hatred. For Weight-watchers, maintaining a strict diet is about restricting the desire.

The most important factor in restricting something is the recognition of evil. That is why we are given the Torah. It contains within it that wondrous power that enables us to understand the enemies and the obstacles on our way to attain spirituality.

All of us must overcome many difficulties in life, to the point where we feel that there is no purpose to our work, as long as we do not understand where the truth is. As long as we do not make that restriction, we cannot even begin to know where the truth is. However, once we attain spirituality, we're in good hands, and no longer need the explanation because we can see everything for ourselves.

Before we receive the right aim from Above, we must labor in physical actions, even if for ourselves, hoping to change our situations. But the effort is not needed in and of itself, because the goal of Creation is pleasure, and effort means pain or the absence of something. If we could switch to the aim to bestow to the Creator, or receive spiritual pleasure without any effort, that would be wonderful. There is no necessity to look for hardship in our world.

However, if the effort is pleasurable, it stops being an effort. It is like a mother who feeds her baby and enjoys it. If the effort to think of the Creator was first laborious and false, suddenly it becomes enjoyable, vital and important. From the moment it becomes a pleasure, no effort is required. The effort is needed only to cross that spiritual barrier.

When we begin to practice spirituality, our work changes and we receive a different kind of reward, though people around us will not notice it. If, for example, spiritual music were to be performed by the best musicians, they would make it sound like any other music. People who do not practice spirituality might consider a spiritual composition less elevated than it is, placing it on the level of nice, but ordinary music.

CHAPTER 4.3
FROM A KABBALIST'S NOTEBOOK

My rabbi used to write everything he'd learned from his father. When I came to study with him I began to ask the questions that had been bothering me all along, but he kept avoiding answering me. And then one day he let me read a certain notebook so that I would find in it what was important and interesting to me. He added that these writings would support me for the rest of my life, even when he was gone, and that I would understand what I must understand when I read them.

The year was 1981; he gave me a notebook that I copied, then read it and used it for the next ten years. In 1991, a day before he passed away, he gave me the original manuscript. He said: read it, it's for you. He asked me to come earlier the next morning to help him put on his *Teffilin* (a portion of the Pentateuch written on a piece of parchment and put into special boxes that orthodox Jews put on their heads and arms every morning except on Saturday and on holidays). He knew what was going to happen in advance, but I did not, and when I arrived, it was too late. He was already semi-conscious and perished right before my eyes.

The essays and the writings that he'd given me are priceless. Every time I read them, I learn something new. My perception of the words grows deeper every time I read them, and my understanding of my inner state deepens.

These essays were written from the highest spiritual attainment possible. Any reader can find his or her own inner state, learn what must be done at any given moment, and discover what the author wanted to reveal at that very moment.

I recommend reading these essays or even a few lines of them every day before going to sleep. Rabash used to open the notebook for just a few seconds every night; that was enough for the expansion of the Light in the soul.

One of the deepest and most important articles of the rabbi is entitled, "There is None Else Beside Him." This article should be on the desk of every person who wants adherence with the Creator. It contains the entire teaching of Baal HaSulam, his approach to Creation, and everything one must always feel and keep in mind. This article is the first in the book, *Shamati*" (I heard) that I published after his demise.

"It is written that 'there is none else beside Him,' meaning that there is no other power in the world with the ability to do anything against Him. And what man sees, namely, that there are things in the world that deny the Household of Above, is because He wills it so.

And it is deemed a correction, called 'the left rejects and the right adducts,' meaning that which the left rejects is considered correction. This means that there are things in the world that from the beginning aim to divert a person from the right way, and divert him from holiness.

And the benefit from these rejections is that through them a person receives the need and complete desire for God to help him, since he sees that otherwise he is lost. Not only does he not progress in his work, but he sees that he regresses, and he lacks the strength to observe Torah and *Mitzvot* even if not *Lishma* (for Her name, for the name of the Torah). That only by genuinely overcoming all the obstacles, above reason, can he observe Torah and *Mitzvot*.

But he does not always have the strength to overcome above rea-son, that otherwise he is forced to deviate, God forbid, from the way of the Creator, and even from *Lo Lishma* (not for Her name). And he, who always feels that the shattered is greater than the whole, meaning that there are a lot more descents than ascents, and he does not see an end to these predicaments, and he will forever remain outside of holi-ness, for he sees that it is difficult for him to observe even as little as a jot, unless by overcoming above reason, but he is not always able to overcome. And what shall be the end of it all?"

Explanation: We can see from the beginning of this essay that the Creator is the sole Ruler of Creation. He created man with certain properties, gave him all the necessary forces, and placed him under the optimal circumstances for progress toward the purpose of Creation. But the Creator doesn't help us—quite the contrary. He confuses us with all kinds of entanglements: discharge from work, disease, domestic prob-lems, and a variety of failures.

Furthermore, He does it in concealment, without us knowing it is He Who stands behind all that. An individual must go though quite a long period of being treated that way by the Creator. One has no choice but to go through these trials to gain experience that will lead to eventual completeness, eternity, and adhesion with the Creator.

That time comes to its end when "**he reaches the decision that no one can help him but God Himself. This causes him to make a heart-felt demand of the Creator to open his eyes and heart, to bring him nearer to eternal adhesion with God.**"

The desire of the Creator is that when we ascend in the spiritual worlds, we will acquire all the properties of these worlds, become like the Creator in each and every world, and replace Him. However, this is impossible to accomplish without the help of the Creator. We are unable to do anything by ourselves. All the pains and troubles that we experi-ence happen because our properties-desires are opposite to those of the Creator, meaning they are opposite to the Light.

That oppositeness of form makes us see a reality that doesn't re-ally exist. It is only a consequence of the reflection of our level of ascent to the Upper Light. We only see our own properties. When the Light comes from Above, we do not feel it, but only our own corrupted properties. In order to feel the Light, we must first get rid of our egoism, the obstruction blocking us from the Light.

When one cries to the Creator for help, one suddenly finds "that all the rejections he had experienced had come from the Creator.

That means that the rejections he had experienced were not because he was at fault, for not having the ability to overcome, but because these rejections are for those who truly want to draw nearer to God. And in order for such a person not to be satisfied with only a little, namely, not to remain as a little child without knowledge, he receives help from Above so that he will not be able to say that "Thank God, I observe Torah and perform good deeds and what else could I ask for?"

And only if that person has a true desire will he receive help from Above. "And he is constantly shown how his faults in his present state; that is, he is sent thoughts and views, which work against his efforts. This is in order for him to see that he is not one with the Lord. And as much as he overcomes, he always sees how he is found in a position farther from holiness than others, who feel one with the Lord.

But he, on the other hand, always has his complaints and demands, and he cannot justify the behavior of the Creator, and how He behaves toward him. And it pains him that he is not one with the Lord, until he comes to feel that he has no part in holiness whatsoever.

And although he is occasionally awakened from Above, which momentarily revives him, but soon he falls into an abyss. However, this is what causes him to realize that only God can help and really draw him closer.

A man must always try and cleave to the Creator, namely, all his thoughts will be about Him. That is to say, that even if he is in the worst state from which there cannot be a greater descent, he should not leave His Domain, namely, think that there is another authority that prevents him from entering into holiness, and which has the power to either benefit or harm.

That is, he must not think that there is a matter of the power of the *Sitra Achra* (Other Side) that does not allow man to do good deeds and follow God's ways, but he should think that all is done by the Creator."

The Creator sends us troubles in order to bring us back to the purpose of Creation. Normally, if we are happy, we don't even care if the Creator exists, but it is precisely during the "good" situations that we must adhere to the Creator. That is why He sends us troubles, so that we will remember Him. If we feel bad, we are compelled to think of the Creator. Thus, our work is mainly to think of the Creator when we feel good, as well as when we feel bad.

Kabbalah speaks of man's most subtle feelings. We never expect the blow; it always comes unexpectedly when we are disconnected from the Creator. Providence operates individually on each and every one of us, even when we don't remember about Him. He sends us special messages to remind us of Him. That is why we are told that we must always aim our thoughts at the Creator. That is all that's needed.

"...he who says that there is another power in the world, namely shells, is in a state of "serving other gods." It is not necessarily the thought of heresy that is the sin, but if he thinks that there is another authority and Force apart from the Creator, by that he is committing a sin.

Furthermore, he who says that man has his own authority—meaning that he says that yesterday he himself did not want to follow God's ways, that, too, is considered to be committing the sin of heresy. It means that he does not believe that only the Creator leads the world."

There isn't even a single thought in us that does not come from the Creator. That is how it was predetermined in the design of Creation and there is nothing we can do to change it.

So who am I? "Self" is the one that feels what comes from Above. In the beginning, we are confused by the thoughts that come to us from Above. It is the result of the instilling of spirituality into our corporeality.

After some time, things begin to fall into place and take effect. One begins to understand that there actually cannot be any other way.

An ascent is one's consent with the Creator's actions. In that state, one feels complete, full and eternal, separated from the body and connected only with spirituality.

"But when he has committed a sin, and he must certainly regret it and be sorry for having committed it, but here, too, we should place the pain and sorrow in the right order: where does he place the cause of the sin? That is the point he should be sorry for.

And a man should then feel sorry and say: 'I committed that sin because the Creator hurled me down from holiness to a place of filth, to the lavatory, where the filth is.' That is to say, God gave him a desire and a craving to amuse himself and breathe air in a place of stench. (And you might say, as it says in the books, that sometimes a man incarnates in the body of a pig, that he receives a desire and craving to take livelihood from things he had already determined were litter, but now he again wants to revive himself in them).

And also, when a man feels he's in a state of ascent, and tastes some good flavor in the work, he must not say: 'Now I am in a state where I understand that it is worthwhile to worship God.' Rather, he should know that now the Lord has fancied him, and for that reason He draws him near, which is the reason why he tastes a good flavor in the work. And he should be careful never to leave the domain of holiness and say that there is another operating force besides the Creator.

(But this means that the matter of finding favor in the eyes of the Lord, or the opposite, does not depend on man himself, but everything depends on God. And man, with his external mind, cannot comprehend why now the Lord likes him, and later He does not.)

And likewise when he regrets that the Creator does not draw him near, he should also be careful not to be sorry for himself for having been distanced from the Creator, for by so doing he becomes a recipient for his own benefit, and he who receives is separated from the Creator. Rather he should regret his exile of Divinity, for inflicting sorrow upon Divinity.

One should take as an example when some small organ of a person is sore. The pain is still felt mainly in the heart and mind, which are the generality of man. And certainly the sensation of a single organ cannot resemble the sensation of a person's full stature, where most of the pain is felt.

Likewise is the pain that a person feels when he is detached from the Lord, since man is but a single organ of Divinity, for Divinity is the general soul of Israel. Therefore, the sensation of a single organ does not resemble the sensation of the general pain. Divinity regrets that there are parts of it that are detached from her, which she cannot provide for.

(And that might be the meaning of the words: "When a man regrets, Divinity says: 'It is lighter than my head'). And if man does not relate the sorrow at being distant from God to himself, he is saved from falling into the trap of the desire to receive for himself, which is the separation from holiness.

The same applies when one feels somewhat closer to holiness, when he is happy at having merited favor in the eyes of the Lord, he must say that the core of his joy is that now there is joy in Divinity, from having being able to bring her private organ near her, and not send it away.

And man rejoices at having been endowed with the ability to please Divinity. And this goes by the same token, because joy that an individual feels is but a part of the joy that the whole feels. And through these calculations he loses his individuality and avoids being trapped by the Other Side, which is the will to receive for himself.

Although the will to receive is necessary, since 'that is the whole man,' anything that exists in a person apart from the desire to receive is attributed to the Creator. Nevertheless, the will to receive pleasure should be corrected to a form of bestowal.

That is to say, the pleasure and joy taken by the will to receive should be intended to bring contentment Above, because there is plea-sure below. For that was the purpose of Creation, to benefit His cre-ations. And this is called the joy of Divinity Above.

For this reason, man must seek advice as to how he can cause contentment Above. And certainly, if he receives pleasure, contentment shall be felt Above. Therefore, he should long to always be in the King's palace, and to have the ability to play with the King's treasures. And that will certainly cause contentment Above. It follows that his entire longing should be for the sake of the Creator."

The Creator is benevolent to us, but we feel His Goodness as cruelty when it comes through our egoism. It is expressed in disease, stress, and other difficulties. We cannot be thankful to the Creator when we feel bad. If we only knew how bad the Creator feels, that His Benevolence is turned into the opposite, or how happy He is when we are happy, then we would operate entirely differently.

In other words: all our thoughts, all our actions, and anything that happens should always be directed at the Creator. That is the only way to exit the ego and attain spirituality.

CHAPTER 4.4
QUESTIONS & ANSWERS

THE STUDY

Question: Why do Kabbalists describe the Upper World for us?

Answer: They do this to help us begin to feel them. Man was created to feel the Upper Worlds and to feel the Creator. We, who cannot see the beginning of Creation, the reason for it, are unable to see its end and ultimate purpose. Therefore, we are also unable to understand the meaning of our lives.

If a researcher from another world were to examine a day-old lamb and a day-old child, he would determine that the human infant has very little prospect of evolving successfully, whereas the lamb, which can already walk and understand its surroundings, is certainly headed for a brighter future. The alien would assume that nature gave the lamb everything necessary for life and therefore it would evolve much more successfully than the infant.

That is what any alien would think of our world. It would reach this conclusion because it would not be able to see the final state, after the completion of the development of each species. It would miss the part when the human infant makes a breakthrough and reaches far beyond the evolution of the lamb. If we do not (as is our current situation) see the final goal, our purpose, if we stay confined to our own world, we will continue to believe that our lives begin and end in this world.

That is why Kabbalists repeatedly mention in every book that even if one does not understand what one is reading, but seemingly 'just' reads, by that one is still unconsciously extending the spiritual Light that surrounds us. That Light gradually purifies us and prepares us to feel spiritual powers. Then, at a certain moment, first unaware and then aware of it, one begins to feel the spiritual world and can see and understand the reasons for one's life and the evolution of the soul over the generations. In addition, one receives new spiritual powers in order to learn how to ask for additional spiritual powers from the Creator.

Q: Can anyone become a Kabbalist?

A: If a person studies with a spiritual teacher and with the right method of study, that person will eventually become a Kabbalist. We become the vessels over which we perform experiments, representing the model of the Creator that is the subject of our studies. We can feel spirituality to the extent that we equalize our forms with that of the Creator.

There are two phases to the spiritual progress: the first is the attainment of spirituality, a process called "the construction of the screen." The second indicates how to use that screen. In order to build and utilize these two formulas, one needs a teacher, a group, and the right books to study from.

Q: Psychiatrists believe that the sixth sense is a hallucination. Can you clarify that point?

A: All the stimuli that our senses receive come to our brain. They are processed by a fixed program imprinted in the brain, and the final outcome is expressed in our emotions and sensations. The brain can even send out signals based on past memories. If the mind begins to create imaginary feelings and hallucinations, then whether or not one is aware of it, it is a defect in the system, meaning a disease.

However, in the wisdom of Kabbalah, we feel our surroundings and at the same time can examine reality from the side, because we learn how to feel both ourselves and the origin of our feelings, meaning the Creator. It is a personal understanding; there is no one who can testify to its correctness or describe it accurately. But the wisdom of Kabbalah is the most practical science there is. All knowledge is acquired through experimentation.

Direct contact with the Creator is what enables us to see and understand the actual reality and the negligible part that we can perceive in the limitations of our world.

Q: So how can one see if one is wrong?

A: If one is in contact with a real Kabbalist, it will become evident that one's feelings are not founded on actual knowledge, a system, or a control mechanism, all of which are constituents forming the wisdom of Kabbalah.

The ability to study reality systematically, through scientific observation, and to assess the results with other Kabbalists who went through a similar process of revealing the concealed, plus the continuity and the scientific observation and experimentation, all these differentiate the wisdom of Kabbalah from mental disease and the hallucinations of mediums.

In the 19th century, humanity was looking for redemption in art. In the 20th century, it was power and scientific advancement. Today, people find that their lives depend on guidance from Above, and if they want to participate in the guidance, they must reach its roots in the Upper World.

We will begin to feel the need to understand the Upper Roots of life. Our own lives will compel us to seek redemption and the capability to affect the processes in the world. Mankind will find that it is impossible to exist without the ability to intervene in the Upper Guidance. Thus, the collective law of reality will compel us to evolve spiritually because it is our nature to be lazy and egoistic, and pain is the only way we can be motivated to act.

The wisdom of Kabbalah enables us to reduce or even avoid suffering and to be cured before we feel illness. The study of Kabbalah renders us with spiritual forces, understanding, and the ability to know what to do in this world. Thus, we are able to avoid problems, disease, and other trials.

Q: How can you explain the fact that despite the bliss and divine pleasures of Kabbalah, there isn't any "Kabbalah rush"?

A: The fact that the coarsest souls descend to our world in this generation does not necessarily imply that they are aware of what they need for their correction. Every generation consists of layers of all the souls in previous generations. This is the reason the public is still passive.

An ordinary person does not want to live in dreams about the future because the body only feels the present. The ordinary person aspires for no more than animate pleasures. No one is in a hurry to take on the laborious work of spiritual correction. However, if one realizes that this is the only way to redemption, it will be impossible to abandon the study of Kabbalah.

Even if humanity does find someday that there is a means to attain spirituality, everyone will relate to it differently, depending on his or her kind of soul. Some will begin to take an occasional interest, some will begin to learn on their own, some will study with Kabbalists every now and again, and some will even study regularly. But only a few will devote themselves to the study of the wisdom of Kabbalah because their souls demand it.

Ultimately, it makes no difference which route we take: the important thing is that each and every one of us must know that it exists, that it is available, and that we are aware of its purpose.

Kabbalah appeals to a wide variety of people: there are many who seek blessings from the wise, some study the Torah as history, and some look for secrets in the letters, like treasure hunters. But within the wisdom of Kabbalah are people who are closer to the center, to the desire to cleave to the Creator, and there are others who are farther from that goal.

The latter kind studies Kabbalah like a science and seeks knowledge within its pages. It is like the circular ripples that form around a stone thrown in the water. Anyone who hears about the wisdom of Kabbalah will find a unique approach to it, in a position that matches the desire of one's soul for correction. Those who have not come to Kabbalah yet, have not come to it because their time hasn't come.

Q: Is it okay for adolescents to take Kabbalah classes?

A: Yes. I recommend the articles from the book, *Matan Torah* (*The Revelation of Godliness*).

Q: What is our attainment based on?

A: Our attainment is based on sensations, contact! This is the best way to research the goal of attaining spirituality in our world. That is because all our senses are expressed in the sense of touch. The other senses—sight, sound, smell, and taste—are incomplete and are a consequence of the *Bitush* (beating) of the Surrounding Light against the screen.

This beating results in the five vessels of the *Partzuf*: Moach, Atzamot, Gidin, Bassar and Or, which are (respectively) *Keter, Hochma, Bina, ZA,* and *Malchut,* uniting within a single vessel, meaning one attainment of the Light. When the Direct Light comes straight from Above downward, from the degree of *Keter* (*Moach*), through the degree of *Malchut* (*Or*), it strikes the screen and raises Returning Light back to the degree of *Keter*. That means that if the Light reaches the degree of *Or*, all the

Sefirot in the *Partzuf* become one, resulting in all the senses being filled with Light as well as information.

Because the other senses operate from a distance, as opposed to the sense of touch, they are not filled with the entire amount of knowledge, and are therefore not completely real and do not reach all the way to *Malchut*.

Q: Can one be forced to study Kabbalah?

A: There is a spiritual law that states, "There is no coercion in spirituality." Any kind of coercion, or even a command, that might rob someone, directly or indirectly, of one's freedom of choice, is wrong. Coercion robs us of the most important thing the Creator gave us—free will. It is by choice that we will understand our essence and draw near to Him by correcting it. Therefore, coercion is against the true nature of Creation.

Q: During our studies, we sometimes encounter situations when we have no answers to the most essential questions, but at the same time are unable to formulate any questions. Why does that happen?

A: It happens when one does not feel the text from within, when it has not yet been discovered by one's senses. In these cases, one does not respond to what one hears.

Q: What is the difference between knowledge and faith?

A: The only thing we need in this world is faith. Faith is the sensation of clearly feeling the Creator.

Knowledge is something that appears to be outside faith for someone who is still unable to feel the Creator. For that reason, knowledge is a limited vision of the world, whereas faith is complete. When one refuses to take the path of knowledge and uses only one's egoistic vessels, one begins to feel spirituality, and that feeling is called faith.

Q: **What can you say about a person who wants to study Kabbalah, but whose course in life is quite ordinary?**

A: It means that the person has been chosen from Above. It can also be the consequence of pains suffered during former cycles of existence.

LETTERS & LANGUAGE

Q: **Are there letters and words to express our feelings?**

A: We have to have some means of expressing our feelings, so for that purpose we have a certain code, a language. We can use it any way we like. The world of *Ein Sof* is described using only four letters *Yod* (י), *Hey* (ה), *Vav* (ו), *Hey* (ה). These letters are the four *Behinot* (phases): *Aleph*, *Bet*, *Gimel*, and *Dalet*. Over the course of their descent to our world, they unite and form letters, and words and their combinations, until they become an entire language in our world.

Q: **Is there any power to the letters?**

A: All the words were built by forces that are marked by letters. However, we cannot say that the letters have any power of their own. It would be more correct to say that the letters *symbolize* power.

All the fundamental forces, the properties with which the world was created, are marked by the twenty-seven letters of the Hebrew alphabet (twenty-two basic letters and five final letters). Each power has its own unique attribute, and when these join together they form the active force of reality. In the essay about the letters in the *Zohar* is an elaborate explanation of the combination of two Lights, the two properties—*Hesed* and *Hochma*.

In other words, the consequence will be the same; there is no contradiction. Everything begins with the letter *Yod* (י), because that is the point from which all the letters are drawn, and in fact, any drawing begins with the letter, *Yod*.

Q: **Is Kabbalah the only way to attain the Creator, and if so, does that mean that everyone must learn Hebrew?**

A: It doesn't matter which language one speaks as long as one wants to attain the Creator by correcting oneself through equalizing with His Properties. The knowledge one receives does not come in words, and yet is completely understood because it penetrates all the senses and the consciousness. That knowledge is spiritual, and is how Kabbalists communicate information among themselves.

THE DAILY ROUTINE

Q: Do Kabbalists live ordinary lives?

A: The wisdom of Kabbalah necessitates that every person take an active part in this world: work, raise a family, learn and teach. In addition to the normal routine, one must also attain the purpose of Creation—a spiritual contact with the Creator. The Creator created this world and everything in it precisely as it is to assist us in learning how to reach His spiritual degree based on the existing reality. That is why the wisdom of Kabbalah does not rely on fasting, abstention, or deprivation of any sort. There is no coercion and no punishments in this world or in the next.

My teacher, and I as his successor, do not take students who wish to pay us for study, instead of working. The wisdom of Kabbalah does not support that form of study. Such a phenomenon arose during the time of the exile when people refrained from working, and rich Jews supported the poor so that they could study Torah.

Rabbi Yehuda Ashlag (Baal HaSulam) sent his children to work right after they finished their formal studies (around the age of eighteen). My rabbi worked many years as a construction worker and in road works and other hard labors. The purpose of Creation is to mold it to resemble the Creator in its properties. It is therefore obvious that in the external sense, nothing is going to change and we will continue to work both physically and mentally.

Q: Every now and again we run into questions that concern the right way to bring up our children. How does Kabbalah regard this matter?

A: There are many ways to educate in our world, but none of them is perfect because twenty or thirty years pass before we see their consequences. In most cases, it is then too late to change patterns of behavior. The entire process of education in Kabbalah is based on the transformation of the system for each person passively, without pressure. At the same time, we continuously give extensive explanations about the system and the benefits offered by spirituality.

It is essential to emphasize that this system leads to proper behavior and enables us to see the consequences of actions beforehand, thus preventing wrongdoing. We can only lead our children to understand what Kabbalah is by personal example; this is the only way we can teach them what they can attain should they want to study it. The choice to study or not study is theirs alone.

THOUGHTS

Q: How do our thoughts affect our environment?

A: Contemporary science finds that the will of the experimenter affects the results of the research. Among other things, astrophysicists have begun to internalize the idea that the entire universe is, in fact, a single thought. That stems from the fact that the Creator did not create anything but the egoistic desire to receive and feel His Light, which is felt as pleasure. The Light itself fills the entire reality evenly. The way one feels this reality depends only on the desire itself, just as a hungry person will find the most wonderful flavors in a mere slice of bread, whereas a satiated person will not be impressed with even a banquet fit for kings.

There are many implications to our subjective approaches towards certain subjects. For example, if we look at a cup of juice from an egoistic perspective, the pleasure embedded in the cup bears an egoistic nature because we use it to soothe our thirst. But if we understand that the juice only gives us a limited amount of pleasure, which was actually given to us so that we could receive it for the Creator, this awareness turns the egoistic pleasure to a spiritual one. The Light of the Creator would be expressed in a corporeal object.

And so it is with everything in our world: if we regard everything through corrected desires, we will be able to see the spiritual objects around us reflected in corporeal objects of this world.

This ability depends solely on man himself; if his egoistic properties have been corrected only as far as the world of *Assiya*, he will only be able to see the world of *Assiya* reflected in the world around him. If he has corrected his selfish desires to the degree of the world of *Yetzira*, he will also be able to see it reflect in our world, and so on. In the end, one begins to see and feel all the spiritual worlds like round spheres, with ourselves in the middle. Outside the system there is the Source, the Creator.

That is why it is said that all the worlds were created for man and all the worlds are inside man. Outside us there is only the Creator. We cannot feel anything outside ourselves, only what is inside us, meaning our own reactions to the activities of the Creator around us. We refer to these reactions as "worlds." Thus, worlds are actually degrees of sensation of the Creator.

We call "this world" or "Our world" a state where we have no feeling of the Creator as a Source, but only see His material reflection. That sensation of the Creator is the most distant and detached from spirituality. There are five degrees of sensation of the Creator, or five worlds. They begin with our world—the zero degree—and end in our complete attainment of the Creator in the world of *Ein Sof*.

The only way for us to feel anything outside us is to equalize in form with it, as with the example of a radio receiver. Hence, the degree of our sensing the Creator testifies to the degree of our equivalence of form with the Light.

If we feel our environment only through the senses we received at birth, that sensation is called "this world." If we succeed in changing, correcting our desires to match those of the Creator, we begin to feel Him to the extent of our correction. The measure of that sensation is called "one's spiritual world," or "one's spiritual degree."

Part Five: Religion, Prejudice and Kabbalah

CHAPTER 5.1
A RELIGION OR A SCIENCE?

Kabbalah is often associated with tradition and even with religion. In most cases, this is a result of the difficulty in finding logic in the old customs and the various prohibitions in the Mitzvot (commandments). It is a difficulty expressed directly or indirectly by antagonism toward religion. This is the reason for the important need to clearly distinguish between Kabbalah and religion.

Every religion relies on a certain prophet, a person who was connected with spirituality and circulated his knowledge among people. This argument is at the basis of every religion, meaning that everything begins with the sublime truth, the revelation of the Creator before the prophet, who was the founder, be it Judaism or any other religion.

The wisdom of Kabbalah is a method to attain the Creator that is available for all. It allows any person to come without any mediators and to reach a spiritual contact with the Creator. People who have reached spiritual attainment described how they did this step by step so that others might follow them to a similar conclusion. One's spiritual connection with the Creator is based on one's own discovery of Him.

Though the wisdom of Kabbalah does not deal directly with studying this world, it is still the basis of every science in our world. The study of Kabbalah gives one the ability to see how spiritual forces find their expression in this world, how they climb up and down, to and from our world with a variety of forms we call, "phenomena" and physical, chemical, and biological processes, as well as moral and other processes.

Because we are unable to learn all those processes as one collective, we study them as separate, specific sciences. Nevertheless, everything is connected and dependent on every other force and element of nature.

After all, the subject matter is one, and we just separate the research into pieces to make it easier on us.

The wisdom of Kabbalah ties all these phenomena of spirit and matter together. This means that from the point of view of Kabbalah, music, astronomy, biology, and medicine externally express a unique law of the inner makings of nature. A Kabbalist who feels the Upper World finds that there is only one law, expressed in many different ways in our world.

The wisdom of Kabbalah contains every necessary component of every science: it consists of researches, records of the results of experiments, continuity and consistency, repetition of the experiments, and accumulation of data. It is a science that deals with the study of the universe, the study of the reality we live in. It is a science that studies nature's only law. Today, we are capable of perceiving only a negligible part of the collective law of reality in the degree of our world. We call that negligible part, "this world."

CHAPTER 5.2
KABBALAH IN OUR LIVES

During the 6,000 years of their existence, souls descend to our world in a certain order and clothe the physical bodies of our world, which is the lowest degree of Creation in the universe. There is a clear and accurate order of the descent of the souls, from the finest with the least amount of egoism, to the coarsest, most egoistic souls.

The first souls to descend are those with the least amount of egoism, whose mere existence in this world is enough to correct them, and they do not need any external influence to guide them. After that, souls begin to come with a need for a guidebook, which we know of as "the written Torah."

Although we have received the four parts of the Torah with their entire spiritual scope, including the wisdom of Kabbalah, over the years it has been used in many ways. At the same time, varying circumstances were organized from Above to keep the *Mitzvot*. For example, the ruin of the temple eliminated the possibility of keeping many of the *Mitzvot* that are connected with the temple and the land.

Although the souls that come to our world grow coarser and need further correction, the number of practical *Mitzvot* decreases. That is because these souls cannot be corrected by merely performing *Mitzvot*. These souls need a special guide to the wisdom of Kabbalah, because this is their final correction. These are souls that were purer in the past, but have sunk deeper and deeper into egoism over the cycles.

Therefore, the last correction should result in an exit from this world into the spiritual world. This is only possible with the help of changing our internal properties from egoism to altruism, not by any mechanical acts.

It is said: "A *Mitzva* without an aim is like a body without a soul." It is only the aim that determines the value of the action. A mere mechanical act, an aimless one, is also a lifeless one. It does not produce any spiritual influence and brings no result.

However, observing *Mitzvot* mechanically is still necessary for the (Jewish) collective because it preserves their identities from generation to generation, and prepares souls for their personal correction in one of the future cycles, for the realization of the aim *Lishma* (for Her name).

Keeping the *Mitzvot* in the physical body purifies the spiritual "still" of man. Man's soul consists of four parts of Creation; these correlate to the name of the Creator: still, vegetative, animate, and speaking. A person who keeps *Mitzvot* physically is turned from an "ordinary still" into a "holy still." We mustn't underestimate the level of this spiritual degree. It is that which keeps the Jews a nation.

A person in that degree is in the first degree of correction, though unaware of it. This person does not feel the spiritual world, just as a stone cannot feel spirituality. Rabbi Zidichev wrote in his book about the verse in Psalms 34, 15: "Depart from evil, and do good." This means that without understanding the wisdom of Kabbalah, man is like an animal, keeping the *Mitzvot* automatically, just like an animal eats its food. Even if he is proficient in every detail of the *Mitzvot*, he must still give some time to study the Kabbalah, the core of the Torah, for without it, one is no better than an animal.

Just as everything comes from the ground, so from this degree it is possible to attain higher degrees. That is why Kabbalists do not object to keeping *Mitzvot* in the physical body, but maintain that it must be accompanied by a spiritual intent, an aim that gives one the ticket to the spiritual world. However, it is only according to one's altruistic aim that one can rise to higher degrees in the spiritual worlds.

Although we have received the entire Torah, its hidden part, the *Zohar*, which was written at the time of the Talmud, was only discovered in recent generations. The Talmud was necessary to keep *Mitzvot* and was therefore immediately publicized, whereas the *Zohar*, because it was not necessary to the public, was concealed by the Kabbalists until they decided it was time to disclose it.

Because souls of a different kind descend to our world in every generation, they also require a different kind of leader to correct their souls. The Creator sends a number of Kabbalists in every generation. By being simultaneously in this world and in the spiritual world, they can create the necessary conditions for the correction of the souls of that generation.

That is the reason for the coming of the soul of the Holy Ari, the great Kabbalist of the 16th century, to our world. He was the Kabbalist who wrote the contemporary interpretation of the *Zohar*, thus creating a solid foundation for a clear and understandable study of the Kabbalah for every person. Rabbi Yeshaiahu Halevy Ish-Horovitz (known as the Holy Shlah) said of the books of the Ari, that their appearance is tantamount to the giving of the Torah to the nation of Israel.

Rabbi Avraham Azulai writes in his book, *Ohr Chaim* (*Light of Life*), that "The concealment of the wisdom of Kabbalah from Above so that not everyone could practice it, was done for only a limited period of time, until the year 5330 (1570 by the Gregorian calendar). But since that year, the concealment has been lifted and it is permitted for everyone to study the *Zohar*."

It also says that "only if the masses study the wisdom of Kabbalah will the Messiah come, and not as a result of anything else, as others think..."

The *Zohar* itself mentions more than once that only the lessened value that we ascribe to the study is the cause of all our anguish and that of the last generation. It also says that this is the reason for our spiritual exile. However, the truth is that the only reason we suffer is that we are not correcting ourselves through the wisdom of Kabbalah; that is why we are marching on the path of pain.

CHAPTER 5.3
UPROOTING PREJUDICE

Nothing is created in vain in this world. Everything is created in order for us to attain the purpose of Creation. The true picture of the world is one of completeness and fullness, with nothing that is redundant, not even a single thought or operation.

Everyone is doing precisely what he or she is meant to be doing, and at the same time people are realizing the purpose of Creation. The vast majority does it unconsciously, but a few do it consciously, after making a free choice between their egoistic and altruistic activities, having decided in favor of the latter. The task at hand is to reach an agreement with the design of Creation and carry it out consciously and willingly. We shall all come to that over the course of our reincarnations.

If we could be aware of our previous lives and the possible combinations of souls and their divisions, we could calculate for ourselves the right combination of the parts of the collective soul—what the ratio should be and which parts they should be combined with in order to correct them. We would see and understand the reason for everything that happens.

Kabbalists see the collective picture either fully or partially. For example, the Ari explains about reincarnation in his book, *Shaar Hagil-gulim* (*The Gate of Reincarnations*). He not only saw the entire picture of the cycle of correction of souls, but was also given permission to describe it. The only sign by which it is possible to determine if one is permitted to study Kabbalah is the genuine desire for spirituality.

Studying the Kabbalah is not meant to be used for any magic or witchcraft; it is also not intended to turn one into a great rabbi or sage. Its purpose is to promote one's spiritual development and attain the Upper Worlds through hard labor. The consequences of our efforts will be measured by our ability to dedicate our every ambition to bestowal upon the Creator.

When speaking of physical performance of *Mitzvot*, it is important to mention that it can only be performed in this world, because that is where we perform physical acts without a spiritual intent, without any intent. *Mitzvot* with a spiritual aim mean *Zivug* with the Upper Light—spiritual reception of Lights into one's altruistic vessels. These operate in order to bring contentment to the Creator. Only a Kabbalist can reach that, and hence the name Kabbalist—one who can receive (in Hebrew, Kabbalah means "reception") the Upper Light.

Therefore, it is the duty of every individual to realize that the true performance of *Mitzvot* is the spiritual performance. That is our real objective. Those who settle for a mechanical observation of *Mitzvot* correct themselves only on the level at which they exist, meaning the level of our world. For that reason such a person is called "holy still"—"still" because this person has no desire for spiritual development, and "holy" because he or she still performs the *Mitzvot*, even if with egoistic intentions, under the limitations of this world.

Because such people still follow the Creator's Will, Kabbalists never object to the keeping of corporeal *Mitzvot*, but only emphasize that mere physical performance is not enough to attain the purpose of Creation.

Furthermore, certain spiritual acts should be performed in order to assist our ability to receive the Upper Light. These are called "the commandments of the Creator." But here arises a problem: one is capable of performing only those operations that may yield personal gain. If the reward for efforts made is uncertain, the ego will not allow even the slightest effort to be made.

The widespread objection to the wisdom of Kabbalah is because it argues that people may perform the *Mitzvot* in an incomplete manner. Therefore, dissenters claim that Kabbalists object to keeping the *Mitzvot*, when in fact Kabbalists claim that they should indeed be kept, not merely on the physical level, but with proper intent.

Kabbalists say just one thing: "Start learning of the wisdom of Kabbalah!" Through the study of the soul of the Torah you will begin to understand what is essential for us, and why we were created.

CHAPTER 5.4
QUESTIONS & ANSWERS

KABBALAH & SCIENCE

Question: Are there certain habits or customs around studying the wisdom of Kabbalah?

Answer: The wisdom of Kabbalah does not require practicing any customs or rituals. Drawings or pictures of the worlds, *Sefirot*, or Gimatria, are simply visual aids. The essence of the wisdom of Kabbalah is the individual experience of the Creator and the spiritual world.

The wisdom of Kabbalah is not mysticism. It is a science that explores the entire reality, unlike every other science that explores only our world.

Q: Does modern science accept this perspective?

A: A science that studies the senses, including the theory of relativity, maintains that everything perceived by our senses is only valid regarding ourselves. But our picture of the world is relative because the concepts of time and space do not exist, as they, too, are relative. If these terms were not already within us, we would perceive them differently.

We might say that man is like the black box in a plane. It is a closed system. We only perceive what reaches this box, what we feel and sense. We call this combination of sensations "Our world," or "This world," or simply, "the world."

We cannot perceive anything that might or might not exist outside our borders, outside this box. We cannot even imagine that there is anything outside it, (meaning outside our senses).

Q: But is there reliable knowledge as far as Kabbalah is concerned?

A: Of course, but that is not all. Kabbalah not only gives us reliable knowledge of the construction of all the worlds and their laws, the history of mankind and phenomena we cannot even begin to imagine, but also allows us to put this knowledge into practical use. It is written in the Torah that "There is not a blade of grass below that has not an angel above." This means that everything in our world has a spiritual root. If we understand these laws and how the spiritual worlds are built, we can influence what happens in our world.

This knowledge requires a deep perception of knowledge, but without it we cannot accurately define what we need. Without this, we would lack a certain kind of information that we are seeking.

Q: Scientists maintain that the world has existed longer than just a few thousand years. What does Kabbalah has to say about it?

A: Kabbalah does not say otherwise. I have written in my book (*Interview with the Future*) about global warming and cooling periods that lasted thirty million years each, and Baal HaSulam did the same in his essay *The Solution*.

Q: How does Kabbalah relate to the "Big Bang" theory?

A: In the 16th century, the great Kabbalist, the holy Ari, wrote in *The Tree of Life*: "Behold, that before the emanations were emanated and the creatures were created, the Upper Simple Light had filled the whole existence. And there was no vacancy, such as an empty atmosphere, a hollow, or a pit, but all was filled with simple, boundless Light." Thus, the "Big Bang" theory was known to Kabbalists long before the astrophysicists learned about it.

Q: Will science understand the sixth sense in the future?

A: While in his five senses, one is completely limited in his feelings—unable even to simply picture that there might be another sense. Man will never be able to imagine it, much less create it, because he will never feel a desire for something that is not already in him, just as we never feel the need for a sixth finger on our hand.

That is why all the tools man builds and all the research systems only enhance our existing senses but under no circumstances will they yield new ones. Our sensory organs provide us with everything we need for that purpose, and other sensory organs would require another Creation. We are limited by the physical boundaries of our Creation, hence we could never picture what exactly we are missing.

Regardless of how advanced our technology, we will still be unable to break the boundaries of our Creation. Our five sensory organs create a clear framework of understanding, and because our fantasies are, in fact, the figment of our imaginations, it is based on those five senses.

If I ask you, for example, to describe something that is like nothing that exists in our world, as if I were a creature from another world, you would still comprise it from elements that exist in our world.

Though our space is only a substance we can feel in a certain manner, there are other worlds and other creatures that we cannot feel, although they exist in the same dimension we do. I am deliberately using the term "dimension," in our limited understanding, to demonstrate how incapable we are of feeling what our sensory organs are not meant to understand.

In fact, even the word, "dimension," is meaningless. In a different sensation the dimension also becomes something completely different.

For example, try to imagine what we would see instead of the ordinary universe if we could see with X-ray eyes. This demonstrates what a drastic change a single alteration in our senses can produce on our picture of the world.

Q: You always write that it is time that the wisdom of Kabbalah became known to everyone. Why is it that you are now so preoccupied with it, and isn't there a danger that every person who discovers the wisdom of Kabbalah will misuse it?

A: Kabbalah is a science, but it is not a science for the experts alone. Anyone can utilize it just as we utilize the results of every other science. The difference between Kabbalah and science is that everyone needs the Kabbalah. If one does not practice this science, one does not receive from life its single most important asset, the one thing that will remain forever. Everyone must know that science and the Source of the power of that knowledge. They must know just how able Kabbalah is to change our concepts of the construction of the world, man's purpose on earth, the evolution of the creatures and man's unique role in it.

Kabbalah renders a complete and fundamental knowledge of the world. The goal of the Kabbalists is to bring as many people as possible into Kabbalah, because if humanity continues to follow erroneous and experimental roads, and keeps fumbling in the dark, it is headed toward horrendous disasters.

When a child puts its finger in the fire he cries bitterly in pain. He or she immediately feels that this is something that should not be done. But in the end the burning heals. By the same token, it is not necessary that we burn our planet in order to understand that it was not worthwhile to put our finger in the fire.

Humanity was created in such a way that it would come to know the Kabbalah as a science and not through experimentation. Kabbalah reveals before us the fact that there are forces and connections in nature and which consequences each act yields.

HUMANITY

Q: When will mankind be able to understand the uniqueness of Kabbalah?

A: Humanity is always pushed forward by disillusionment. Any technological, medical, or other kind of progress is made when humanity is disappointed with past methods. When a certain amount of anguish is accumulated, mankind is forced to understand that the existing methods cannot be a solution to any problem.

Let us take an example from our own lives: over the past several decades, the number of psychoanalysts has increased many times over, but the number of patients has increased even more, and so has the number of suicides. This combination is like a new trend that will soon pass, giving way to bitter disillusionment.

We are trying to prepare for that time by developing various methods for those who are already aware, or will soon be aware, of the necessity for Kabbalah. They should have enough material to enable them to change themselves through it. Anyone who marches on the right path should help those along the way and prevent them from taking dead-end roads. This can be done by circulating books, audios, video files, and cassettes.

Those who are truly interested should be referred to Kabbalah. It is important not to force or compel anyone to study Kabbalah, because people must first ripen for it.

JUDAISM

Q: What kind of connection exists between Kabbalah and the role of the Jews in realizing the goal you described?

A: There is a pyramid-like division in this world: still, vegetative, animate, and speaking. The same division also exists in our souls. The Jews are considered to be the chosen people because they were given the opportunity to reach spirituality before other nations. It is not that Jews are any better than others; it is simply that they are the first of mankind to be obligated to correct themselves and attain the spiritual world. There is a certain type of soul called "Jewish," from the Hebrew word *Yehudi*–meaning "unique," or "unified" (with the Creator).

The Kabbalah maintains that this is the most egoistic type of soul. It is no coincidence that the Jewish people are described as "stiff-necked" and insubordinate.

The collective spiritual vessel (soul, *Adam*) broke into pieces because it was easier to correct small egoistic parts than the entire egoism all at once. The first parts to correct are called "Jews." Afterwards, the other parts mingle with them and begin to approach the Creator. In the end, all the parts merge into a single vessel filled entirely with Light.

This is why there is no such thing as a "Jewish nationality." If a person feels a genuine need to draw nearer to the Creator and attain spirituality through Kabbalah, that person will be regarded as a Jew. This means that the name "Jewish" correlates to one's natural desire, not to a birth nationality. This is how it was in the past, and only later came the determination of who was considered to be a Jew.

Q: Why was the Torah (including Kabbalah) given only to the Jewish people?

A: Our world is divided into certain groups of people called "nations" or "peoples." All the worlds are built according to a single principle, namely the "pyramid principle." Because there is the law of the "opposite value between Lights and vessels," the Torah was given to correct the stiffest part of the world–the Jews. In the Torah they are regarded as "stiff-necked," the most egoistic of all peoples. That is why the Torah and the wisdom of Kabbalah were given to them of all nations.

The Jews are to be the first among the nations to correct themselves, and other nations are to follow in their footsteps. That is why it is said that the Jewish people should become the carrier of the Light for the other nations. The hatred of other nations towards the Jews stems from a spiritual root that demands that they correct themselves first.

The correction of all other nations and their physical and spiritual peace and well-being depends on the success of the correction of the Jews. This is described in great detail in the *Introduction to the Book of rahoZ* (item 66 through the end).

Q: How is the perception of the Creator among Kabbalists different from the perception of the Creator among religious people?

A: A religious person believes that there is a superior force that governs man and determines all the laws that man must follow. Kabbalah is different in that it adds to the above the opportunity of man to feel his Creator.

GOD

Q: Where is God in the wisdom of Kabbalah and what is His function?

A: Reality consists of two elements: the Creator and Creation, or as we normally call it, "the soul." The reason for the existence of the soul is to achieve complete unification with the Creator. Man's desire is to receive pleasure from the Creator. Every property of the soul is defined by a specific term.

Kabbalah uses technical terms when studying the collective law of the universe. In Kabbalah, we do not use the word God because we use technical terms to study Creation, but the meaning still refers to the Supreme Force, the Upper Light, or the Creator. Every degree that is higher than another is regarded as the "Creator" of the lower degree, because it creates, controls, develops, and influences the inferior degree.

It is enough to open any Kabbalah book to see the nature of the Creator-creature relationship. A creature has a clear, concise and well-defined sensation of the Creator, and partakes of His Actions. Eventually, the creatures attain the same spiritual degree as the Creator and become His partners.

OTHER RELIGIONS

Q: Are there parallels to the wisdom of Kabbalah in other religions?

A: There is no parallel to the wisdom of Kabbalah in other religions because the wisdom of Kabbalah is not a religion, but a science. It is not related in any way to religions, faiths, or clairvoyance of any kind, not even to Judaism. Any believing Jew, when asked if is proficient in Kabbalah, would reply negatively, and see no need to be.

One does not need the wisdom of Kabbalah to perform religious commandments. Besides, the study of Kabbalah increases one's egoism; increases one's desire for knowledge, and relies on self-discovery and understanding of the spiritual world, whereas religion relies on self-restriction, coercion, and settling for the limitation of desires.

Q: Do other religions also have ways to attain the spiritual worlds?

A: All other religions speak of internal psychological processes, or processes that relate to one's animate body and the power that revive it. Animals, too, have bodies that operate according to certain laws, and their bodies are not that different from our own. Animals can also, to a certain extent, predict the future, and even more so than people. They can also feel the other.

If there is anything that relates to attaining spirituality in other religions, it is only what has transferred to them from the Torah. The primary question that all religions ask is how to use man's intent to improve his animate and social properties, as well as life in this world.

Q: What does idolatry mean?

A: Idolatry means using egoistic desires. There are only two ways to use the desire for pleasure that the Creator created—either for the Creator, or for oneself. It is not only impossible but unnecessary to change the desire to enjoy. The only thing that must be changed is the *intention* of that desire.

The directing of the desire must be changed. This is called "the correction of the desire," and it is our goal and the only purpose for our being in this world, the lowest of all worlds (states of being). One can either work for the Creator or for self; there is no in-between.

Part Six: Genesis

CHAPTER 6.1
THE SEVEN DAYS OF CREATION

It is written, "In the beginning God created the heaven and the earth. Now the earth was unformed and void, and darkness was upon the face of the deep; and the spirit of God hovered over the face of the waters. And God said: 'Let there be light.' And there was light. And God saw the light, that it was good; and God divided the light from the darkness. And God called the light Day, and the darkness He called Night. And there was evening and there was morning, one day" (Genesis 1:1-5).

This is how the book of Genesis begins. Every one of us, when hearing these verses, is moved in some way. Over the years, we have been exposed to various interpretations of the verses of the Torah on a literal level. However, we rarely settle for such simplified interpretations that leave many questions open. We want to analyze the Torah scientifically, logically. What does the Torah really talk about? And most importantly: What does it do for us?

All the Holy Scriptures speak of one thing only—the Upper World and how it was created. They do not simply reveal what one finds there, but teach one to see that world. The gradual revelation of the Upper World is called man's "spiritual ascent," or "the degrees of one's spiritual rise." The books tell us of the spiritual worlds in several languages.

The wisdom of Kabbalah is a science that teaches the structure of the Upper World. It utilizes for that purpose the language of *Sefirot*, *Partzufim*, drawings and schemes. The Torah describes the Upper World for us in ordinary language.

Besides the Kabbalah, there is also the language of legends and the language of *Mitzvot* (commandments, precepts). Let us try to translate the language of the Torah to the language of the wisdom of Kabbalah.

The Torah describes for us how the Upper World was created, its structure, the design of its development, and after that it depicts the process of man's creation. However, the Torah does not refer to anyone in our corporeal world. Rather, it refers to the creation of the will to receive, called "soul" or "Man" (*Adam*) to fulfill this desire, this Creation, with total, eternal and complete pleasure.

The desire for pleasure is the only Creation. Besides that, there is only the Creator. Thus, everything besides the Creator is no more than various degrees of the will to receive pleasure. That is also the situation in our world: the difference between all creatures and objects is only in the different levels of their will to receive pleasure, and that is what determines the properties of each and every creature.

The desire to receive is divided into five sublevels, marked as:

1. The tip of the letter *Yod* (·), which correlates to the *Sefira* of *Keter*.
2. The letter *Yod* (י), which correlates to the *Sefira* of *Hochma*.
3. The letter *Hey* (ה), which correlates to the *Sefira* of *Bina*.
4. The letter *Vav* (ו), which correlates to the *Sefira* of *Tifferet*.
5. The letter *Hey* (ה), which correlates to the *Sefira* of *Malchut*.

Together these letters form the word *Yod* (·), *Yod* (י), *Hey* (ה), *Vav* (ו), *Hey* (ה), and that is also the name of the Creator, because Creation feels the Creator inside it and names Him accordingly. The five parts of the desire are called *Sefirot*, and their names are *Keter*, *Hochma*, *Bina*, *Tifferet* and *Malchut*.

The Creator wishes to fill Creation with pleasure to the brim, to the full sensation of perfection and eternity, because that is the Creator's state of being. That means that what the Creator wishes to give us is His own state of being. He is perfect and unique, and because of His Perfection, He wants to give His State, meaning His Perfection to Creation. Hence, the purpose of Creation is the attainment of the Perfection of the Creator and the ability to receive what He wants to bestow.

The seven days of Creation are felt by humanity as 7,000 years. The first six stand for the first six days of the week, during which humanity corrects itself unconsciously at first, and finally consciously, through great efforts. In the end it reaches the seventh millennium, or the seventh day, the Sabbath, a state where the Light of the Creator fills the corrected properties with bounty and delight.

The number seven itself bears special significance in Kabbalah. The system that manages our world consists of seven parts. That is why things in our world are divided by seven or seventy: the seven days of the week, the seventy nations of the world, man's soul, which also consists of seventy parts, and the length of a human's life, lasting approximately seventy years.

The entire path of mankind consists of six days, representing the 6,000 years of correction. We have now entered the year 5766 in the Jewish calendar. The conscious correction of the world began in the year 5755 (1995), not so many years ago. In the years we have left before the end of the 6,000 years, the Jews and all of mankind must complete the correction, and in the seventh millennium we will receive the reward.

When you read these lines, you must wonder if there is a way to shorten our way to the purpose of Creation. Well, we not only can, but we must intervene in the process that was meant to last 7,000 years, and accelerate it. Those who can reach this process individually will reach the Upper World and the sensation of the complete and sublime reality before the others.

But even during the process of correction, if we go through it consciously, through our own efforts, we will feel it as a creative process, as a romantic desire, and not as perpetual beating and torment.

The First Day of Creation

"And God saw the light, that it was good; and God divided the light from the darkness" (Genesis 1:4). In the process of Creation, we must equalize ourselves with the acts of the Creator. Hence, our first act should be dividing our thoughts between good (heaven) and bad (earth). This process is called "The recognition of evil," meaning the understanding of what is evil.

One begins to analyze which of his properties belongs to spirituality and which to corporeality, using Kabbalah books and the environment of a group of Kabbalists. The separation of these properties forms the first step toward correction. That is the first day of man's Creation within himself.

The Second Day of Creation

After separating the egoistic from the altruistic properties within us, we must begin the job of correcting our egoism. That is done through a special Light of the Creator. There are two kinds of Light that stem from the Creator: the Light of Wisdom and the Light of Mercy. When we use the property of the Light of Wisdom (earth), the egoistic property of reception, we absorb everything within us. After all, that is our nature.

However, in the property of the Light of Mercy, called "water," we acquire the attribute of bestowal. The water (bestowal) permeates the earth and generates in it the ability to cultivate life. The property of bestowal corrects the egoism and enables us to use it correctly for our own good as well as for the good of others. Through the corrected egoism, we begin to feel the Upper World and the Creator. We also see our former lives and our paths toward the purpose of Creation.

Only an eternal soul that passes from body to body can let us see our past lives. If we have not corrected our souls, we cannot see anything beyond the boundaries of our world.

The Third Day of Creation

Water gathers over the heavens and the earth is exposed. A part of the earth appears under the water. After the correction performed through the water, the earth becomes suitable for evolution of life on it. It combines the properties of the water and the earth.

Life cannot exist when there is only water, just as it cannot exist in a completely dry land. The correction of one's soul and use of the properties of the Creator and the creature inside us is built through finding the right combination between the altruistic and egoistic properties of "heaven" (the attribute of bestowal) and "earth" (the attribute of reception).

That correction is called "the middle line." Our primary egoistic nature is called the "earth line," or the "left line." The "right line" designates the property of the Creator, water, altruism, and the attribute of bestowal. The middle line is what one must create in order to "choose life."

This means that one must take the exact amount of water, and water the earth in such a way that the two lines will complement one another and create something new. The combination of these two properties will produce the "Tree of Life." A spiritual individual feels the entire Creation and lives in all the worlds simultaneously, eternally and happily. Such a person identifies with his or her eternal soul, not with a transient body, considering the "self" as the soul, and the body as mere "clothing."

This transition from sympathizing with the body to sympathizing with the soul is a totally psychological transition and occurs to the extent that one acquires the property of *Bina*.

The Fourth Day of Creation

On the fourth day the planets appeared: the earth, the sun and the moon. Thus, the phases of correction were created—the days, months, and years. Correction occurs in both the collective Creation and in each and every specific particle. Creation itself is called "soul" or "*Adam*," and its specific particles are called individual souls, or people. Each individual soul goes through the same phases of correction that the collective soul experiences.

The Fifth Day of Creation

"And God said: 'Let the waters swarm with swarms of living creatures, and let fowl fly above the earth in the open firmament of heaven.' And God created the great sea-monsters, and every living creature that creepeth, wherewith the waters swarmed, after its kind, and every winged fowl after its kind; and God saw that it was good" (Genesis 1:20-21).

When the attribute of bestowal—water—joins the attribute of reception—earth—it gives the attribute of reception many forms of reception. These different forms are the parts of Creation that were made on the fifth day.

The Sixth Day of Creation

"And God said: 'Let us make man in our image, after our likeness; and let them have dominion over the fish of the sea, and over the fowl of the air, and over the cattle, and over all the earth" (Genesis 1:26).

What does it mean to create "man in our image after our likeness?" It is said in the Torah (Genesis 1:27): "in the image of God created He him." Image (*Tzelem*) is a part of *Bina* that descends from it into the soul and gives it the properties of the Creator.

In other words, *Partzuf Bina* is the mechanism of providence in charge of all the souls that need correction. In order to correct *Malchut*, *Bina* produces a special mechanism that permeates *Malchut* and enables it to perform the correction. That aiding device that every soul in *Malchut* receives from above is called "image." The image is, in fact, the collection of the Properties of the Creator.

Without the knowledge of the design of Creation, without feeling as part of Creation, meaning the ability to sense the spiritual worlds, we do not know how to behave or where to turn. We do not even understand what it is that we must do.

In order to have these attributes, which are necessary for spiritual progress, *Bina*, the highest spiritual degree must demonstrate what we must do and how. That is the mission of the image, the aiding mechanism of *Bina*. This mechanism clothes our souls and produces all the necessary corrections. That is why it is said that through this image, man is created within us.

The Seventh Day of Creation

"And the heaven and the earth were finished, and all the host of them. And on the seventh day God finished His work which He had made" (Genesis 2:1-2). Our work revolves around the acquisition of the trait of *Bina*. One corrects oneself through these properties and thus ascends higher. *Adam* performed these corrections six times within him. These corrections are named: *Hesed, Gevura, Tifferet, Netzah, Hod* and *Yesod*. These gradual corrections are referred to as six days or the 6,000 years of Creation. *Malchut*, the last *Sefira*, is unable to correct itself.

However, once it receives the properties of the six higher *Sefirot*, it is able to adopt their traits. Hence, the essence of the seventh day is that everything that accumulated during the previous six days enters *Malchut*. The Sabbath is a special day because on that day the souls fill with the Upper Light. The only condition is that we must "stay out of the way" in this process. That is expressed symbolically in the rules of the Sabbath.

CHAPTER 6.2
ABRAHAM THE PATRIARCH

In Genesis: "Now the Lord said unto Abram: 'Get thee out of thy country, and from thy kindred, and from thy father's house, unto the land that I will show thee. And I will make of thee a great nation, and I will bless thee, and make thy name great; and be thou a blessing. And I will bless them that bless thee, and him that curseth thee will I curse; and in thee shall all the families of the earth be blessed.'

So Abram went, as the Lord had spoken unto him; and Lot went with him; and Abram was seventy and five years old when he departed out of Haran. And Abram took Sarai his wife, and Lot his brother's son, and all their substance that they had gathered, and the souls that they had gotten in Haran; and they went forth to go into the land of Canaan; and into the land of Canaan" (Genesis 12:1-5).

"And the Lord appeared unto Abram, and said: 'Unto thy seed will I give this land'; and he built there an altar unto the Lord, who appeared unto him" (Genesis 12:7). "And there was a famine in the land; and Abram went down into Egypt to sojourn there; for the famine was sore in the land" (Genesis 12:10).

Does the Torah speak of immigrating to a better country, meaning Egypt, and does the Creator Himself compel Abraham to go there? Why did the Creator choose Abraham? At that time he was the same as all the others who lived in the area spreading from east of Syria to Mesopotamia. Abraham did not go to Egypt right away. Rather, he first went to Beit-El, made a sacrifice to the Creator, and seemed to be soothed afterwards.

It is written that this was followed by a famine, and only then did he go down to Egypt. A question comes to mind: was it the famine that made him go to Egypt, or was it the Creator?

If we relate to the Torah as a historic narrative, we will see that it is not that different from the history of other nations. But the Torah does not deal with the past, it deals with *us*. It deals with each and every one of us; with who we are and what we are and what we must do with our lives. That is how the Torah explains the entire system of Creation.

Man contains everything that exists in all the worlds inside him, including our own world. Besides man, there is only the Creator. Man is the representative of Creation and of all the other worlds.

The Creator turns to Abraham, meaning to a specific attribute in us, which is like all other properties ("Nations") in man (the name Abraham means the "Father of the Nation" in Hebrew—*Av Ha'am*) and tells him: I now separate this specific trait in you, which is called Abraham, and you must leave your country, meaning your situation, all the desires that you are currently in, from your homeland, and break free from the desires you were born with.

In other words, you must exit your original state, the state you were born into. It is neither good nor bad, but you must leave it, leave the home of your father. I (the Creator) am inside your primary egoistic desires and you must leave them and go to the land that I will show you. There is where you will find Me. The words, "that I will show thee" mean desires that the Creator will show and in them He will appear. The Creator only appears before Abraham in order to compel him to take the path at the end of which He will appear before him in completeness. In that state, the entire Creation will appear before Abraham and he will obtain the opposite properties: eternity and completeness, and the degree of the Creator Himself.

The Creator appears before every single one of us. We have all felt an inner voice, an inner power, at least once in our lives urging us to live in a different way. We feel the desire to think more of timeless, meaningful things, leaving all the petty dealings and routines in life, and slowly rising above them all.

As for Abraham, there is no interest whatsoever in speaking of him as a person who lived 5,000 years ago and was picked out by the Creator. Rather, I prefer to focus on the quality of Abraham that is in each and every one of us. How does the Creator turn to it and use it to attract us, saying "Leave your desires, the substance you were created in and have been immersed in, and go to another desire, one that I will show you"?

The Creator does not show us that we must ascend spiritually. Rather, He says that we must first go down to Egypt, to the gutter of our darkest and fiercest egoistic desires. These desires are so egoistic that they are like those of the Egyptians, who knew how to use egoism so perfectly that they could mummify their bodies and preserve them for centuries. They made idols of their dead and remained tied to their bodies after death.

The Creator does not tell Abraham that he must aspire upward in order to cross to the other desire, which is where he will find the Creator, Who will then fill him with Light.

That means that the most perfect state is when Abraham has already been through Egypt. The Creator doesn't even say that Abraham must go through Egypt, He simply tells him to go there. This sounds like an unreasonable commandment. After all, Abraham is an ordinary person who lives his daily life in the bosom of his family, a shepherd.

Suddenly, he is compelled to experience terrible states of decline in order to attain the spiritual state, and those situations are called "Egypt." One never wants to go down to Egypt, so Abraham builds an altar and thanks the Creator for having noticed him, choosing to remain where he is. Though Abraham goes to Beit-El, he thinks that there he is closer to the Creator, but in fact the Creator drives him away from there.

Abraham goes as far as Beit-El. He is like a man who attains spirituality and begins to be attracted to the books that concern that subject. He reads them, perhaps even begins to study Kabbalah, and thinks that this is the House of the Lord (Beit-El). When he sacrifices to the Creator and begins to examine what life really asks of him, what the Creator and his inner voice want him to do, he suddenly begins to feel hunger. That hunger is so intense that it drives him off to Egypt.

Similarly, during the preliminary reading of the books before him, man begins to feel ever-growing pains, accompanied by a greater still spiritual hunger. He begins to see himself through his innermost feelings as lower and lower and meaner than ever. The world appears so petty that this feeling is the same as when one feels when he goes down to Egypt, meaning to his lowest desires.

The phase when one feels oneself is the best and most vital for one's progress. The intensity or quality of the sensation is of no importance; it can be good or bad, uplifting or depressing. One cannot obtain the correct desires under the direct instruction of the Creator without being in Egypt.

Our initial desires are very small, and even if we stretch them to the limit they can only bring us as far as Beit-El. That is, we can practice the ordinary Torah and feel as one who has already entered the house of God, and the Garden of Eden. But in fact, this is not the case! The Torah should bring us first to the recognition of evil, to the feeling that we are complete egoists, and that all our desires are completely opposite to spirituality.

If we experience that state, if we understand and internalize it, not only because that is what the books say, then we can accept that that is also our own situation. Our recognition of our egos must be an emotional, tangible experience. To the extent that we feel this way, we will begin to want to correct ourselves. Therefore, recognizing our egos as evil is a very long phase.

The exile in Egypt is not intended for Abraham, but rather for Jacob and his family (Josef and his brothers), who went down to Egypt. The exile was to be 400 years long, but in fact it lasted less than that. Baal HaSulam writes that because they did not complete the 400 years, the entire nation that left Egypt was forced to experience another exile, the one that has been ongoing for the past 2000 years.

In order to feel who you are and what your properties are, you must feel at least a little bit of what spirituality is like. You must experience these feelings to the fullest and examine them in every way. When the process is completed, you will be granted exodus from Egypt.

Abraham is only the first phase. When we begin to study the wisdom of Kabbalah, we begin to feel that we are much worse than before. However, this feeling passes. It is a small entrance to Egypt. Afterwards Abraham returns to Beit-El

On the second visit to Egypt, he takes his family with him. This means that once he has accumulated a substantial amount of desires, and has already acquired a clear notion of the way, he must go toward spirituality. At this stage, he is already in a certain degree of spiritual development, and has already absorbed it. Only after that is he granted the second descent to Egypt.

Abraham immediately went there, but only reached as far as Beit-El. That is because we can only be pushed ahead by pain.

We are indeed immersed in our egoistic desires. "Thy country, and from thy kindred, and from thy father's house" are one's entire being. We cannot exit these states, at least we think we can't, because it is our nature, and we cannot imagine a different way of thinking, much less a different way of acting. We cannot imagine what is not within us to begin with, what we never felt, and even what our fathers and our forefathers never felt.

Because of that, it is only possible to bring us out of that state and throw us into the state of acquiring new desires through immense spiritual hunger. That hunger can only be developed and amplified in a group with a teacher and some very special books.

If one reads these books in the wrong order, it is very easy to be misled and deviate from the right path, which means a temporary halt in spiritual evolution. We must always maintain a careful watch, verifying that we are on the right track. But in fact, if we stand still, yet at the same time want spirituality, then the Creator Himself will push us, using that hunger.

Abraham is a spiritual property that seems to be the basis of all our properties. It is a general spiritual attribute that is the first to be approached by the Creator. People don't come to the wisdom of Kabbalah because they were sent here, but because the Creator approached them first. He begins to haunt them and make them hungry, and only then they come.

We will never chase something without a reason or a special need for it. Only the sensation of hunger pushes us out of our country. Love and hunger rule the world, meaning that the feeling that we're missing something is the only thing that pulls us. That sensation is called "Abram," and it is to him that the Creator turns and says, "Do you really want to fulfill your feelings and attain the truth? If you do, you must leave this feeling altogether and move onto another feeling called 'Egypt.'"

That means that you really must examine your egoistic desires from within. If you correct them, you will attain Me; I will be revealed to you in *them*. The Creator appears precisely in those desires we call "Egypt." Only afterwards are they corrected.

Let us take this man, Abraham. In a different degree we might have referred to him as a prophet. A prophet is a person who has attained such a degree that he is now in direct contact with the Creator. There are prophets who only speak to the Creator, meaning they attain the level of spiritual speech.

Naturally, they do not hear any horns blowing in the sky, as the Torah writes, and the voice of God does not sound from Mount Sinai from gigantic speakers to the whole of mankind. It is the inner voice of one who obtains evident contact with the Creator. There are prophets who see and hear, and there are those who only see and hear afterwards.

The books of the prophets demonstrate the versatility of the connections of the prophets with the Creator, and how and when He appears before them, meaning in which degree one can reach which prophet. The prophecy degrees, as all other degrees of our forefathers, are inside us. Each of us must experience them all. We must go the entire way while being in our corporeal world. Everything that the Torah speaks of must be attained by us from beginning to end.

Only then is one completely united with the Creator and reaches the final point of development that constitutes the purpose of Creation and its preliminary design.

In fact, the Torah provides us with this entire plan, but tells us about it in a special way. The Torah can be perceived as a historic narrative, or as pictures from people's ordinary lives, both are of course completely incorrect. Our Torah is Holy; it is not just another novel.

Is *Sefer Yetzira* (*Book of Creation*) that Abraham wrote studied equally with the *Zohar*?

The *Book of Creation* that Abraham wrote was written in précis, as though in brevity. The book writes simply: "This world was created in apparent, semi apparent and concealed form, in thirty-two paths of wisdom." It can take years to understand even the first sentence properly. This book was written succinctly, as though according to a certain code. It is written for a person in the same spiritual degree, or close to it but lower, but it is not meant for us.

The rest of the Kabbalists, especially the more contemporary ones, address us directly. The farther the generation is from the time a certain Kabbalah book was written, the more the book has the right to be discovered in our time. Since the Ari, there is a clear directive from Above to open everything and teach everyone.

As a result of that spiritual commandment, books are written in a language that is much easier to understand, so that the need for interpreters decreases. However, we still need teachers. Without a teacher it is impossible to understand anything, although the material itself is already much more accessible.

If the Creator turns to you, you feel it as that unique property called "Abraham." That inner voice that you feel addresses you is called "the Creator." The effort to understand it, the voices, and indeed yourself, that is what the Torah aspires to, nothing more.

Part Seven: The Inner Meaning

CHAPTER 7.1
PRAYER

A talk at a banquet in memory of Rabbi Yehuda Ashlag,
Baal HaSulam marking the 40th anniversary of his departure

It is written in the Torah that prayer is the "work of the heart." This refers to desires that come from the heart that one cannot control. We are built in such a way that, in most cases, we are unable to expose and know precisely what our desires are. Even our own prayers are concealed from us.

The words written in the prayer book describe situations that we must go through on our own. If we work on ourselves to correct our thoughts and desires, we will be able to reach the same desires and pleas as those of the members of the Great Assembly, the authors of the Jewish prayer book who published it some two thousand years ago.

There are dozens of phases of recognizing evil that we must go through if we want to equalize with the desires of the members of the great assembly. We will have to understand its makings, and that we are all made of egoism, which is the root of all evil. We must not only understand it, but feel it in our every bone.

But for that we need the revelation of the Creator. That is because everything is learned by comparing it with its opposite. The gap between the properties of the Creator and our own will enables us to feel our insignificance compared to the greatness of the Creator. We must perceive and feel Who He is and that everything depends on Him. It is not enough to point to the heavens and say, "I believe." Faith is the sensation of the Creator inside me, and my presence inside the Creator.

There are several states to the soul:

1. Before we come into the world.

2. When we receive additional egoism, something the souls feel as clothing in a corporeal body. Because of it, all the worlds of the soul contract to the dimensions of "our world."

3. When the souls feel themselves and the entire spiritual world after the end of correction.

The situation the souls are in before they descend to our world is called the world of "*Ein Sof.*" In that state, the soul receives the unlimited Light of the Creator. Afterwards, it receives additional egoism which weakens the contact between the soul and spirituality until the soul is finally clothed in a human body.

Now it no longer feels spirituality and therefore does not believe that it exists, meaning one does not feel the Creator. In other words, the soul no longer feels something that not long ago was its entire world.

"This world" is the sensation of the current state we are in. This name refers to that part of reality of the system of Creation and the Creator that I now feel through my ego.

The next degree is higher because it is attained by correcting my senses, and therefore the perception of reality is wider in my next degree from the degree that I have attained thus far. Because of that, this degree is called my "next world." When I reach tomorrow, I will feel myself again as being in this world and name the degree I have now attained, "this world," and I will name what will appear as my tomorrow regarding my present state, my "next World."

There are a few letters of Baal HaSulam that we must study and memorize until we recall them by heart. At the right moment, we will be able to remind ourselves of them and identify our situation, seeing the letters merge into one:

- The Creator is the Source to which we all aspire.

- The Torah is the Light that feels man every minute.

- Israel is man himself, the desires that he aims at the Creator.

We must ask then, how can these three terms, which seem completely disconnected, be one and the same thing? The purpose of Creation is to bring man to exist both in his corporeal envelope and in this body, while attaining complete adhesion and sameness with the Creator. To be more precise, all the worlds will combine inside us to a point where we and the Creator will form one reality as we merge and unite with Him, taking His Paths, and keeping His Commandments.

In order for us to attain that perfect and eternal state, meaning the purpose of Creation, we are given the Torah in this world. That is why the Torah was only given to man after he came into this world, after he had sunk into egoism, into his corporeal body. The Torah was given to people, not to angels, because man consists of evident and total egoism.

If we take upon ourselves the path of Torah, we will eventually be able to neutralize our egoistic bodies, meaning our desires, in a way that they will no longer stand between us and the Creator. Then we will become one with the Creator just as it was before our souls came down to this world and received the addition of egoism.

Furthermore, by correcting egoism and precisely because of it, we will climb up the spiritual ladder and reach the degree of the Creator. All creations except for man lack egoism; therefore, they have no tools for climbing. As a result, they remain in their preliminary states.

Precisely for that reason all creations except for man are regarded as "still." Even angels, which are forces operated by the Creator through which He governs Creation, are not independent forces with their own desires, but are simply forces that carry out His Will. It is mankind's egoistic desire that enables us to reach the degree of the Creator by changing the form (intent) of the will to receive.

An angel is like a robot that performs a certain task in the spiritual world. It merely transfers something from one place to another. It doesn't ascend or descend in spiritual degrees like us, nor does it even "grow" in the spiritual sense. It is simply a spiritual force that operates at every spiritual degree.

The soul is a part of the Creator within each of us. Once we are wrapped in the egoistic shell, we can no longer feel spirituality, much less the Creator, because our every sense is immersed in egoism, the opposite attribute of spirituality. Replacing egoism with altruism is like taking off our egoistic "coats" and beginning to feel the entire Creation until nothing separates us from the Creator. In that state, the three terms—Creator, man, and Israel—unite.

Our purpose is to extinguish the egoistic obstacle that stands between our souls and the Creator. Of all Holy Scriptures, the Kabbalah is the most efficient in attaining that goal. It is the study with the most powerful spiritual Light that shines during the study.

There are no movements in the spiritual world. The difference between two worlds is only in my inner feelings and what my inner coating allows me to see. We never feel anything but the Creator, but we always feel Him behind our filters, meaning across from our egoistic properties. Our feeling of the Creator and Creation will intensify to the extent that we can extinguish these filters.

The degree of egoism that we remove from ourselves, or the extent of our correction, is called "the degrees of the spiritual ladder," or "worlds." Thus, the worlds are actually the measurements of the sensation of the Creator.

The egoistic obstruction of our ability to sense Creation exists only inside us. There are no obstructions from the perspective of the Creator. He treats mankind with perfect benevolence; He does not hide Himself. It is only we who feel or do not feel that concealment. We hide the worlds from ourselves as though behind an egoistic veil.

Revoking egoism does not happen all at once. Rather, the Creator first gives us periods of time called "life in this world," which are lives that are opportunities for us to ascend. Other than our initial awakening to spirituality, the rest is up to us. Any new life helps us remove some of our egoistic natures and draw nearer to the Creator.

These periods repeat themselves until we finally correct ourselves in a way that our desires (named *Guf* in Kabbalah) will no longer be a hindrance between us and the Creator, until we cleave to the Creator with our every trait, regardless of the world we're in.

After physical death (something that Kabbalah regards as one's separation from the egoistic cover), there is a rebirth in our world from the corrected parts of the collective soul. They blend and merge in a new order because they are all parts of the collective creature and all the covers are actually egoism.

The egoism, *Adam ha Rishon* (the only creature), broke into many pieces, or separate souls, in order to make the correction of the collective soul possible. That is because it is easier to correct each part separately than to correct the entire body. That is the reason for the reincarnations in the world and their unique order of correction.

At the end of correction, all the souls will regroup into a desire, a single collective soul that will receive the entire Light of the Creator, and thus perfection will appear.

In order to help the process of correction, the Creator brings down to our world special souls in addition to the ordinary ones, which do not leave our world after they complete their corrections. Rather, they stay and continue their spiritual work in both worlds to support us in the process of our corrections. These people, representatives, or messengers of the Creator, write books and lead and tutor students.

Once their task is accomplished, they depart to the spiritual world, but the possibility to connect with them and ask them questions remains. It is even possible to feel how they "clothe" us and act through us, depending on our spiritual degrees.

Anyone can feel within the connection with these righteous people. These states are defined as "the impregnation of the soul of the righteous." We feel them even now, indirectly, because we are following in their footsteps and learning by their books.

In fact, the only world (spiritual state) that actually exists is the world of *Ein Sof*, a world of absolute adhesion with the Creator. All the other sensations we feel are but sections of that complete, unlimited, and eternal feeling, known as the world of *Ein Sof*.

One of the sections of the world of *Ein Sof* is called "*Adam Kadmon*." After that comes a section called "*Atzilut*," then comes the world of "*Beria*," then "*Yetzira*," and finally "*Assiya*." The smallest section of this sensation is "this world."

The world of *Ein Sof* grows narrower in its perception by the egoistic senses of the creature, right down to the degree of our world. I can therefore define my progress and the spiritual world I am in according to the expansion of my sensations. It all depends on the "band width" of my sensing abilities.

Everything we learn is relative to the attaining person, beside which there is only the world of *Ein Sof*. There are a great many corrections that *Malchut* of the world of *Ein Sof* (the creature, or the soul) must perform. There is nothing in our world that was created without a reason.

For example, Baal HaSulam brings a tiny insect in the wood that spends its entire life in search of food and no one pays it any heed. And not only every insect, but every single atom of that insect bears a tremendous value to the attainment of the collective end of correction.

The Creator did not create anything in vain, and everything happens only according to the process of nearing to the ultimate goal. Events happen with or without our consent, regardless of how we view them. But whether or not we understand what happens and why, things still move toward the completion of the design of Creation, and the revelation of the full purpose of Creation to the creatures in this world.

Just as there are different people and different nations and nationalities, so the various parts of *Malchut* of *Ein Sof* differ in their measure of desire (and in that alone), thus creating the various degrees of nature: still, vegetative, animate, and speaking. Everyone is interested in the difference between men and women in terms of the correction they must perform, but no one wants to know what is the correction that a stone must perform.

Even the stone was created in Our World, and it, too, must reach the goal of Creation. The correction of all of nature depends on the correction of mankind. It is the work of man that enlivens nature toward the end of correction. Animals and plants were not given the Torah because they have no free choice and their egoism is not under their control, hence, it is not for them to correct it.

And as for people, not all were given the same measure of practical laws of the Torah in Our World. The nations of the world were given seven Mitzvot (precepts), while the Jews were given 613 Mitzvot. This refers to the physical performance of the Mitzvot, meaning in the degree of the spiritual still. Different people perform the Mitzvot in different ways, depending on the number of corrections each soul must perform in this world.

Men and women also have corrections to perform that correlate to the origin of their souls, but the inner pull toward the Creator does not depend on one's gender. Many believers and non-believers alike never ask a single question about Creation, correction, and the purpose of Creation.

They have not received a desire for spiritual change from Above and only perform the operations they were taught to perform mechanically. There are differences between Jews and non-Jews in these mechanical operations, just as there are differences between men and women and children under thirteen years of age, or older than thirteen.

However, when we attain the spiritual world, we see that the only difference between people is that those who seek spirituality do so because the Creator gave them that desire. It is their time to grow spiritually, while others have not yet been given this desire.

Thus, it is forbidden to classify people by any external signs such as nationality or gender. The question of whether or not this or that person should study Kabbalah is irrelevant. Those who were summoned from Above, meaning those who feel a desire for Kabbalah, study.

How do we come to the world? It is as though the Creator takes a tiny part of Himself and adds egoism to it. After the complete desire that the Creator created is broken into tiny egoistic particles, they are gradually corrected and create the Upper Worlds: *Atzilut, Beria, Yetzira* and *Assiya*. The finer the fragments, the higher the worlds they comprise.

The soul of *Adam ha Rishon* consists of the most egoistic desire, the core of every creature, the *Malchut* of the world of *Ein Sof*. That soul also breaks into tiny particles, which are our souls.

When we begin to study Kabbalah and ask, "Does everything depend on the Creator or on me?" and, "Is He the doer or am I?" we tend in the beginning to define the private and collective providences erroneously. Before we begin to act we must be certain that everything really does depend on us. But afterwards, we must tell ourselves that everything depended only on the Creator. If we keep to this thought, we will take the right path.

Some things can only be felt but cannot be explained, since it is impossible to express in words how spirituality is clothed in corporeality. We can explain corporeal science and spiritual science, but not how one world clothes the other. All Kabbalistic explanations end in the explanation of the breaking of *Adam ha Rishon*.

It is not that Kabbalists do not want to explain more elaborately; it is simply that one can feel and attain these things, but not understand them. It is also not possible to convey in words a feeling that was never felt by another.

Egoism is a very powerful spiritual force, and it is all that we can feel. We haven't any idea of what we are trying to rid ourselves because we must look at ourselves from the outside, experience something different than ourselves, and compare ourselves to something external, objective.

The only reason we can see other objects in this world is that they also, like us, consist of egoism. Otherwise, we would not be able to feel them. Egoism consists of many types and degrees, and its tiniest and simplest part is that which feels only itself.

That is precisely how we originally feel ourselves in the world. We are such small egoists that we feel absolutely nothing but ourselves, just like small children. When we mature a little, our egoism will reach beyond the limits of our world, and we will feel the Creator. That kind of egoism will be called "spiritual."

At that stage we will stop wanting the petite and petty pleasures of our world, called "Minute Light," and crave only the spiritual desires of the Light of the Creator. We will want the Creator Himself and nothing less!

Our actions follow our desires, whether we are aware of it or not. The mind serves only as an aid to analyze and examine our desires. That is why it cannot exceed them. As human beings, we actually follow our desires and emotions. That means that we first act, and only then "perceive," meaning analyze intellectually.

The Creator implements His Guidance through our actions. This is how we can understand and analyze our actions and act in the future according to the conclusions we draw. Whether I remember what I did and act more wisely in the future, or learn through pain depends only on the Creator. He teaches us every single moment, but we are unable to make any corrections. We must only understand that we are comprised of pure, unadulterated selfishness that we will never be able to resist.

The Creator does everything else for us except give us this understanding. The further we advance in spirituality, the worse we feel about our own natures. The more evident the Creator becomes, the more we perceive our egoism, compared to Him. This is the process of spiritual advancement.

If, for example, we correct ninety-nine percent of ourselves, we still see the one remaining percent as if through a magnifying glass that makes it look as big as the ninety-nine corrected percent. We perceive that tiny grain as a horrible sin. Such people are called "righteous." The greater the Light that shines on us, the more we can perceive the bright and the dark inside us.

Therefore, when we do some work or when we study, we attain both the Creator and ourselves. If all that we can feel is our own baseness, we will despair because we cannot feel the Creator. Then, our entire world grows dark before us. But when these desperate states are over and we perceive their spiritual origin, meaning the Creator, we already have a spiritual contact with Him. Now we can ask and even demand of Him, or be mad at Him, because we understand that everything comes only from Him.

When we feel the Creator in addition to ourselves, we no longer despair because we know our situations are given from Above, that they pass, and that they are necessary for our spiritual growth.

The Creator does not care how we turn to Him. It is only important that we recognize His Existence and that He is the one who sends us all these strange desires. He does that so that we will constantly feel different things about Him, and consequently evolve.

Baal HaSulam wrote in one of his prophecies that the Creator told him that a new world would be built through him, and that from that moment he, Yehuda Ashlag, would begin to carve a new road through his books, a road for readers to follow to reach the Creator.

As a result, Baal HaSulam began to write his book, *The Study of the Ten Sefirot*. He understood that he would not be able to write anything if he were not connected to people because of his sublime spiritual degree, though physically he was no different than any other person. For that reason, Baal HaSulam pleaded before the Creator to lower him to a level from which he could write to people, and the Creator granted his wish.

The Study of the Ten Sefirot begins with describing the four phases of Direct Light, meaning the four phases of the creation of the initial desire. It is a description of the situation that preceded Creation. In a different place, Baal HaSulam writes that he did not write anything that he himself did not fully attain. This tells us what his actual spiritual degree was.

In one of his letters, Baal HaSulam writes that the soul of Rabbi Shimon Bar-Yochay, author of the *Zohar*, the soul of the Ari, and his own soul are one and the same soul that keeps returning to our world in order to make the method of the study of Kabbalah suitable for its time. This is needed because every generation a new type of soul comes down to our world, requiring a new system of correction. Some are high souls that descend to this world in order to correct it and show us the way to the purpose of Creation. These special souls are sent to us in order to save us, and this is how we should relate to the great Rabbi Yehuda Ashlag, as the personal messenger of the Creator.

CHAPTER 7.2
THE MEANING OF THE JEWISH HOLIDAYS

Over the years, we have been presented with a number of interpretations regarding the meaning of the Jewish holidays. Some were easier for us to accept, and some seemed less acceptable to our rational understanding. In this chapter we briefly explain the significance of some of the holidays from the perspective of the Kabbalah.

All the holidays represent specific phases in one's path of discovery and understanding of the Upper World, the Creator, leading to the state of complete unification with Him. *Pesach* (Passover), for example, represents our exit from the sensation of the material world to the sensation of the spiritual world.

It happens when we begin to feel an external, broader world beyond our physical world. We begin to see how spiritual forces affect us, altering the course of physical events and processes in our world.

Pesach is the only holiday that is still connected with our material world, or rather, with our exit from it. All other holidays signify a process of discovery and understanding of the spiritual world far beyond our

THE PATH OF KABBALAH

own. In order to advance toward the spiritual worlds, we must be well versed in the rules that govern them.

The holiday of the giving of the Torah (Pentecost, *Matan Torah*) stands for the acceptance of the "guidebook," the laws by which our spiritual ascent is performed.

During *Rosh Hashanah* (the Hebrew New Year) and the ten days that follow until *Yom Kippur* (Day of Atonement), we build within us a new *Sefira* out of the ten each day, thus creating the vessel of the soul. Afterwards, during the holiday of *Sukkot* (Tabernacles Feast), this vessel fills with the Upper Light.

Because this vessel is empty at first, it produces a feeling of absence and lack. Over this period of ten days, we ask for pardon from the Creator, examine ourselves, and draw conclusions about our progress thus far. This process finds its expression in prayers.

So what actually is the meaning of the Hebrew New Year (*Rosh Hashanah*)? From which point do we begin our count? *Rosh Hashanah* is the day of the creation of *Adam*. The Creator created the soul and called it *Adam* in order to grant it eternal delight. The Creator did not create anything but that desire to receive pleasure. The Kabbalah calls this desire, "the will to receive delight and pleasure."

Thus, all that exists is the Creator and the desire to receive pleasure that He created. But pleasure from what? From the Creator! The creature's sensation of the Creator *is* pleasure. In Kabbalah it is called "Light," and the desire to receive the Light is called a "vessel."

600,000 rays stretch from the spiritual object called *Adam*. Each ray produces a tiny soul at its end, and we are all interconnected through the soul of *Adam*. This spiritual object was created on *Rosh Hashanah*, hence the great importance of this holiday.

The creation of the world began on the first day and extended over the next five days, or over the next five spiritual degrees. *Adam* was created on the sixth day. *Adam*, who was at the highest spiritual degree on the sixth day, did not wait for the seventh day (Sabbath) and received the entire Light of the Creator into its inner vessel (described as the eating of forbidden fruit).

Adam's soul tried to attain the purpose of Creation all at once, but failed and consequently broke into 600,000 parts. The parts continued to break and split into thousands of even smaller parts, all of which exist in souls, meaning inside people living in our world. Each of these particles must complete its individual correction through many cycles. Then these particles will unite into one collective soul, an enormous spiritual structure called "*Adam.*"

The autumn holidays stand for the process of the unification of the soul with the Creator. First, during *Rosh Hashanah* there is a process of complete detachment of the soul from the Creator. This process is entitled, "Sawing off" (*Nesira*), because this process seemingly cuts this entire system in two.

Over the next ten days until *Yom Kippur*, the soul that was separated from the Creator receives its ten *Sefirot*: *Keter, Hochma, Bina, Hesed, Gevura, Tifferet, Netzah, Hod, Yesod, Malchut*, and gradually begins to adopt the properties of the Creator. The word *Sefira* comes from the word, "sapphire," meaning "sparkling."

After that, on *Yom Kippur*, all ten *Sefirot* gather into a collective soul. After *Yom Kippur* begins a process called "Sweetening," a process of correction. This occurs by changing the egoistic attributes of Creation to the altruistic attributes of the Creator. Because the properties of Creation become identical to those of the Creator, He begins to fill the ten *Sefirot* of Creation with His Light, which the soul experiences as immense pleasure.

That process occurs during the holiday of *Sukkot*, though only a portion of the Light can enter the soul before the end of correction. As a result of the filling of the soul with Light, Creation attains the spiritual degree called *Simchat Torah* (Rejoicing in the Torah).

That day is also called *Shmini Atzeret* (the eighth day that stops), because it is forbidden to receive Light for more than seven days before the end of correction. Filling Creation with Light is executed according to the extent of correction it has attained, meaning the extent of sameness with the properties of the Light it has acquired. When Creation becomes completely identical with the attributes of the Light, it is filled with it completely.

The process of the creation of the soul begins with having completely opposite properties to the Light's. Then, the vessel of the soul is gradually corrected to finally adopt a completely altruistic desire, identical to that of the Light. The more alike the soul and the Light become, the more Light it receives, and the holidays symbolize this process in our world.

The Day of Atonement (*Yom Kippur*) is also considered a holiday, and the ten days between *Rosh Hashanah* and *Yom Kippur* are days of thought and contemplation. During that time, many uncorrected desires are collected and then corrected and filled with Light. Therefore, these are good days, and must be met with joy, corresponding to their spiritual purpose.

Yom Kippur completes the process of creation of the ten *Sefirot* of the soul and renders the soul capable of receiving the Light of the Creator. This means that the soul is now prepared, yet still empty. This emptiness is symbolically consistent with the five prohibitions of *Yom Kippur*: eating and drinking, bathing, wearing perfume, wearing leather, and performing sexual intercourse.

These prohibitions are joined with the ordinary Sabbath prohibition, as the soul/vessel is not yet ready to receive the Light of the Creator. On the Sabbath, the soul climbs to the world of *Atzilut* by the power of spiritual forces that come from Above, not by its own strength. Because it reaches such a high level of spirituality, but with help, the soul must refuse to receive the Light that fills that world, if it wants to extend its stay. That is the symbolic reason for the prohibitions of the Sabbath.

The soul rises on *Yom Kippur* to an even higher degree than it does on the Sabbath. Accordingly there are five additional prohibitions, because the soul consists of five parts (*Sefirot*): *Keter*, *Hochma*, *Bina*, *Zeir Anpin*, and *Malchut*, and each *Sefira* has its own limitations in the world of *Atzilut*.

Yom Kippur designates the completion of the creation process of the soul. It then becomes capable of receiving the Creator's Light. On that day we reach a spiritual degree where the vessel can receive the entire Light of the Creator, meaning at this stage it is ready, but still empty.

The days between *Yom Kippur* and *Sukkot* are days of detachment from the previous situation. The Surrounding Light begins to gradually enter the soul on *Sukkot*. It is called "Surrounding Light" until the holiday of *Sukkot*, because it remains outside the soul. But once inside, it is regarded as "Inner Light."

These are special days when the Light of the Creator enters the soul and fills it completely on the day of *Simchat Torah* (Rejoicing of the Torah). All during the seven days of the holiday, the seven *Sefirot* of our soul fill with Light. Filling means good days, happy ones.

A soul that has been completely filled with Light matches the spiritual degree of the holiday of *Simchat Torah*. The entire Upper Light that is to ultimately fill the soul is called "Torah." When that process is carried out, the spiritual degree of a soul that can perform it is called "*Simchat Torah*."

When we read these lines, we must ask: "Why does it take seven days to fill the soul, and not five or ten days, for example?" Where did this division into seven parts, or *Sefirot*, come from?

In fact, this division is a result of the partial filling of the soul with this Light. The final correction and fulfillment of the soul will only occur at the end of correction. Because the *Sefirot* that are to receive the Light of Wisdom are as yet inoperative, the number is only seven.

THE PATH OF KABBALAH

During these holidays, a very powerful spiritual Light comes from Above. It surrounds our entire universe and our souls. It is called "Surrounding Light" and it yields a spiritual ascent, protects, raises, and cleanses us. That is why these days are also called "Days of Good Will," meaning the Creator regards our actions favorably on these days, provided we use them to advance toward Him.

The actual reception of the Light is postponed until *Sukkot* and *Simchat Torah*. These are two contradicting situations of Creation: on the one hand, there are the holidays of *Rosh Hashanah*, *Yom Kippur*—"terrible days" when the real desire for perfection and spiritual growth evolves. On the other hand, there are the holidays of *Sukkot* and *Simchat Torah*, when the corrected soul is filled with the Upper Light. It is recommended to read Kabbalah during this time, because there is a very strong Light that shines from Above.

It is written in the prayer of *Rosh Hashanah* that "Prayer, almsgiving and repentance cancel the punishment." That means that even if one is meant to suffer pain, anguish and torments, these three operations prevent the punishment from being dealt.

Such an operation cannot be in the spiritual world as it can be in ours, when one asks a question and receives an answer. An operation in the spiritual world relies on the correction of the intent, and only afterwards one receives the reward.

Therefore, all our requests should focus on asking for help in the process of seeking correction, and not for personal assistance in this or that inconsequential issue. The request for spiritual strength must focus on our ability to correct our intention and thus draw nearer to the Creator. Thus, it all depends on directing our spiritual efforts in the right direction.

We can now understand that prayer is, in fact, the creation of the spiritual intent of the soul. Almsgiving is called "a screen" in Kabbalah, meaning something that limits the use of egoism. It is called "almsgiving" when there is a screen that can direct this spiritual intent only toward spiritual ascent (altruism) and not toward greed (egoism).

Repentance is when the intent and the screen are used for spiritual ascent, or progress toward the Light, and a return to *Ein Sof*. It is a return to the Creator. By doing so, one extinguishes all the barriers and misery, and steps into the realm of the Upper Light.

All the phenomena and the events we now perceive as negative, the anguish we experience, happen only because of the absence of the Light of the Creator around us. Therefore, if we reach a higher spiritual degree, we will naturally be able to feel and receive the Upper Light, and thus avoid the judgment of the Creator.

The *Sukkah* (the *Sukkot* hut) stands for the zone, or vessel of the soul, its structure and attributes. We must create that spiritual system called *Sukkah* within us. This system will reflect our interrelations with the Light that surrounds us. The soul cannot receive the Upper Light until it is corrected, and it therefore remains outside the soul in the form of Surrounding Light. The wisdom of Kabbalah helps us to gradually correct our soul and induce the gradual permeation of the Light into our soul.

In order for the Light to be able to permeate the soul, it must acquire identical attributes to those of the Light. Spiritual sameness of the properties of the soul with the Light is physically expressed in the rules of construction of the *Sukkah*. Constructing the *Sukkah* is a very meticulous process, especially with regard to the thatch that covers it.

The wisdom of Kabbalah teaches us the external appearance and the measurements of the *Sukkah*, as it teaches us about all other Mitzvot— the laws of the Upper World we carry out in our world as a reflection of the spiritual laws. When Kabbalists perform these Mitzvot in the spiritual realm, meaning in their souls, they feel the holidays as sublime, eternal, and an entire form of existence.

The Upper Light can only permeate the soul when our spiritual desires correlate to its properties. This is parallel to a radio receiver tuning its inner frequency to match a specific wavelength in order to find a specific station.

Turning the "dial" of my transmitter toward the Light of the Creator is a little more complex than that. First, I must truly want to feel the spiritual world. That desire must be extremely powerful. This spiritual desire does not appear all at once; it often takes many years to prepare and cultivate its every detail.

It is only possible to feel the Light of the Creator in a vessel that was created by specific rules in a unique, concise and clear method. The wisdom of Kabbalah elaborates on that method in great detail in the most significant book that Baal HaSulam, the greatest Kabbalist of the previous century left us, *The Study of the Ten Sefirot*.

There is no contradiction between the fact that the vessel of the soul is created between *Rosh Hashanah* and *Yom Kippur* and that now we say that it may take months or years to prepare. That period only represents the creation process of the vessel of the soul in our world. We can describe our entire existence during all the cycles from the first to the last, as one year, at the end of which we are equipped with a spiritual vessel of identical attributes to those of the Upper Light and filled with Light.

The creation process of the soul begins with a spiritual degree called *Rosh Hashanah*. The next correction correlates to a spiritual ascent to a degree called *Yom Kippur*. Five days pass from *Yom Kippur* to the beginning of *Sukkot*, during which the preparation of the five parts of the Upper Light, *Nefesh*, *Ruach*, *Neshama*, *Haya*, and *Yechida*, are performed. The Upper Light permeates the soul during the seven days of *Sukkot* because the vessel of the soul consists of seven *Sefirot*: *Hesed*, *Gevura*, *Tifferet*, *Netzah*, *Hod*, *Yesod*, *Malchut*.

The Upper Light can only permeate the soul (*Malchut*, represented by the citron, *Etrog*) when it is connected with a superior spiritual object (*Zeir Anpin*, represented by the palm branch, *Lulav*) and the origins of the Light, *Netzah* and *Hod* (represented by the myrtle and the willow, *Hadas* and *Arava* respectively). Just as there is a need to tune the radio receiver to receive the outer wave, so the soul must be attuned internally to match the properties of the Light, the Creator, and only then will Light permeate and fill it.

In order to direct the soul toward reception of the Upper Light, the receiving vessel (*Malchut*, the citron) must be connected with the giver (*Zeir Anpin*, the palm branch), which symbolizes the Creator. The myrtle and the willow stand for the attributes of the Creator that the soul must acquire.

If the correction of the soul is completed, and it adopts the properties of the Creator (meaning if the soul places itself under the Surrounding Light of the Creator through a series of spiritual actions) it is influenced by it in a special way called "embrace."

There is a "left embrace" and a "right embrace." The Song of Songs writes about it (2:6): "Let His left hand be under my head, and His right hand embrace me." This state correlates to the preparation of the vessel to be filled with Light before *Sukkot* ("Let His left hand be under my head"), followed by the spiritual unification with the Creator and the filling with Light on *Simchat Torah* ("and His right hand embrace me").

Our bodies are a reflection of spiritual forces and connections. Just as one force influences another in the spiritual world, so these forces express themselves in our physical body parts. Each part of the body has its appropriate properties, and the interconnections with other parts, just as in the spiritual world.

HBD, HGT, NHY (*Hochma-Bina-Daat, Hesed-Gevura-Tifferet, Netzah-Hod-Yesod*) are three parts of the spiritual "hand" that seemingly embraces the soul and surrounds it from three sides: the arm and the forearm, which are of equal length, designate the two long sides of the *Sukkah*, and the third, short side of the *Sukkah* is like the palm of the hand. All the properties and measurements of the *Sukkah* derive from the properties of the Surrounding Light and the soul, which must be completely identical if they are to unite. Thus, the Light will fill the soul entirely

351

and they will unite, a state called "spiritual *Zivug*" (mating). We call that state, *Simchat Torah*.

The *Sukkah* no longer exists on *Simchat Torah*, because the Light has already entered the soul and filled it entirely, hence the complete feeling of joy expressed in this joyous festival. This holiday (spiritual state) occurs when the soul is filled with joy because it fills the Creator with joy.

On *Pesach* and *Sukkot*, Kabbalists are especially meticulous and keep even the most strict commandments, because these two holidays symbolize the two most crucial moments in the evolution of the soul and the attainment of the purpose of Creation—the process of the discovery and reception of the Upper Knowledge, the Creator. This is the essence of the wisdom of Kabbalah. These two moments (*Pesach* and *Sukkot*) symbolize the beginning and the end of one's spiritual way, hence their special significance. This is the reason why Kabbalists are so careful about keeping the *Mitzvot* that correlate to these holidays.

CHAPTER 7.3
THE RECEPTION OF LIGHT ON HOLIDAYS

Any increase in the Light is a holiday. Every soul that attains spirituality receives the Light from the world of *Atzilut*. Its power depends on the degree of the soul. The ordinary level of Light is called a "weekday." The next degree of intensity is called "*Rosh Hodesh*" (the first day of the month). Each weekday designates a different kind of Light.

On *Rosh Hodesh Partzuf* ZON (*Zeir Anpin* and *Nukva*) of *Atzilut* rises to *Partzuf* YESHSUT (*Israel Saba ve Tvuna*), meaning it climbs one degree, and illuminates a completely different quality of Light. The next level up is called *Shabbat* (the Sabbath).

Every minute and every hour bear their own unique shades in spirituality. The influence of the Light on the souls in our world is a perpetual state. As a result, there is an ongoing process of correction and movement. Without the constant change and influence of Light, the vessel would remain immobile. A vessel moves under the influence of affliction, the consequence of the absence of Light in the vessel, or the permeating of Light into it.

ZON of *Atzilut* determines the movement of all souls. There is constant abundance extending from ZON, which souls perceive incorrectly due to their egoism. The purpose of the correction of the souls is to change the bad feeling into a good one, meaning to correct the vessels from egoism to altruism. The more correct the soul is, the more it perceives the Creator as Absolute Goodness.

We cannot perform independent corrections, but must realize what kind of enemy our egoism really is, and then ask for help from the Creator. The revelation of the Creator brings us to a higher quality experience. The change in our perception of reward and punishment will make punishment feel like pleasure.

If we were no longer able to feel pain in our bodies, we would not know if a disease were spreading in our bodies. We would not do anything to cure it, because we would not feel the symptoms that indicate it. Sometimes it is worthwhile to endure pain for the purpose of future benefit. If we realize that bitter medicine is a necessary means to health, the medicine will not taste bitter but sweet.

Any "low" spiritual or mental feeling indicates a malfunction in one's soul, and must be cured. Neutralizing the sensation of pain will produce harmful results because the body will be denied its alarm system to warn of a deteriorating mental state.

The month of *Adar* is a special month. It is the month of the holiday of *Purim*, the greatest of all festivals. It is customary to drink alcohol on *Purim* to complete intoxication and absolute detachment from reality, until one stops feeling any concern or worry. It comes to remind us of our future state of absolute pleasure and wholeness, when the mind is disconnected and only emotion remains active.

But why do we need to disconnect the mind in order to feel whole? What happens to a person when filled with delight? Is there any room left for thoughts, or cold reasoning?

Most of the people who turn to Kabbalah come from society's middle class, whether socioeconomic or educational. A college professor, for example, devoted entirely to scientific research, does not need any religious coatings. Logic is king, and science *is* religion. Often scientists are even more fanatic in their beliefs than religious fanatics.

We must teach people to look within and discover the ten *Sefirot* inside them. The first, *Keter*, is the attribute of the Creator. The others are measurements of exposure of the Creator to the creature, meaning *Malchut*. We must be taught to differentiate between these properties and ourselves.

As *Malchut* corrects itself, it increases its ability to resemble itself to the upper nine *Sefirot* and contain itself in them. Consequently, it (*Malchut*) will eventually cleave entirely to the Creator.

When a cell in the body stops "thinking" of the body and begins to function independently, "chewing" everything up without giving the body what it must, this is considered a cancerous cell. Every cell in the body knows what it is destined to become when it matures. If something goes wrong inside, cells know how to restore their functioning to normal; they are connected with the collective system of the body.

If we behave that way toward the Creator, the universe and mankind (which are one and the same thing), we will function correctly and our health will be in order. Otherwise, we become like a cell that thinks only of itself, thus turning from a healthy cell to a cancer cell.

When we begin to study Kabbalah, we are told to start in a state of *Lo Lishma*. We approach such a person with kind and gentle words, because in that state one is categorized as "women, children and slaves," meaning with egoistic properties. The "women" state signifies the will to receive, the "children" state signifies wanting to perceive everything unconsciously and the "slaves" state represents the pursuit of pleasures (slaves to pleasures). These are internal states that every person experiences, regardless of sex, age, or religion, because every person possesses all the spiritual states within and must therefore experience and correct every single one of them.

When we begin to acquire independent wisdom and understanding, even if we are still immersed in egoistic properties, we can already observe ourselves from the side. At that point we are being gradually introduced to the real meaning of bestowal (altruism, giving) and what really lies behind the term "for the Creator," also called "in order to bestow."

The only way to liberate ourselves from our egoism is to bring ourselves to a state where we cry out to the Creator. Otherwise, our Pharaohs will not let us out of Egypt. Every situation must be meticulously analyzed, until we understand precisely how to operate our reason in order to analyze our feelings. If we do not do that, these situations will repeat themselves until we understand that and cry to the Creator to take anything He wants, if only to set us free from the one and only enemy that prevents us from approaching the Creator, namely our own egoism.

Both situations—deep depression and extreme pleasure—are extreme situations that do not allow us to analyze our situations correctly. We must try to do it independently, while asking: "Why was I given this situation?" "What can I do about it?" If we delve deeply into the thought that these situations were given us by the Creator, our anguish will cease to be a torment and will turn to pleasure. It depends on our perception of the greatness of the Creator. There is nothing more that we should consider!

CHAPTER 7.4
A HOLIDAY AS A MEANS FOR CORRECTION

All the corrections in *Partzuf Zeir Anpin* of *Atzilut*, which is our root, occur in a spiritual process entitled *Sukkot*.

Man, meaning the soul, or spiritual vessel, is a simile for *Zeir Anpin* of *Atzilut*. The origin of the Light that the soul receives is the interaction between *Bina*, ZA and *Malchut* of *Atzilut*.

All the operations that ZA must perform are connected with the *Mitzvot* that relate to the *Lulav* (palm branch) that symbolizes it, and the *Etrog* (citron) that symbolizes *Malchut*. One must combine these properties within, and this inner work happens entirely inside the *Sukkah*. The

Sukkah is the Surrounding Light of *Bina* that surrounds ZA, which is where one absorbs the Inner Light.

Rabbi Yehuda Ashlag explained that there are two different terms relating to the *Sukkah*, namely "Clouds of Glory" and "Clouds that Hide." The hiding clouds are those constituents of the thatch, made of remnants of plantation and branches. Those who can build a thatch within themselves to protect against the pleasures from Above, will begin to see the clouds of glory instead of the clouds that hide them from the Creator and His Revelation.

One's work during the building of the thatch symbolizes the building of the spiritual screen to filter the pleasure that comes from sensing the Creator. This type of work is called MAN de Ima (MAN of *Ima*); it is a prayer to receive the Light to resist one's egoism. If one's request is granted, this Force fills the vessel and renders ability to receive the Upper Light (of Wisdom) using the screen.

This Light contains extensive knowledge about our place in the world, what happens with and around us, and our current degree. When we attain the properties of a certain spiritual degree, we are called by its name. When we attain a higher one, our names will change accordingly.

As we climb higher in the spiritual degrees and as our names change accordingly, we acquire new attributes and expose ourselves to increased degrees of sublime abundance. That is why people sometimes think that if they change their names artificially, they will be influenced by a greater spiritual abundance.

Each and every soul that descends to our world has but one destination: to reacquire the spiritual degree from which it descended to our world, to materialize in a biological body. We must attain the roots of our souls while we are still in our physical bodies, during one of our lifetimes. We must reach the same spiritual degree from which our souls came, despite the obstacles and the obstructions that physically stand before us.

Some souls are obliged only to attain their previous degrees. They rise through the 6,000 degrees called the "6,000 years" and stop there. That is why it says that after 6,000 years the world will come to its end.

However, there are special souls that, after attaining their degrees, must rise even higher, along with the worlds of BYA to the level of *Partzuf SAG* of the world of *Adam Kadmon*. This degree is called the 7,000th, or seven thousand years. There are also souls that must attain the degree of *Partzuf AB* of *Adam Kadmon*, called "8,000 years," or that of *Partzuf Galgalta*, called "9,000 years."

There are also very special souls that attain the degree called "10,000 years," meaning they transcend in their emotions and attainments to the world of *Ein Sof*. Such a soul comes to our world very rarely—perhaps once every ten generations. Only the greatest among the Kabbalists belong to this type of souls.

Performing *Mitzvot* that relate to the *Sukkah* signify one's adhesion with the Creator in the highest degree. How does that happen?

Zeir Anpin, which consists of six *Sefirot*, defines six directions: north, south, east, west, up, and down. *Malchut* receives Light from each of these *Sefirot*, which are the six properties of *Zeir Anpin*. That is why the citron is first attached to the palm branch before one can offer the blessings. That is how the *Mitzva* of the *Sukkah* and the *Lulav* are performed.

However, it is absolutely forbidden to think that by performing this physical act, one performs a spiritual act as well! One cannot perform anything spiritual with one's hands or lips. A spiritual act can only be performed by a person who has acquired a screen over egoistic desires and can receive the Light of the Creator for the sake of the Creator.

The way to acquire that state is called "the wisdom of Kabbalah" and it can only be acquired under the strict guidance of a Kabbalistic teacher. It is impossible to become a Kabbalist by studying on one's own. Even the greatest Kabbalists had teachers without which they would not have attained their spiritual powers. Once the beginning Kabbalist receives the right direction from his teacher, and obtains preliminary contact with the Creator, he can intensify this contact to the point where he can even ascend higher than his teacher.

The holiday of *Sukkot* lasts seven days, the length of time it takes for the Light to go from *Bina* to the seven *Sefirot* of *Zeir Anpin*. Every day represents a new spiritual state, a new Light that permeates the corresponding *Sefira*. The seventh day indicates the transition of the Light from *Zeir Anpin* to *Malchut*.

The day of the reception of the Torah by *Malchut* is called *Simchat Torah* (Rejoicing of the Torah). This is because the entire Light that *Malchut* receives descends to the souls, and this Light is called "Torah."

This Light is not a part of the *Sukkah*. Rather, it is a separate holiday. A *Sukkah* is a transition of Light by means of the screen through *Zeir Anpin* during the seven days of *Sukkot*. *Simchat Torah*, however, is the permeation of the Light of the Torah, meaning the Light of *Zeir Anpin* into *Malchut* and their complete unification.

The night before *Simchat Torah* is called *Hoshana Raba*. This is a special night when all the Surrounding Light gathers around ZA, but because it is around and not inside ZA, it is considered a "nocturnal state" before it is turned into Inner Light when it permeates *Malchut*.

Any act performed with the intent to bring contentment to the Creator is a spiritual act. If the very same act were intended toward self-gratification and egoism, this act would be opposite to spiritual, meaning corporeal.

A beginning student of Kabbalah finds it hard to perform the physical *Mitzvot*, which every orthodox person does very easily, but effort should still be made to do them. The difficulty in performing these *Mitzvot* arises because the Kabbalist regards every act and every thought in terms of its impact on one's progress.

The Kabbalist evaluates these actions according to how helpful they are in helping us attain our goal of bonding with the Creator. And since the connection with the Creator is attained through the intent and the inner effort that is directed against the egoism, it is hard for us to do anything physical that is seemingly connected with spirituality.

This is because there isn't even a single act that one can perform in this world that actually affects spirituality. Our contact with God passes only through our hearts. However, physically performing *Mitzvot* is a must, because that, too, is the Will of the Creator.

There is, however, one type of effort that does help us advance toward attaining spirituality. It is the effort to maintain thinking about the Creator's existence while studying Kabbalah, and the need to remember that the Acts of the Creator are taught solely to attain the purpose of Creation.

Egoism allows us to move only when it sees some benefit to it, when the act produces pleasure. We need to pray to the Creator to receive the strength to act against our egoism. That is our direct contact with the Creator, the only straight path to Him. That contact grows gradually clearer and more solid, and we begin to understand what happened to us and why, and what we must do next. At that point, our efforts become a springboard to attain the next degree.

What is the "secret" and what is the "Wisdom of the Hidden?" A secret exists only if one has not yet uncovered it. Today's secret may be known tomorrow. But it is our work to unravel the secret, and the teacher's job to point us in the right direction and motivate us to search.

It is impossible to measure effort itself, since it is a personal thing that relates to one's emotions, and we cannot describe feelings. Thus, it is impossible to feel something that another feels.

In general, an effort is an egoistic activity, when one tries to receive pleasures from this world. One unconsciously changes one's pleasures in an endless pursuit of tiny sparks of Light that keep changing their appearance.

And what is labor, according to Kabbalah? It is when one tries to do something against one's ego, and fails. Then, after trying every possible option and failing, the prayer to the Creator forms within, the real prayer to Him. That prayer is the one *true* labor.

The Creator alone can deliver us from our egoism. We cannot do it for ourselves. If we still think there is a chance that we can attain spirituality by ourselves, even if it is the most remote possibility, it is a sign that we have not yet run out of options, and our egos will not allow us to raise a real prayer, a heartfelt cry from the bottom of our hearts for help. Ego will not surrender itself to the Mercy of the Creator before it is certain that, without attaining spirituality, it will simply die, and that the only way to attain it is with the help of the Creator.

Kabbalah is like no other way, because it is impossible to predict the next step. It is always like stepping into total darkness towards a new revelation. Thus, one cannot build one's future steps relying on past experience. If we could do it, we would rely on our minds and reason, and not on the negation of the reason and the adoption of faith in the Creator, with faith above reason.

We can only see if we are directing our efforts in the right direction by constantly returning our thoughts to the Creator. We must bear in mind that every new sensation is sent by the Creator because He wills it so. He puts obstacles in our way only to the extent that we can overpower them.

It is different for every person and cannot be compared, but the only thing we can arrive at is the "recognition of evil," the recognition of our own egoism. We can see the enemy face to face; we do not have to fight windmills. This phase is general and everyone experiences it, but it is experienced differently by every individual.

There is no direct link between the intensity of the egoism and the length of time it must take to correct it. Even people who study and work in the same group have different desires. In one person they might grow, while in another they might stay the same or even decrease, and no external interference will help. It all depends on the extent to which one can ask for help of the Creator. However, this is something that is very hard to do because the ego senses it as humiliation.

Still, there is no other way! Without His Help, without the Light that permeates the vessel, the vessel will not become altruistic. A vessel without the properties of the Light is a completely egoistic will to receive delight and pleasure that cannot perform any spiritual movement.

When one has tried every way possible and failed, it will be clear that one's situation is hopeless. Only then will egoism surrender and the person be willing to receive any help. In order to reach that state, one must constantly increase the importance of spirituality, giving it increasing favor over corporeality. This should be done even if, in the beginning, this comes from ego, or the desire to benefit from spirituality.

We must use every tool at our disposal. Afterwards, when our egoistic desires decrease, we will find ways to help us preserve the desire to study Kabbalah. Our incentive will first be the desire for honor, then for power, but in the end we will be left with one wish only—to experience the Creator.

Once attained, it will become of greatest importance to do everything for the Creator. Ultimately, it will not even be important if we actually do something for Him, because the knowledge that we directed everything toward Him will be the pleasure.

We must not underestimate the forces and the means we have. We must remember that the Creator works on us through the world we presently inhabit.

CHAPTER 7.5
FROM THE INTRODUCTION TO THE ZOHAR

Introduction to the Book of Zohar (item 10): "Now we can understand the fourth inquiry: how is it possible that from His Holiness will emerge the chariot of defilement and shells, since it is at the other end of His Holiness and how can it be that He supports and sustains it?

"Indeed, we must first understand the essence of defilement and the shells. Know, that it is the great will to receive, of which we said that it is the essence of the souls by creation. And because they are willing to receive the entire filling that is in the thought of Creation, it does not stay in that form within the souls, because if it had, they would have had to remain eternally separated from Him, because the difference in form would have separated them from Him.

"And in order to mend the separation that rests upon the vessel of the souls, He created all the worlds and separated them into two systems, as the verse goes: 'God hath made even the one as well as the other,' which are the four worlds of ABYA of holiness.

"Opposite them are the four worlds of the impure ABYA. And He imprinted the will to bestow in ABYA of holiness and removed from them the will to receive for themselves, placing it in the system of the impure worlds of ABYA. For this reason, they have become separated from the Creator and from all the worlds of holiness.

"For that reason the shells are called 'dead,' as the verse goes: 'sacrifices of the dead' (Psalms 106, 28). And the evil are attracted to them, as our sages say: 'The evil are called dead when they are still alive,' because the will to receive, imprinted in them in oppositeness of form to His Holiness, separates them from the Life of Lives, and they are remote from Him from one end to the other.

"This is so because He has no interest in reception, only in bestowal, whereas the shells want only to receive for their own delight, and have nothing to do with bestowal, and there is no greater oppositeness than that. You already know that spiritual remoteness begins with some difference of form and ends in oppositeness of form, which is the farthest possible distance in the last degree."

If there is complete detachment between the Creator and the creature, how can He support and guard it? The Creator intentionally formed Creation with opposite traits to His own. Thus, He assigned his creatures with the task of correcting these traits. In order to help them, He built two opposite systems of worlds to serve the creatures.

The one that takes the right side, that of holiness, or the desire to bestow, is called "living" and "righteous." Those that take the left side, that of uncorrected desires, meaning egoism, are considered "dead," and "evil." All these states refer only to spirituality, when the Light is either in the vessel (still, vegetative, and animate), or removed from it (only the still degree).

When we say "evil," we are referring to people who have already attained the revelation of the Creator, have entered the worlds of BYA, and are now climbing on the 6,000-rung ladder toward the Creator. Though they are now working in order to bestow, they might still fall into egoism and reception in order to receive. These two situations must be experienced in every single degree.

The "evil" state compels us to advance toward holiness and correct the attributes of the left line. But the more egoism we correct in our current degree, the greater portion of egoism we receive in the next. Then we must perform the same operations in the spiritual degrees and correct the next lot of desire to receive. The situations are much more acute and profound in spirituality, but at the same time, the power we receive to handle them is greater, too.

We always choose the desire that gives us the most pleasure in every situation. This conduct was imprinted in us from Above and is unchangeable. But what we can change is the intent, meaning that we can invert the direction of the pleasure toward its origin. Thus, the focus should be on feeling the source of the pleasure!

The will to receive in itself is not egoism. If I want to receive because the Creator gives me pleasure, and I please Him by receiving, it is considered giving, not receiving. If I don't care who gives me pleasure, even knowing that it comes from the Creator, but take everything to derive the greatest possible pleasure from it, then my desires are egoistic and corrupted. Our world is still far below that of the impure desires, meaning even below the corrupted desires.

The pure and impure worlds complement each another. They are both necessary for spiritual progress. The individual is in between them, in the middle part, *Tifferet*. That is the only neutral place.

Above it there is holiness, and below it, impurity. There is nothing to correct in holiness, but it is impossible to correct the impure forces. Only in the middle third of *Tifferet* is it possible to connect the upper and the lower parts, and thus correct them.

CHAPTER 7.6
QUESTIONS & ANSWERS

TORAH & MITZVOT

Question: What is the connection between Mitzvot and the purpose of our existence?

Answer: Mitzvot are rules, meaning characteristics of spiritual degrees. For that reason the number of Mitzvot that were given to Israel—613—and the nations of the world—7—indicate the sum of spiritual degrees reaching from our world to the world of Ein Sof, from complete disconnection from the Creator leading to complete adhesion with His properties.

It is said that, "A Mitzva without an aim is like a body without a soul." This relates to a spiritual altruistic vessel, to the sensation of a spiritual Light, meaning the Creator. For that reason, it is good that people keep the Mitzvot, but it is certainly not a spiritual act. The only way to operate in the spiritual world is by corrected spiritual intentions, even without performing any physical activity.

However, man's purpose is to combine the mechanical performance of Mitzvot with the spiritual performance, so that all 620 spiritual degrees will be included in the mechanical performance. Thus, one combines all the worlds within, beginning in our world and ending in the world of Ein Sof. That is why that spiritual degree is called the "end of correction."

The importance of Kabbalah is that it shows how to create within us the right intent when we perform the Mitzvot. Kabbalah adds the spiritual aim to the mechanical act, but this by no means negates the physical performance of Mitzvot. The purpose of Creation is not to fly into the spiritual world, but to feel the spiritual worlds by means of our world and experience them simultaneously. We do this by adding the spiritual dimension to the mechanical operations we perform.

Q: What does it mean to fully keep the Mitzvot?

A: A complete performance of a *Mitzva* means keeping it at its root. In other words, it is the ascent to the degree from which the *Mitzva*, the spiritual property came, using the corrected properties. The ascent to the spiritual degree means that the vessel of the soul must be emptied from its previous filling in order to receive a new one. The beginning of a new spiritual degree happens through a process called "Impregnation."

The refining of the soul from its spiritual past is called the "stripping of corporeality," but this does not refer to the corporeal past. Being emptied from the past is necessary because *Keter* of the inferior becomes *Malchut* of the superior when changing from absence to existence (during the spiritual ascent) and vice-versa.

Q: Why must we perform all 620 Mitzvot, if each of them is a law in a certain spiritual degree on the ladder between the Creator and us?

A: Each spiritual degree contains all the other degrees inside it. Each of the 620 degrees between man and the Creator consists of 620 parts and all of them must be corrected in every degree, according to their spiritual level. The difference between the degrees is only in the intensity of their altruistic power.

Q: Why are there Mitzvot that were given hundreds of years after the giving of the Torah?

A: Moses, the great Kabbalist, told his people about the structure of the spiritual worlds. We know that what he conveyed to them became the book of Torah.

This book offers two options: the first is when we feel only our world and learn Torah, and especially the wisdom of Kabbalah. In that state, we unconsciously extend Light from the spiritual worlds, which gradually corrects us.

The second is when we already perceive the spiritual world through feelings. Then, the wisdom of Kabbalah becomes a guide that shows us precisely what we should do next and how. It teaches us the operation of every system in the Upper Worlds.

The growing coarseness of the souls that descend to our world during the 6,000 years requires every generation to have its own Torah, one that suits the soul of that generation. The Torah is the means to correct our egoism, as it says: "I have created the evil inclination, I have created for it the Torah as a spice." For that reason, Kabbalists presented new Mitzvot in every generation in the form of customs and laws. They determined that the customs of Israel are laws.

On the other hand, when there is no need to perform something in our world, we witness events that affect our ability to perform them. Such events include the ruin of the first and second temples, exiles, and other catastrophes. As a result, people were unable to perform many of the Mitzvot connected to the temple or the sanctity of the land.

Q: Can we talk about the construction of the third temple and what it means?

A: In every generation, different kinds of souls descend to this world. The first souls to descend were the finest, purest, and consequently the simplest. These souls had such a small will to receive that they had no desire to evolve in the physical world. Consequently, it took many years for anything significant to happen.

However, over the years these souls accumulated hardships and pain, which increased their will to receive; they grew coarser. The increase of the will to receive compels people to seek answers to questions and needs that awaken in them. This search produces the development of science, medicine, culture and technology.

Our generation and the generations to come belong to a time generally entitled "the last generation." This is the generation that precedes the collective correction of the souls. In this generation, egoism grows so intensely that it awakens needs for every corporeal thing that exists, as well as the need to understand and control the spiritual world.

For that reason we are witnessing a growing importance and interest in certain mystical sciences. Bookstores are loaded with books, films and magazines about extraterrestrials and other such phenomena. But these are merely midway points on the way to the ultimate question: "What is the meaning of my life?" Although this question was asked in the past, the intensity behind it today is far greater.

The temple represents the corrected state of the soul because it correlates with the state of the temple. It is said that the temple will be built only when relationships between people have been corrected (altruism).

But why did the Creator do it that way? Why must man nullify his ego and think only of others and never of himself? Does the Creator need it? He doesn't need it whatsoever; we do! Doing that, we create an objective outside ourselves and disconnected from ourselves. These are the only conditions that allow the building of a temple.

Q: What does the blessing for the food mean in terms of Kabbalah?

A: The Talmud speaks of a big group of *Tana'im*, Kabbalists who buried their deceased teacher. After the funeral they sat by the river and had a meal of bread and salt. All of a sudden they realized they could not bless the blessing for the food without their teacher. Regrettably, they had not succeeded in learning this blessing from their teacher.

So what is the blessing for the food? The blessing for the food is the reception of pleasure in order to please the Creator. It is when there is mutual respect between the guest (man) and the host (the Creator). One who receives should do it with the intent of giving pleasure to the Creator. Doing that raises the recipient to a spiritual degree. If his intention is not taken into account, and one enjoys without thinking of the host, one remains at the level of our world. This spiritual act (receiving in order to give pleasure to the Creator) is called "the blessing for the food."

Q: So is it correct to say that the important thing is the intent with which you bless the food?

A: Yes, but not only with regards to the blessing for the food. It is written in the Torah that, "A *Mitzva* without an aim is like a body without a soul." This means that every act, every *Mitzva* that has no reciprocal connection with the Creator, a mutual giving, is tantamount to a body without a soul, a dead body, meaning one that has no spiritual content. However, keeping *Mitzvot* even on this level is still important because it is a preparation period, when one can keep the *Mitzvot* on this level until attaining the spiritual world.

Q: Which is more important: the sentiment, or the mistakes we might make when we pray?

A: The sentiment is more important; mistakes don't matter. If you take only a few lines from the prayer book and feel them deeply, that would be much better than any mechanical prayer.

Q: Do things happen to us only by the Will of the Creator, or are there other forces?

A: The Torah states clearly that, "There is none else beside Him." This means that there is only one supreme force, namely the Creator. Everything we perceive as a struggle between opposing forces in nature stems from one guidance, the Creator that leads Creation. The Creator is the sole ruler; He is one, unique and unified.

Moreover, the idea that there are other forces contradicts the essence of Judaism. The concept that it is not the Creator who governs the evil forces is intended to justify our existence. The Torah clearly states the heavy punishments that will befall the chosen people by the Creator if they do not follow the path of the Torah.

Catastrophes have happened more than once throughout our history, and each time the Creator warned us about it in advance. The Talmud speaks of the foretokens of the ruin of the first and second temples before they actually happened. It is written in the Torah and in the *Zohar* that in order to reach perfection in a good way, we must study Kabbalah.

HOLIDAYS

Q: What is the meaning of *Yom Kippur* (Day of Atonement)?

A: *Yom Kippur* is the day when the construction of the spiritual vessel is completed. Reality consists of Light and vessel. The Light is the Creator, the pleasure, and the vessel is the creature, the soul, or *Malchut*. The Light is in complete rest and never changes. The Light's only purpose is to delight His creatures and bring mankind to eternal bliss.

The entire process of the making of the spiritual vessel, from its current lowest of states, to the highest, eternal and complete, is expressed in this world in the "Ten Penitential Days" between New Year and the Day of Atonement. During these ten days, the soul, which originally consisted of nothing but a desire to receive, begins to gradually acquire the attribute of the Light, beginning on the first day of *Rosh Hashanah* (the first day of the year), until the Day of Atonement. The will to receive changes in ten ways, ten *Sefirot*, the foundation of the correction of the soul.

At the end of those ten days, the soul completes its correction and is ready to receive the Light. On the tenth day, the Day of Atonement, it is forbidden to display any desire to receive, emphasized by the prohibitions on eating, drinking, and the other limitations on this day of fasting. That day completes the final correction.

After the Day of Atonement begins the preparation for the reception of the Light by the (by now) totally corrected vessel. The reception of the Light is executed on the seven days of *Sukkot* by the performance of the *Mitzvot* of the *Lulav* (palm branch), the *Etrog* (citron) and the other *Mitzvot* necessary to extend the Light into the vessel.

Finally, the holiday of *Simchat Torah* (Rejoicing of the Torah) sums up the process and the Light of the Creator fills the prepared vessel entirely. The Torah symbolizes the Light, and the *Simchah* (joy) symbolizes the reception of the Light in order to bestow upon the Creator.

This correction doesn't have to be on these precise dates; in spirituality it can happen any time. We only denote this process in our world on specific times of the year.

Q: Who is the subject of the Torah?

A: The entire Torah, without exception, speaks of the individual. Each person is regarded as an entire world. There are rivers in this world, lakes, mountains and forests. There are people, nations, men and women, children, slaves, stars, moon and sun. Everything we can think of exists inside this creature. It is the only thing that the Creator created; outside it there is only the Creator. Everything that happens to this creature happens within it. Everything we perceive with our five senses—sight, sound, scent, taste and touch—comes from the Creator Who surrounds us.

Thus, the Torah speaks of each and every one of us; it is a personal guide to the perception of the Creator. That is why whatever we read in the Torah must be immediately ascribed to ourselves, out inner state. We must relate the characters to our properties, the events in our world are actually relationships between the hereditary, intellectual and emotional attributes. They were originally created by the Creator and we acquired them from Him and from no other, because there are no others! There are only different clothes that appear as different people through which the Creator works on each and every one of us.

MISCELLANEOUS QUESTIONS & ANSWERS

Q: What is *Eretz Israel* (the Land of Israel)?

A: *Eretz Israel* is an inner desire for spirituality. If one is also in the physical land of Israel, one's physical body unites with the soul. This is the state of the end of correction. If one is not in *Eretz Israel* in the spiritual sense, but only physically, one feels uncomfortable in this country, and is driven off. That person will constantly face external enemies until deciding to correct oneself from within. But when this is done, these external enemies immediately become friends.

We must act on the inner (spiritual) level and on the outer (corporeal) level simultaneously. If something is dear to us, we will not give it up that easily, and if we still do not appreciate the spiritual land of Israel, it is because we haven't acquired it, and we are therefore unable to appreciate the corporeal *Eretz Israel*.

There is a tight link between the root and the branch in our world. If we knew the spiritual meaning of *Eretz Israel*, what it is connected with and what it is identified with, we would not even consider giving it away, just as a parent would not give up a child.

Q: War and peace—are they in the hands of the Creator?

A: This depends much more on our desires than on the desires of politicians. I am not referring to the Kabbalists, but to the desires of people in general. Their desires can change everything Above, and politics will change accordingly.

Q: Is humanity headed toward unity?

A: Of course humanity is ultimately headed toward unity! In the end, mankind will realize that without unity, it will be impossible to lead a peaceful and secure life.

Q: Can writers, poets and composers call their works their own?

A: Yes, of course they can.

Q: Is a Kabbalist obligated to be respectful toward figures that other peoples consider holy?

A: Even the laws of the literal Torah, not only Kabbalah, state that one must be respectful to everybody.

DETAILED TABLE OF CONTENTS

OUR OTHER BOOKS

A Guide to the Hidden Wisdom of Kabbalah (with ten complete Kabbalah lessons): provides the reader with a solid foundation for understanding the role of Kabbalah in our world. The content was designed to allow individuals all over the world to begin traversing the initial stages of spiritual ascent toward the apprehension of the upper realms.

Attaining the Worlds Beyond: is a first step toward discovering the ultimate fulfillment of spiritual ascent in our lifetime. This book reaches out to all those who are searching for answers, who are seeking a logical and reliable way to understand the world's phenomena. This magnificent introduction to the wisdom of Kabbalah provides a new kind of awareness that enlightens the mind, invigorates the heart, and moves the reader to the depths of their soul.

The Science of Kabbalah: is the first in a series of texts that Rav Michael Laitman, Kabbalist and scientist, designed to introduce readers to the special language and terminology of the Kabbalah. Here, Rav Laitman reveals authentic Kabbalah in a manner that is both rational and mature. Readers are gradually led to an understanding of the logical design of the Universe and the life whose home it is.

The Science of Kabbalah, a revolutionary work that is unmatched in its clarity, depth, and appeal to the intellect, will enable readers to approach the more technical works of Baal HaSulam (Rav Yehuda Ashlag), such as *Talmud Eser Sefirot* and *Zohar.*

Although scientists and philosophers will delight in its illumination, laymen will also enjoy the satisfying answers to the riddles of life that only authentic Kabbalah provides. Now, travel through the pages and prepare for an astonishing journey into the Upper Worlds.

Introduction to the Book of Zohar: is the second in a series written by Kabbalist and scientist Rav Michael Laitman, which will prepare readers to understand the hidden message of *"The Zohar"*. Among the many helpful topics dealt with in this companion text to *The Science of Kabbalah,* readers are introduced to the "language of roots and branches," without which the stories in *The Zohar* are mere fable and legend. Introduction to *The Book of Zohar* will certainly furnish readers with the necessary tools to understand authentic Kabbalah as it was originally meant to be, as a means to attain the Upper Worlds.

Kabbalah for Beginners: By reading this book you will be able to take your first step in understanding the roots of human behaviour and the laws of nature. The contents present the essential principals of the Kabbalistic approach and describe the wisdom of Kabbalah and the way it works. *Kabbalah for Beginners* is intended for those searching for a sensible and reliable method of studying the phenomenon of this world for those seeking to understand the reason for suffering and pleasure, for those seeking answers to the major questions in life. Kabbalah is an accurate method to investigate and define man's position in the universe. The wisdom of Kabbalah tells us why man exists, why he is born, why he lives, what the purpose of his life is, where he comes from, and where he is going after he completes his life in this world.

The Kabbalah Experience: Never has the language of Kabbalah been as clear and accessible as it is here, in this compelling, informative collection. The depth of wisdom revealed in the questions and answers of this book will inspire reflection and contemplation. Readers will also begin to experience a growing sense of enlightenment while simply absorbing the words on every page.

The Kabbalah Experience is a guide from the past to the future, revealing situations that all students of Kabbalah will experience at some point on their journeys. For those who cherish every moment in life, the author offers unparalleled insights into the timeless wisdom of Kabbalah.

About Bnei Baruch

Bnei Baruch is a non-profit group centered in Israel that is spreading the wisdom of Kabbalah to accelerate the spirituality of mankind. Kabbalist Michael Laitman PhD, who was the disciple and personal assistant to Kabbalist, Rav Baruch Ashlag, the son of Kabbalist Rav Yehuda Ashlag (author of the *Sulam* Commentary on *The Zohar*), follows in the footsteps of his mentor in guiding the group.

Rav Laitman's scientific method provides individuals of all faiths, religions and cultures the precise tools necessary for embarking on a highly efficient path of self-discovery and spiritual ascent. The focus is primarily on inner processes that individuals undergo at their own pace. Bnei Baruch welcomes people of all ages and lifestyles to engage in this rewarding process.

In recent years, an awakening of a massive worldwide quest for the answers to life's questions has been underway. Society has lost its ability to see reality for what it is and in its place easily formed viewpoints and opinions have appeared.

Bnei Baruch reaches out to all those who seek awareness beyond the standard view. It offers practical guidance and a reliable method for understanding the world's phenomena. The group's unique method not only helps overcome the trials and tribulations of everyday life, but initiates a process in which individuals extend themselves beyond the standard boundaries and limitations of today's world.

Kabbalist Rav Yehuda Ashlag left a study method for this generation, which essentially 'trains' individuals to behave as if they have already achieved the perfection of the Upper Worlds, here in our world.

In the words of Rav Yehuda Ashlag, "This method is a practical way to apprehend the Upper World and the source of our existence while still living in this world. A Kabbalist is a researcher who studies his nature using this proven, time-tested and accurate method. Through this method, one attains perfection, and takes control over one's life. In this way, one realizes one's true purpose in life. Just as a person cannot function properly in this world having no knowledge of it, so also one's soul cannot function properly in the Upper World having no knowledge of it. The wisdom of Kabbalah provides this knowledge."

The goal-orientated nature of these studies enables a person to apply this knowledge on both an individual and collective basis in order to enhance and promote the spirituality of humankind, and indeed the entire world.

HOW TO CONTACT BNEI BARUCH

Bnei Baruch
1057 Steeles Avenue West, Suite 532
Toronto, ON, M2R 3X1
Canada

E-mail: info@kabbalah.info

Web site: www.kabbalah.info

Toll free in Canada and USA:
1-866-LAITMAN
Fax: 1-905 886 9697